McCAWLEY AND *TRETHOWAN*: THE CHAOS OF POLITICS AND THE INTEGRITY OF LAW

VOLUME 2: *TRETHOWAN*

In the second part of this two-volume study, Ian Loveland delves deeply into the immediate historical and political context of the *Trethowan* litigation which began in New South Wales in 1930 and reached the Privy Council two years later. The litigation centred on the efforts of a conservatively-inclined government to prevent a future Labour administration, led by the then radical politician Jack Lang, abolishing the upper house of the State's legislature by entrenching the existence of the upper house through the legal device of requiring that its abolition be approved by a state-wide referendum.

The book carefully examines the immediate political and legal routes of the entrenchment device fashioned by the State's Premier, Sir Thomas Bavin, and his former law student, colleague and then Dean of the Sydney University law school, Sir John Peden. It places the doctrinal arguments advanced in subsequent litigation in the State courts, before the High Court and finally in the Privy Council in the multiple contexts of the personal and policy-based disputes which pervaded both the State and national political arenas.

In its final chapter, the book draws on insights provided by the detailed study of *McCawley* (in volume one) and *Trethowan* to revisit and re-evaluate the respective positions adopted by William Wade and Ivor Jennings as to the capacity of the United Kingdom's Parliament to introduce entrenching legislation which would be upheld by the courts.

McCawley and *Trethowan*: The Chaos of Politics and the Integrity of Law

Volume 2: *Trethowan*

Ian Loveland
Professor of Public Law, City, University of London

·HART·
OXFORD · LONDON · NEW YORK · NEW DELHI · SYDNEY

HART PUBLISHING

Bloomsbury Publishing Plc

Kemp House, Chawley Park, Cumnor Hill, Oxford, OX2 9PH, UK

1385 Broadway, New York, NY 10018, USA

29 Earlsfort Terrace, Dublin 2, Ireland

HART PUBLISHING, the Hart/Stag logo, BLOOMSBURY and the Diana logo are trademarks of Bloomsbury Publishing Plc

First published in Great Britain 2021

A catalogue record for this book is available from the British Library.

A catalogue record for this book is available from the Library of Congress.

Library of Congress Control Number: 2021011467

ISBN: HB: 978-1-50994-827-7
ePDF: 978-1-50994-829-1
ePub: 978-1-50994-828-4

Typeset by Compuscript Ltd, Shannon

PREFACE

This book is the second in a two-volume project examining aspects of Australia's constitutional history. This second volume follows on seamlessly from the concluding chapter of the first book, which ended with an analysis of the judgment of the Privy Council in *McCawley v The King*. The primary focus in this book is the litigation at all its various stages in *Trethowan v Attorney General for South Wales*,[1] a case which is one of the two seminal entrenchment cases to which most British law students are introduced during their LLB or GDL studies. The other, the South African case of *Harris v Donges (Minister for the Interior)*,[2] was one I explored in a book published by Hart Publishing some 20 years ago.[3] That book, and these two volumes, were written because I came to the view very early on in my career as a constitutional law scholar that the UK's constitutional arrangements were grotesquely unsatisfactory, principally because of our unhappy attachment to the idea that sovereign lawmaking power lies with bare majorities in the two Houses of Parliament (or even just the Commons if Parliament Act legislation is in issue), and that it is therefore possible for seismic changes to constitutional arrangements to be made by legislators who may represent at best only a large *minority* of the population, and who cast their legislative votes on the basis of palpably ill-informed consideration (or even no consideration at all) of the issue before them.

Harris and *Trethowan* are both offered up to British law students as vehicles for exploring the supposed legal impossibility of entrenching any political or moral values in a form that would safeguard them from alteration through that normal lawmaking process. The simple lesson generally offered up is that, as a matter of law, *Harris* and *Trethowan* offer no assistance to achieve that objective. The purpose of this project is not to rebut that conclusion, but rather to offer an antidote – a supplement might be a more appropriate and less pejorative term – to the cursory treatment that many supposedly seminal constitutional law cases are accorded in terms of their sociological and political contexts.

The book has been written primarily for a British and American audience for whom Australian political and legal history is a very unfamiliar terrain, and to whom Jack Lang, Thomas Bavin, John Peden and Bert Evatt are likely unknown names. I hope at least to introduce those (and other) characters – some of them politicians, some lawyers and many both – and their careers and ideas to the book's readers, on the basis that the personal is not just political but also constitutional.

[1] [1930] 31 SR (NSW) 183 (New South Wales Supreme Court); [1931] CLR 394 (High Court of Australia); [1932] AC 526 (Privy Council).

[2] 1952 (2) 428 (AD).

[3] (1999) *By due process of law? Racial discrimination and the right to vote in South Africa.*

However, in the final chapter of this volume, I have returned to the contemporary British context, and drawn on the study of *McCawley* and *Trethowan* and their various contexts to revisit arguments as to the legal possibility and political desirability of entrenching certain moral values within our constitutional law. That is done, I should say, in the spirit of inviting discussion rather than proposing a solution. That final chapter does assume that readers have at least a rudimentary familiarity with the basic principles of British constitutional law. For the benefit of those who do not, I have occasionally made reference to passages in my own constitutional law textbook to offer some background explanation of the matters being discussed.

I do not doubt that there are errors in the text, arising from the inadequacies of my own research or understanding; and such errors are, of course, entirely my responsibility.

Ian Loveland
London, 2020

ACKNOWLEDGEMENTS

This is the second part of a two-volume study, the first part being: *McCawley and Trethowan – a study of the chaos of politics and the integrity of law: Volume 1 – McCawley.* As in that first volume, I would like to record my thanks to Kate Whetter at Hart Publishing for commissioning the project; to Professors George Williams and Sean Brennan for hosting me as a Visiting Professor at the School of Law at the University of New South Wales in July 2019, a visit which gave me the opportunity to consult a wider range of primary and secondary sources than are available in London; and to Professor Anne Twomey for offering me her insights into certain aspects of my research. Thanks are also owed to the Robert Menzies Bicentennial Fund at King's College London, which graciously provided a grant towards the cost of that visit. I must also record my gratitude to the law library staff at City, especially Conor Jackson and Robert Hodgson, who have been unfailingly helpful in responding to my requests for assistance in tracking down obscure source materials.

BRIEF CONTENTS

DETAILED CONTENTS

ABBREVIATIONS

BC	*Brisbane Courier* (newspaper)
CAG	Commonwealth of Australia Gazette
HCD	House of Commons Debates
HLD	House of Lords Debates
HRA	*Historical Records of Australia*
HRD	House of Representatives Debates
JRAHS	*Journal of the Royal Australian Historical Society*
JRHSQ	*Journal of the Royal Historical Society of Queensland*
LD	*Labour Daily* (newspaper)
NSWLAD	New South Wales Legislative Assembly Debates
NSWLC	New South Wales Legislative Council Debates
ODNB	*Oxford Dictionary of National Biography*
QGG	Queensland Government Gazette
QLAD	Queensland Legislative Assembly Debates
QLCD	Queensland Legislative Council Debates
SAR	*South Australian Register* (newspaper)
SMH	*Sydney Morning Herald* (newspaper)
SD	Senate Debates
VPLA (NSW)	Votes and Proceedings of the Legislative Assembly (of New South Wales)
VPLC (NSW)	Votes and Proceedings of the Legislative Council (of New South Wales)

TABLE OF CASES

New South Wales

Queensland

Australia

Canada

European Community/Union

South Africa

United Kingdom

TABLE OF LEGISLATION

New South Wales

Queensland

Australia

United Kingdom

[1] Strictu sensu this is of course a United Kingdom statute and is categorised as such in vol 1. I have treated it here as (by 1930) Australia's indigenous constitution.

1

The Immediate Political Roots of the *Trethowan* Controversy

> I had made the mistake of allowing the personal friends and relatives of Labor politicians to be nominated. Some of them were not, in fact, Labor men and never had been. The result was that there were defections when the test came, and we were defeated …
>
> Jack Lang, Premier of New South Wales, on his failed 1926 attempt to abolish the Legislative Council

The entrenchment argument which had been fought out so bitterly in Queensland in the first two decades of the twentieth century was revisited shortly afterwards in New South Wales. The heart of that dispute lay in large part in the cut and thrust of party politics between a faction-ridden Labour Party led by Jack Lang and a Nationalist/Country Party coalition headed by Sir Thomas Rainsford Bavin, and in particular in the very different views taken by those two politicians and their respective parties of the proper role of the Legislative Council within the state's governmental system.

I. Fact and Faction in New South Wales Party Politics During the First World War and its Aftermath

Billy Hughes's departure from the national Labour Party over conscription was mirrored in New South Wales by the state's sometime Premier, William Holman.[1] Born in London in 1871, the son of actor parents, Holman emigrated to Sydney as a teenager. He worked as an apprentice cabinetmaker, combining his trade with great enthusiasm for literature, the arts and radical politics. He formed a close relationship with Hughes, both joining the nascent Labour Party and showing flair for oratory and organising. Holman's political ambitions were almost derailed by a fraud conviction in 1896 arising from his connection with a newspaper, *The Daily Post*, but the conviction was subsequently overturned.[2] Two years later, Holman was elected to the Assembly. Vigorously active as a politician, Holman also qualified for the Bar, and built a small practice focused mainly

[1] http://adb.anu.edu.au/biography/holman-william-arthur-6713. The most substantial biography is Evatt (1940) *Australian Labour leader*.

[2] Evatt (1940) op cit ch 13.

on trade union clients.[3] Holman had not supported federation, and after 1901 directed his energies to state politics. He became deputy leader of the state party in 1905.

Much as the Queensland Labour Party had used its growing Assembly representation to press non-Labour governments to promote reformist legislation, the New South Wales Labour Party also successfully exploited the balance of power it held while a minority party in the 1890s and early 1900s:

> Hughes and Holman … played off the Free Traders against the Protectionists to see which would give the greater concessions in return for support in Parliament … They were great days. Reform after reform went on the statute book. They were all obtained at the point of the pistol … They forced the Dibbs government to abolish plural voting. From Reid they obtained a Factories Act, a Coal Mines Regulation Act providing for daily inspections and abolition of female and boy labour on the pits, an Immigration Act and other reforms.[4]

Labour's election to government in New South Wales lagged slightly behind its Queensland counterpart. The party was the official opposition after the 1904 and 1907 Assembly elections, and then – led by James McGowen – secured a majority of two in the (90-seat) Assembly in 1910. McGowen had the unusual distinction of having been born at sea as his parents emigrated to Australia from Lancashire.[5] A boilermaker by trade, McGowen's active trade unionism led him into electoral politics and he was among the first wave of Labour Assembly members elected in 1891. McGowen became leader in 1894. While diligent, McGowen was not especially gifted as either a policy strategist or parliamentary tactician. A kindly biographer suggests that McGowen's: "honesty and loyalty more than counterbalanced his lack of brilliance".[6] Despite his limitations, McGowen remained party leader for almost 20 years.

By 1910, Hughes was striding the national stage and Holman was visibly the power behind McGowen's throne. Holman was largely responsible for the government's legislative programme, most notably – an initiative which solidified his standing with the trade unions and enhanced his own leadership ambitions – the Industrial Arbitration Act 1912, which inter alia empowered the courts to fix wage rates, working hours and other employment conditions in a wide range of industries.[7] Holman succeeded McGowen as party leader and Premier in 1913, and led Labour to a resounding 49–28 success over the Liberals in the 1913 election. While Holman's political ideology on many social and economic policy matters remained firmly on the centre-left, those concerns were increasingly overshadowed by matters arising from the war, to the extent that Holman – infuriating many members of the Labour caucus – essentially abandoned the reformist economic programme on which the election was fought.[8]

[3] ibid ch 23. Holman was Higgins's junior in *Railway Servants*; vol 1 pp 195–96.

[4] Lang (1956) *I remember* pp 27–28.

[5] http://adb.anu.edu.au/biography/mcgowen-james-sinclair-7360. McGowen was unflatteringly described by Jack Lang as: 'indolent by nature and quite happy to allow others to do his thinking"; Lang (1956) *I remember* p27. The 'others' Lang had in mind were primarily Holman and (before 1901) Hughes.

[6] Bede Nairn at http://adb.anu.edu.au/biography/mcgowen-james-sinclair-7360.

[7] Evatt (1940) *Australian Labour leader* pp 297–99.

[8] Evatt (1940) op cit p351 records: "The Assembly failed to carry the following Bills past their initial stages: the Eight Hours Bill, the Fair Rents Bill, the Mines Inspection Bill, the Police Appeal Bill, the Shearers' Accommodation Bill and the state Fire Insurance Bill"; more generally, see ibid chs 67–68.

Table 1.1 New South Wales House of Assembly elections 1904–17

Year	Party	% vote	Seats won	Change
1904	Liberal	44.5	45	
	Progressives[a]	18.5	16	
	Australian Labour Party	23.0	25	
	Independent Liberal	4.6	1	
	Independent	3.0	8	
1907[b]	Liberal	45.5	45	
	Progressives[c]	–	–	
	Australian Labour Party	32.9	32	
	Independent Liberal	10.7	8	
	Independent	10.7	4	
	Independent Labour	0.5	1	
1910	Liberal	42.0	37	–8
	Australian Labour Party	51.1	46	+14
	Independent Liberal	6.9	6	–2
	Independent	1.5	1	–3
	Farmers Party	0.7	–	
1913	Liberal	32.8	28	–9
	Australian Labour Party	46.6	49	+3
	Independent Liberal	3.1	–	–6
	Independent	1.5	1	–
	Farmers Party[d]	13.3	11	+11
	Independent Labour	1.4	1	+1
1917	Nationalists[e]	47.4	52	+13
	Australian Labour Party	42.9	33	–16
	Independent Labour	3.6	1	–
	Independent	4.1	3	+3

[a] The 'Progressives' can best be described as the vestiges of the former Free Traders.
[b] The Assembly was reduced to 90 seats (from 125) for the 1907 election (vol 1 pp 205–206) and I have therefore omitted any 'change' figure for that election.
[c] The 'Progressives' disappeared as a distinct party, most of their members joining the Liberals.
[d] I have included the vote share and single seat won by the Country Party in the Farmers Party figures.
[e] For the purposes of the 'change' column, I have treated the 'Nationalists' as the Liberals + the Farmers, albeit that some Nationalist MPs were Holmanite 'rats' from the Labour Party.

Holman also antagonised many Labour Assembly members and party activists by refusing to nominate any party supporters to the Council, even though the opposition majority there blocked many measures which Labour put to the electorate in 1913:

> Without doubt, Holman had been given a clear popular mandate to carry these proposals into effect. Yet one by one they were defeated in the Upper House or not even carried to finality in the Assembly. The list included: the Bakery Bill, the Baking Hours Bill … the Early Closing Bill … the Industrial Arbitration bill, the Police Appeal bill, the Rural Tenants bill, the Shearers Accommodation bill, the Trades Union Amendment bill and the Workers Compensation Amendment bill.[9]

Holman's refusal was seemingly rooted in personal pique. He had promised a financial supporter (Hugh McIntosh – a newspaper entrepeneur) that he would appoint McIntosh to the Council should he become Premier. Before Holman became Premier, the state Labour Party amended its internal rules to require that nominees be approved by the state Executive and indicated that only party members would receive approval. McIntosh was not a party member nor willing to become one. Both Holman and the Executive displayed remarkable stubbornness over the issue, with the result that Labour's legislative programme was substantially curtailed.

The McIntosh dispute much weakened Holman's party position. But by the next state election in 1917, the conscription split had occurred, and Holman, while still Premier, had – like Hughes in the national arena – led many former Labour legislators into (yet another) fusion with the former 'Liberals' to create a state branch of the Nationalist Party.[10] McGowen, expelled from the state Labour Party for supporting conscription, was among them; on losing his Assembly seat in 1917, he was rewarded by Holman with a Council appointment.[11]

Holman's 'National' Government(s)

Holman conducted negotiations with the Liberals assuming that if he led a new party with an Assembly majority he could offer the Governor his resignation as Premier of a Labour government and be promptly reappointed as Premier in a National Party administration. To Holman's astonishment, however, the Governor, Sir Gerald Strickland,[12] indicated that while he would accept Holman's resignation, he would not reappoint Holman as Premier. Strickland's reasoning was that Holman now led a party with no electoral legitimacy, so the appropriate course was dissolution and a new election.

Holman subsequently pleaded his case directly to the Colonial Office, and persuaded the British government to order Strickland to accept him as Premier. The British intervention was ostensibly hard to reconcile with the by then supposedly firm convention that internal colony controversies should be resolved internally, but, given the wartime context, such action is perhaps unsurprising. More surprising was the British government's instruction to Strickland that he should assent to a bill promoted by Holman's

[9] Evatt (1940) op cit p356.

[10] ibid ch 58 provides an illuminating account of Holman's thoughts and actions on the issue.

[11] http://adb.anu.edu.au/biography/mcgowen-james-sinclair-7360.

[12] Strickland, a Cambridge-educated barrister and soldier, was also a Maltese Count, and spent his early life in Malta. He was successively Governor of the Leeward Islands, Tasmania and Western Australia, before becoming Governor of New South Wales in 1915; http://adb.anu.edu.au/biography/strickland-sir-gerald-8700.

new government to delay the 1916 Assembly election for a year.[13] Holman had feared losing an election while voters' memories of his manoeuvrings were still fresh. The fears were ill-founded; Holman led the Nationalists to a convincing victory in 1917, winning 52 seats to Labour's 33.

As a Nationalist Premier, Holman immediately used the Council to bolster his popularity among his new allies and the former Labour politicians who had ratted with him. He prevailed upon Strickland to appoint 23 new councillors in 1917 (including one Hugh McIntosh). Given that the Council then contained only a tiny minority of Labour nominees, there could be no justification for such appointments on the basis that the Council was improperly obstructing the elected government's policy programme. Strickland was effectively sacked as Governor by the British government shortly afterwards in 1917,[14] and replaced by Sir Walter Davison, a career civil servant previously Governor of the Seychelles and of Newfoundland.[15]

The Storey and Dooley-led Labour Parties

Following Holman's expulsion from the state Labour Party, leadership passed to John Storey. Holman took 23 of the party's 47 Assembly members (including most of the Cabinet) with him in the split, which presented significant opportunities for advancement to the remaining 24.[16] Born in New South Wales in 1869, Storey initially worked as a boilermaker. An active trade unionist, Storey joined the state Labour Party in 1891 and was elected to the Assembly in 1901. Storey's opposition to conscription and personal antipathy towards Holman meant he did not serve in Holman's Cabinet, which left him well placed after the conscription split to be elected leader in 1917. Labour's defeat at the 1917 election was hardly unexpected, and Storey retained the leadership, steadily increasing his own and his party's popularity and winning a tiny Assembly majority (which included Holman's seat) in 1920.[17]

As Premier, Storey invoked Holman's mass nomination of new Council members as a precedent to persuade Davidson to appoint 16 Labour nominees. The appointments still left the Labour Party in a substantial minority. In late 1921, the Council had 82 members: only 24 formally took the Labour whip. Nor could Storey be entirely confident as to where the ideological loyalties of those 24 actually lay.

Storey's leadership was marked by yet another schism within the state Labour Party. The members who united – albeit briefly – over conscription now divided over the proper relationship between trade union militancy and parliamentary democracy as to the route

[13] Both episodes are closely examined in Evatt (1936) *The King and his Dominion Governors* ch xvii. Evatt – writing from his then seat on the High Court (p 68 below) – suggests that the British intervention was an improper interference with Strickland's discretion and was driven simply by anti-Labour bias; ibid, especially pp 151–52.

[14] Evatt (1940) op cit pp 194–95: Lang (1956) op cit ch 16. Strickland returned to Malta, founded a new political party and served as Prime Minister between 1927 and 1932.

[15] http://adb.anu.edu.au/biography/davidson-sir-walter-edward-5904.

[16] Nairn op cit pp 38–39.

[17] Labour had 43 seats, as did the informal Nationalist/Progressive coalition, leaving four Independents holding the balance of power. Storey persuaded an independently minded Nationalist, Daniel Levy, to accept the Speakership, which left Labour with a nominal majority of one.

to political progress: the 'convulsions' triggered by Hughes and Holman's defections in 1917 had evidently not been traumatic enough to convince its remaining members of the benefits of maintaining a stable internal identity. Tom Ryan and Ted Theodore had succeeded in uniting the state Labour Party in Queensland to a greater extent than their counterparts had managed in New South Wales. Indeed, to talk of 'a' Labour Party in New South Wales in the early 1920s is misleading in anything but the most formal of senses.[18]

This was partly a consequence of the party's (reflecting the country's) federal structure. The New South Wales and national parties were formally distinct organisations. Similarly, within New South Wales, the party executive and its parliamentary caucus were also discrete bodies, with limited overlaps of personnel and ideology. Notionally, the state party's annual conference was its 'sovereign' in terms of setting policy, choosing its leaders[19] and deciding all the party's administrative rules, including such matters as the composition of the party Executive and the selection of Assembly candidates, the latter task in 1920 being primarily controlled by local constituency associations ('leagues').

It is similarly misleading to speak of *a* 'trade union' influence within the New South Wales Labour Party. More accurately – if still crudely – three distinct union factions jostled for power. To the right[20] – and in 1920 wielding a controlling influence on the party Executive – was the large Australian Workers Union (AWU), in which Theodore was so influential. A second grouping, hostile to the AWU, coalesced around the Miner's Federation, led in the early 1920s by Albert Willis. Willis was born in 1876 in Wales, where he worked as a miner and mines trade union official, acted as a lay preacher and was elected to his local county council. He emigrated to New South Wales in 1911, joined the state Labour Party and rapidly became active in mining union circles. Willis saw the mining unions rather than the AWU as the natural leaders of a 'One Big Union' movement which would pursue an industrial rather than parliamentary road towards socialism,[21] and was briefly expelled from the Labour Party as the Miners Federation jostled for prominence with the AWU. Willis's faction regained sufficient influence for him to be readmitted to the party in 1922; his importance grew from 1924 onwards, when he became chairman of the party's official paper, the *Labour Daily*.[22] A third faction was rooted in the New South Wales Trades Council, a cluster of small unions – the so-called 'Trades Hall Reds' – closely linked with the Communist Party and led by Jock Garden, a man demonised constantly by much of the New South Wales press. Garden was a mercurial figure, who successively held many apparently incompatible leftist political beliefs. He was a Scots émigré, and variously in Australia a sailmaker, Methodist minister, trade union activist and prospective Labour political candidate. In the early 1920s, however, having spent time in Moscow, where he met Lenin, Garden had contributed to founding the Australian Communist Party, where his activities

[18] What follows is a simplistic summary. Nairn (1995) *The "big fella": Jack Lang and the Australian Labor Party, 1891–1949* provides a thorough, authoritative account.

[19] Conference then elected both the leader of the parliamentary party and Cabinet members (albeit that the leader could allocate Cabinet portfolios as he thought fit).

[20] I use the term guardedly.

[21] On the 'One Big Union' movement in Australia – and its various factions – see inter alia Ward (1978) *The history of Australia: the twentieth century 1901–1975* pp 77–78: Nairn (1995) op cit pp 21–25; in respect specifically of Lang's career, see Hagan (1977) 'Lang and the unions' in Radi and Spearritt (eds), *Jack Lang*; Dixson (1971) 'Ideology, the trades hall reds and J T Lang' *Politics* 53.

[22] http://adb.anu.edu.au/biography/willis-albert-charles-9122.

fuelled concerns among more centrist elements of the Labour Party about the prospect of covert communist infiltration.[23]

The New South Wales Labour Party of the early 1920s was an entity in which fragmented organisational structures coexisted with myriad ideological positions and a bewildering melange of personalities, many driven as much by personal rivalries as by coherent political visions. Storey had little success in building party unity in this context. However, his tenure as leader was short-lived. He died in October 1921, having suffered for many years from a debilitating kidney condition. He was succeeded by James Dooley.[24] Dooley, Irish by birth, had worked as a tailor and involved himself in both trade union and Labour Party activity from the 1890s onwards. He was elected to the Assembly in 1907. He had opposed conscription, was elected as Deputy Leader in 1916 after the Holmanites were expelled and served as Treasurer in Storey's administration. Dooley's leadership was marked by even more bitter party infighting than occurred in the Storey era. He was repeatedly attacked from the left on economic policy and trade union issues. Given its internal fragmentation, it is little wonder that Labour lost the 1922 election,[25] to a Nationalist Party which had tempted some former Progressive members to join a formal coalition.

That coalition had no place for Holman, however, who, after his 1920 election defeat, had moved to practise at the English Bar, harbouring unrealised ambitions to be adopted as a parliamentary candidate by the Liberals or Conservatives.[26] The new government was led by Sir George Fuller, a Sydney born and educated barrister first elected to the Assembly in 1889 as a Free Trader. He sat in the Commonwealth Parliament between 1901 and 1913, and served as a minister under Deakin. Fuller returned to the Assembly in 1915, and was a key player in the negotiations leading to the creation of Holman's Nationalist administration.[27]

Table 1.2 New South Wales House of Assembly elections, 1920 (20 March 1920) and 1922 (25 March 1922)

Year	Party	% vote	Seats won	Change
1920	Labour	43.0	43	+10
	Nationalist	29.9	28	–24
	Progressive	15.0	15	+15
	Independent	6.7	3	–
	Socialist	1.0	1	+1
1922	Nationalist/Progressive	43.1	41	+13
	Labour	38.5	36	–7
	Progressive	11.0	9	–6
	Independent	5.3	3	–
	Democrat	1.7	1	+1

[23] See especially Farrell (1977) 'Dealing with the communists 1923–136' in Radi and Spearritt op cit; Nairn (1995) op cit ch 3. On Garden generally, see http://adb.anu.edu.au/biography/garden-john-smith-jock-6274.
[24] http://adb.anu.edu.au/biography/dooley-james-thomas-6000.
[25] A year later, Theodore had led the Queensland party to take 43 of the Assembly's 72 seats; vol 1 p 338.
[26] Evatt (1940) op cit chs 69 and 71.
[27] http://adb.anu.edu.au/biography/fuller-sir-george-warburton-6256.

A Judicial Clarification of Commonwealth–State Constitutional Relations?

Fuller's government was the unsuccessful party in a constitutionally significant 1923 High Court judgment. The prosaic question in *Commonwealth v New South Wales*[28] was whether the Commonwealth government should succeed in a negligence action against the New South Wales government for damage caused to a Commonwealth boat by a New South Wales vessel. The larger constitutional matter Fuller's government raised was whether the High Court had jurisdiction even to hear the claim without the state's consent. The issue turned on the meaning of the Constitution Act 1901 s.75. Prima facie, the text of s.75 (which identified the court's original jurisdiction) indicated that state consent was not required. The relevant subsection (s.75(iii)) provided simply that the High Court would have original jurisdiction, inter alia, in cases: "in which the Commonwealth, or a person suing or being sued on behalf of the Commonwealth, is a party".

The primary premise on which New South Wales relied was that Australian states were 'sovereign' entities in the same sense as nations, and since, as a principle of international law, a nation could not be sued in another nation's courts without its consent, neither could a state be sued in the High Court without its consent. Fuller's government accepted that this was only an interpretive presumption as to the Constitution's meaning, but it was a presumption rebuttable only by the most explicit of textual provisions; ie s.75 would expressly have to have provided that a state could be sued without its consent.

The broader principle which New South Wales was pressing was that because the states were 'sovereign' entities, the Constitution should always be construed – save where the text made it plainly impossible to do so – in a fashion which maximised the respective states' political autonomy. If offered to Samuel Griffith's court (especially prior to Isaac Isaacs and Henry Higgins's appointment in 1906), that proposition would perhaps not have been outlandish.[29] That was perhaps exemplified by Griffith's comment in *D'Emden* that when construing the Constitution the courts should recognise that a state was: "sovereign … within the ambit of its authority".[30] From a legal perspective, this was a remarkably silly observation when it was made, resting on a peculiar equation of sovereignty with mere autonomy. But, given the Court's conclusion and reasoning in *Engineers* in 1920,[31] it is unsurprising that the state's contention received short shrift in the majority (Isaacs, George Rich and Hayden Starke) judgment:[32]

> It may be convenient to refer first to the assertion (which is at the root of the defendant's contention) that an Australian State is a 'sovereign State' … There are two fallacies involved in this. The first is that there is any analogy whatever between the position of the "representative" of a foreign State and that of one of the states of Australia …
>
> New South Wales is not a foreign country. The people of New South Wales are not, as are, for instance, the people of France, a distinct and separate people from the people of Australia. The Commonwealth includes the people of New South Wales as they are united with their

[28] (1923) 32 CLR 200.
[29] Vol 1 pp 172–96.
[30] *D'Emden v Pedder* (1904) 1 CLR 91, 109; vol 1 p 186.
[31] *Amalgamated Society of Engineers v Adelaide Steamship Co Ltd* (1920) 28 CLR 129; vol 1 pp 182–85.
[32] Knox and Higgins concurred for different reasons in separate opinions.

> fellow Australians as one people for the higher purposes of common citizenship, as created by the Constitution. When the Commonwealth is present in Court as a party, the people of New South Wales cannot be absent ...[33]

The majority was equally clear that there was no proper basis to assume that constitutional interpretation should be shaped by a presumption that states should be regarded as somehow equivalent to 'sovereign' entities:

> The conclusion to which we were invited to come in interpreting the Constitution upon the assumption that New South Wales is a "sovereign State" would be both 'mischievous and unfounded'. The term "sovereign State" as applied to constituent States is not strictly correct even in America since the severance from Great Britain ... Still further from the truth is it in Australia. The appellation "sovereign State" as applied to the construction of the Commonwealth Constitution is entirely out of place, and worse than unmeaning.[34]

Although the majority did not spell their reasoning out expressly, the implication is obvious.

While states as colonial governmental entities pre-dated 'Australia's' creation as a colony, they were not sovereign then; sovereign power lay with the British Parliament. The effect of the 1900 Act was that Australian states were now subordinate entities at two levels: firstly, to the terms of the 1900 Act and then – as were the 'national' governmental entities created by that Act – to the sovereignty of the British Parliament. Consequently, there could be no justification for departing from the plain meaning of the Act's text when determining the respective limits of state and national governmental power. The 'sovereign state' might exist in the realm of political rhetoric or popular imagination, but it had no place in Australia's constitutional law, and could not unless the Constitution was amended (whether per s.128 or by the British Parliament).

II. Jack Lang and the New South Wales Labour 'Party' in the Early- to Mid-1920s

Following Labour's 1922 election defeat, Dooley was removed as Leader by the party's state Executive in early 1923, but retained the support of the majority of his Assembly colleagues. He was reinstated in June 1923 after intervention by the national party Executive, but was sufficiently wearied by Labour's constant intra-party factionalism to resign later that year. His resignation opened the door for a new party leader; a man for whom 'state sovereignty' was – for reasons both of principle and pragmatism – an article of fundamental political faith.

Jack Lang,[35] like many Labour contemporaries, rose from impoverished beginnings to a position of middle-class affluence (as an estate agent and property developer

[33] (1923) 32 CLR 200, 209.

[34] ibid 210.

[35] I am indebted to Bede Nairn's analysis of Lang's career, (1995) op cit and to the essays in Radi and Spearritt op cit. Nairn is a far from sympathetic biographer. Lang has offered his own autobiographical accounts of his career, although on Nairn's view Lang's attachment to historical truth is tenuous. See also the comment by

rather than a lawyer),[36] and climbed the ranks of the state Labour Party through assiduous construction of a party machine. Elected Mayor of the Sydney suburb of Auburn in 1909, Lang was returned as Assembly member for Granville in 1913,[37] the year Holman had become leader. Lang's initial speeches and activities placed him notably to Holman's left on economic issues and Australia's war involvement, and there is no indication that he ever contemplated leaving the party to join Holman and Hughes following the conscription split.[38] The defection of some party members to the Nationalists provided Lang with the opportunity to advance his own party prospects; he garnered sufficient support among his colleagues and in the party at large to serve as Treasurer in the Storey and Dooley administrations in the early 1920s. In that office he acquired a reputation for fiscal prudence, and exhibited an overriding concern to produce a balanced budget. Initially rooting his popular support in the local leagues and Willis's union faction, Lang became leader of the state party in opposition in 1923 following Dooley's resignation.

Storey and Dooley's experiences suggest one should use the term 'Leader' of the 1920s New South Wales Labour Party cautiously. The extent of the party's fragmentation is nicely caught by Perks:

> Throughout the life of the Storey/Dooley governments NSW Labour displayed a conspicuous inability to contain its factional conflict. Once [the party was] relieved of office these problems mounted until eventually the whole movement was convulsed.[39]

Lang's leadership bid in 1923 indicated he could chart a successful course through the party's factional infighting. He ran on a combined ticket, with a more right-leaning colleague, Peter Loughlin, as his proposed deputy.[40] Although falling well short of gaining unanimous support from the caucus, Lang's eventual victory by 21 votes to 11 (and Loughlin's by 17–13) is testament to his ability (at that time) to garner support across factional lines,[41] particularly from Willis and the Miners Federation (Lang was later to have Willis appointed to the Council and to a post in Cabinet, Willis having by this point become distinctly less optimistic about the 'One Big Union' route to political reform) and within local party organisations.

Perks: "As for all Lang's memoirs, his own account of himself requires cautious handling"; Perks (1977) 'The rise to leadership' in Radi and Spearitt (1977) *Jack Lang*. I have nonetheless made frequent resort to Lang's own accounts in (1956) *I remember*; (1962) *The great bust*; (1970) *The turbulent years*. As my own journey through writing these books has progressed, I have found that Lang's accounts have acquired increasing credibility.

[36] Manning Clark's assertion ((1993) *History of Australia* p488 that Lang: "amassed a small fortune" is likely an exaggeration.

[37] Spearritt (1977) 'The auburn plute' in Radi and Spearritt op cit.

[38] His account is at Lang (1956) op cit pp 63–65.

[39] Perks (1977) 'The rise to leadership' in Radi and Spearritt op cit.

[40] Loughlin, born in rural New South Wales in 1882, was a police constable's son. He worked initially as a teacher, joined the Labour Party and won an Assembly seat on an anti-conscription basis in 1917. Loughlin became Minister for Lands in Storey's government, and in office and subsequently in opposition became an inveterate, almost obsessive, opponent of communist influence in the party; http://adb.anu.edu.au/biography/loughlin-peter-ffrench-7239.

[41] The manoeuvrings preceding the leadership election are recounted in Nairn (1995) op cit pp 55–60.

The Lang-led Labour Party in opposition from 1923 to 1925 staked out a clearly social democratic policy programme. Both Lang and Willis were consistently and staunchly anti-communist in political outlook, and it seems the voters in the 1925 election had few qualms about returning Lang – revelling in the populist nickname of 'the Big Fella'[42] – to power, albeit with only a two-seat majority.

Table 1.3 New South Wales Legislative Assembly election, 1925 (30 May 1925)

Party	% vote	Seats won	Change
Nationalist	37.0	32	–9
Independent Nationalist	0.6	1	+1
Progressives[a]	11.5	9	–
Australian Labour Party	47.0	46	+10
Protestant Labour	2.1	1	+1
Independent		0	–3

[a] Shortly to rename itself the Country Party.

Lang's electoral success was not repeated by the Labour Party in the (November) 1925 Commonwealth elections. Despite securing a larger share of the total vote than the Nationalists, Labour support (23 seats) was skewed in a fashion that left the Nationalists much the largest party in the House; albeit that, with only 37 of the 75 seats, they would need either formal or informal support from the Country Party (14 seats) to govern. In the Senate, the Nationalists retained their overwhelming majority, with 25 of the 36 seats.

Labour's 1925 national defeat left Lang as one of the party's most important players. That position was strengthened by Theodore's failure to win a Queensland House seat in the 1925 election. Like Ryan before him, Theodore had decided that it was time for him to play on a larger stage.[43] His defeat in the 1925 election was unexpected. Theodore's subsequent decision to leave Queensland and cultivate a safe Labour seat in New South Wales opened yet another fissure in Labour factionalism in both the New South Wales and national fields. It took Theodore over a year to find such a seat, but in January 1927 the sitting Labour member for Dalley retired, Theodore secured the nomination and was returned in a by-election.[44] The next year, allegations surfaced that Theodore's supporters had bribed the previous member to retire (the alleged bribe being the then large sum of £8000).[45] The Stanley Bruce government established a judicial commission to investigate the charge. The commission concluded that the charge could not be proven. The slur nevertheless cast over Theodore's personal integrity was however to become a recurring theme.

[42] A descriptor which spoke to his (atypically large) physical size as well as his political ambition.
[43] The post-Theodore state party succeeded in winning 43 (of 72) Assembly seats in the 1926 state election.
[44] See generally Fitzgerald (1995) *"Red Ted": the life of E.G. Theodore* pp 175–78.
[45] ibid pp 206–15.

Table 1.4 The 1925 Commonwealth election (14 November 1925)

House of Representatives	% vote	Seats won	Change
Nationalists	42.5	37	+6
Country	10.7	14	–
Labour	45.0	23	–6
Liberal[a]	–	–	–
Independent	1.7	1	–
Senate[b]			
Nationalists	45.3	25	+1
Labour	45.0	8	–4
Country	9.4	3	+3

[a] I have treated the 1922 'Liberal' candidates as 1925 Nationalists for the purposes of the change column.
[b] 22 seats contested.

For both personal and ideological reasons, Lang and Theodore became foes rather than friends. Both had ambitions to lead the national party, and neither had or ever would develop the capacity to smooth over rather than exacerbate the constant factional infighting that characterised Labour politics in that era. At this point, their relations remained cordial. Theodore had actively campaigned for Lang in the 1925 state election, eliciting both thanks and an invitation to continue his good works.[46] Theodore, both as Premier and Ryan's Treasurer, had achieved considerable legislative success in Queensland, not least in being the first Premier to achieve the long-standing Labour policy of abolishing a Legislative Council. He presented Lang with a hard act to follow.

Shortly after the 1925 election, leadership of the New South Wales Nationalists passed to Thomas Bavin. Bavin,[47] born in 1874 in New Zealand, pursued a multi-lateral career as a barrister (taking his LLB at the University of Sydney),[48] academic lawyer, journalist and political activist. He became remarkably well connected politically at an early age; he served (when 27) as Edmund Barton's private Secretary when Barton was Prime Minister, and held the same post under Alfred Deakin. Having begun his formal political career in the Progressive party, Bavin won an Assembly seat for the Nationalists in 1917. Although a conscriptionist, Bavin was no admirer of Holman; he quit the Nationalists to return to the Progressives shortly after being elected and was returned as a Progressive in the 1920 election. He subsequently served as Attorney-General in Fuller's merged Progressive/Nationalist government, before becoming party leader in 1925 when in opposition.

[46] ibid p181.
[47] http://adb.anu.edu.au/biography/bavin-sir-thomas-rainsford-tom-86.
[48] He was Isaacs's junior in *Railway Servants*; vol 1 pp 195–96.

The First Lang Government's Policy Programme – And the Legislative Council's Response

Lang's government swept into office intent on implementing a wide-ranging package of progressive social policy reform. Lang promptly removed New South Wales from the Loan Council, considering that the arrangement was in principle threatening to the autonomy of the states and in practice would preclude his government seeking new sources of domestic and overseas finance.[49] Lang consistently portrayed the issue of autonomy as one of 'Sovereignty'; ie New South Wales was a 'Sovereign State' and as such should be immune from either Commonwealth or British control. The High Court's recent conclusion that such nomenclature was 'mischievous and unfounded' was not one that Lang was willing to embrace.[50]

The Lang government's legislative programme included archetypally social democratic welfare and labour relations measures, and also the traditional Labour commitment to abolish – as achieved in Queensland – the Legislative Council.[51] For the first few months of the government's life, the Council was generally acquiescent towards government bills, the majority of members accepting the premise that they could not legitimately block measures clearly put before the electorate in 1925. The government's 44 hours week bill was its most significant industrial relations initiative. The measure was enacted as the Forty-Four Hours Week Act 1925. It was applicable to many industries, and modified (Holman's) Industrial Arbitration Act 1912[52] by imposing the 44 hours maximum as a legislative fiat, rather than simply enabling a court to provide for 44 hours maximum as part of an arbitration award.

The government also secured prompt enactment of the Widows Pension Act 1925. The Act (s.14) set the pension at £1 per week for the widow, plus 10s per week per dependent child under 14.[53] Lang recalled his primary motivation for supporting the measure was his memory of the extreme poverty he had witnessed as a child.[54] Bavin had not voiced any principled objection to the bill at first reading, beyond making the general point that the Lang government's 'humanitarian' policies were being pursued without proper regard being given to their cost.[55] Despite Bavin's moderate stance, and the relative modesty of Lang's proposal, the bill was attacked with apocalyptic hysteria

[49] Lang (1956) op cit ch 46.

[50] Pp 8–9 above.

[51] For an illuminating analysis, see Nelson (1977) 'Legislative record 1925–27. How radical?' in Radi and Spearritt op cit.

[52] P 2 above.

[53] The pension was not a universal benefit. The Act (consistent with Labour's White Australia sentiments) excluded, inter alia, per s.3(3), a widow if "… (e) she is an alien; or (f) she is an Asiatic and was not born in Australia; or (g) she is an aboriginal native of Africa, the Islands of the Pacific, or New Zealand" and per s.13(3)(a). The Act was also limited to 'deserving' widows. An applicant would also be excluded if: "the magistrate to whom the claim for a pension is referred is not satisfied that she is of good moral character and sober habits and that the pension will be properly used for the support of herself and her children".

[54] Lang (1956) op cit ch 42.

[55] *NSWLAD* 26 November 1925 p2587.

by some Nationalist members. The most stirring 'critique' came from a Mr Hill, who informed members that:

> … [T]his is the most soul-destroying, poisonous bill which has ever been submitted to this house. It is nothing more or less than Communistic legislation. The Premier states in the press that he has been fighting communism all his life, yet he comes here week after week submitting communistic legislation to this House.
>
> Mr. LANG: That is a very unjust statement![56]

Unjust it may have been, but the 'communist' charge became a recurrent feature of Nationalist critiques of Lang's policies, even though Lang had no empathy with Garden and his 'Trades Hall Reds' faction.[57] The Lang government again faced such accusations when it promoted a worker's compensation scheme, enacted as the Workers Compensation Act 1926, to provide financial support to employees injured at work. Initially it appeared that the legislation would be made unworkable by a cartel-like agreement by most insurance companies to set rates at unsustainably high levels. The government's prompt response – following Ryan's lead[58] – was to provide such insurance through the state's own insurance bureau, at rates affordable to employers and modestly profitable for state revenues.[59]

In January 1926, the Legislature had enacted the Constitution Act Amendment Act 1926, a brief statute, the key part of which was s.2:

> 2. The Constitution Act, 1902, is amended by inserting at the end of section sixteen the following paragraph:–
>
> The word "person" in this section shall be construed as including a woman whether married or unmarried.

S.16 was the provision which controlled eligibility for appointment to the Council, a status hitherto (perhaps) available only to men.[60] It seems unlikely the Lang promoted the measure because he was a man ahead of his time on gender equality issues. He records his primary motivation as the assumption that any female Council members he nominated would be more reliable allies than male appointees.[61]

[56] ibid p2588.

[57] Theodore's Queensland administrations had constantly faced similar accusations; repeated references to Theodore's supposed 'communistic' tendencies made by opposition members in the Assembly and Council during the passage of the abolition bill were a constant rather than atypical feature of Queensland political discourse.

[58] P 270 n 17 above.

[59] Lang's celebratory account is at Lang (1956) op cit ch 45. A Fair Rents (Amendment) Act was passed in February 1926 which empowered local courts to set long-term rents for tenants of both residential and some commercial premises. The measure antagonised many small- and large-scale landlords by both restricting their income and making it more difficult for them to evict tenants.

[60] The 'perhaps' is deployed because that year a legal controversy raged in Canada on whether the word 'persons' in the provisions of the British North America Act 1867 which defined eligibility for appointment to Canada's Senate should be construed to include women as well as men. In *Edwards v Attorney-General for Canada* ([1928] SCR 276) the Canadian Supreme Court had concluded that it should not be so construed, basing its judgment primarily on an 1867 English case which denied women the vote in elections to the Commons (*Chorlton v Lings* (1868) LR 4 COP 374). That judgment was reversed in the Privy Council ([1930] AC 124), then headed by the Labour Lord Chancellor Lord Sankey. Sankey reasoned that while it might have been acceptable in 1867 to construe a prima facie gender-neutral term such as 'persons' to exclude women, such a construction was: "a relic of days more barbarous than ours" (ibid 128) and should not be accepted in 1930.

[61] Lang (1956) op cit pp 296–97.

Lang also took initiatives not requiring legislation and so denied the opposition the chance to obstruct them in the Council. Foremost among them, achievable by a simple majority vote in the Assembly to change its standing orders, was to alter the Assembly's sitting hours from a 4.00 pm start with no fixed finish time to a 10.30 am to 6.00 pm daily session. The change infuriated the Nationalists, who to a much greater extent than Labour were represented by members with outside commercial and business interests for whom the 4.00 pm start time was very accommodating.[62] A second innovation was a simple executive decision to force the resignation of the Treasury Secretary, Bertram Stevens, who Lang both personally disliked and found insufficiently sympathetic to the new government's economic policies.[63]

The Council's initial quiescence towards Lang's legislative programme was likely shaped at least in part by recent events in Queensland. The prospect of abolition achieved by swamping the Council with Labour nominees was an obvious one. Yet it seemed soon to recede from the minds of many Council members. By early 1926 the Council's anti-Labour majority was becoming distinctly less accommodating to government bills,[64] which prompted the Labour caucus to press Lang to follow Theodore's Queensland example and request the Governor to appoint sufficient Labour members to create a majority that would support legislation abolishing the Council altogether.

The 'Constitutionality' of 'Swamping' the Legislative Council

The issue of appointing legislative councillors threw up another nice illustration of the tension between legal form and political reality in New South Wales's constitution. As a matter of law, appointment lay in the gift of the Governor qua representative of the King. As a matter of politics, notions of responsible government suggested the Governor should act in this issue on the advice – and only on the advice – of his ministers. The various *Instructions* provided to successive New South Wales Governors had, however, retained the proviso that had featured in Denison's *Instructions* in 1855 that a Governor might act in opposition to the wishes of his 'Executive Council' when he thought it proper to do so.[65] There was still no legal basis requiring a Governor to accede to a swamping request.

While Lang's Assembly majority was – at best – precarious following the 1925 election, the Labour Party was in a substantial minority in the Council. Only 20 of the 74 members were formally Labour Party members. Given the party's factionalised state, Lang could not count on those 20 members' unwavering support. Of the remaining Council members, a few had no discernible political affiliation, but most were Country Party or Nationalist. Should party lines hold in the Council, there was little prospect of Lang's government having much of its legislative programme enacted. Lang immediately sought appointment for three close allies following the election, including Willis.

[62] Nelson (1977) op cit pp 75–76.

[63] Nairn (1995) op cit pp 98–99: Lang (1956) op cit pp 260–61.

[64] Nairn records government defeats in the Council on local government franchise measures and an abolition of capital punishment bill; Nairn (1995) op cit pp 102–03.

[65] Vol 1 pp 13–14.

He then turned to a larger ambition, indicating to the Governor that he wanted 25 new Labour members.[66]

By the mid-1920s, the phenomenon of mass appointments to the New South Wales Council was hardly a novelty. Cowper had set the precedent in the 1860s. Reid had taken two such initiatives in the 1890s. Holman – on moving to the Nationalists – had sought 20 new members; and Storey had received 16 appointments in 1921 from Davidson.[67] The Governor in 1925 was Sir Dudley de Chair,[68] a career naval officer, appointed in 1923. de Chair was certainly a conservative in the small 'c' sense, and evidently formed a close personal relationship with the then Nationalist Premier, Sir George Fuller. Nairn suggests that de Chair was 'shocked' by Lang's request, and sought guidance from the Colonial Office in London.[69] The then British government declined to intervene.[70]

In 1925, the political reality of appointing New South Wales Council members had a further layer when a Labour government was in power, since the party's (then) rules required that its putative Council representatives be selected (by the party's Assembly caucus) from candidates shortlisted by the state Executive.[71] There was no guarantee for the Premier that either the nominees or the selected candidates would be men[72] to his political liking. Radi's detailed analysis of the shortlisted candidates suggests that few were Lang men in the narrow sense, and not many more could be regarded as sympathetic to Lang's policy agenda.[73]

In Lang's view, the constitutional position was clear. Under a system of responsible government, the Governor should act on the advice of his ministers so long as they enjoyed the support of the elected Assembly; just as the King should act on the advice of his ministers if they had majority Commons support. Since there was nothing in any sense unlawful about a swamping request, the Governor should simply agree to it. That the Governor might consider such a request politically unwise was neither here nor there.

de Chair's evident 'shock' was at the propriety of granting a request that would (or so he thought) swamp the Council and render it a rubber stamp for the Assembly or, even more problematically, lead it to support its own abolition. Theodore's successful pursuit of that strategy in Queensland should presumably have presented de Chair with a 'precedent' pointing to the propriety of him approving Lang's request, but that consideration seemed not to weigh heavily in his mind.[74] After considerable toing and froing

[66] The summary of the episode is taken largely from Radi (1977) 'Lang's legislative councillors' in Radi and Spearritt op cit; Nairn (1995) op cit ch 5.

[67] Vol 1 pp 61–62, 155–56, and this volume p 5 respectively.

[68] http://adb.anu.edu.au/biography/de-chair-sir-dudley-rawson-stratford-5939.

[69] Nairn (1995) op cit p105.

[70] This being Stanley Baldwin's Conservative administration.

[71] The rules accepted that the Leader could nominate small numbers of Councillors on an ad hoc basis, a power Lang used to have Willis appointed; see Nairn (1995) op cit pp 94–95.

[72] Lang did not avail himself of the possibility per the Constitution Act Amendment Act 1926 to propose any female appointees.

[73] Radi op cit pp 104–09.

[74] Perhaps because Theodore had circumvented any difficulty that might be caused by the Governor's own sense of constitutional propriety by the expedient of having Lennon appointed as Lieutenant-Governor in the hiatus between Goold-Adams's departure and Nathan's arrival; vol 1 pp 316–17.

between Lang and de Chair,[75] and correspondence between de Chair and the Secretary of State for the Colonies, who declined to approve any refusal of Lang's request, the Governor appointed the 25 Labour nominees. After these appointments, the Council for the first time had more members (99) than the Assembly (90).[76] On a strict reading of the Colonial Laws Validity Act 1865 (CLVA 1865) s.1, this might mean that New South Wales no longer had a 'representative legislature'.[77] That legalistic point – and its possible future significance – escaped the attention of the players in and observers of the episode. Reaction to the appointments lay more in the realm of their political (in) defensibility.

The 1926 Abolition Bill

The government's Council abolition bill was initially put before the Council in January 1926. However, Lang soon became concerned that 'his' new appointees would not support the bill in sufficient numbers, and the proposal was withdrawn.[78] The resolution of the 'suicide squad'[79] which Theodore had been able to appoint in Queensland was not matched by the New South Wales nominees. After considering its options, the government determined to press the issue, even though it expected to lose the vote. Lang reintroduced the bill to the Council in late February 1926. The measure was defeated 47–44. Several of Lang's 25 appointees absented themselves from the chamber when the crucial division occurred and two more long-standing Labour members voted with the opposition.[80] On Lang's recollection (which perhaps overstates his control over the nomination process):

> I had made the mistake of allowing the personal friends and relatives of Labor politicians to be nominated. Some of them were not, in fact, Labor men and never had been. The result was that there were defections when the test came, and we were defeated.[81]

One biographer has suggested Lang's stance towards the Council and the Governor was designedly (if covertly) duplicitous.[82] An obstructively conservative Council offered some benefits to a Labour Premier whose own political preferences did not reach quite so far to the left as those favoured by other party members. To have what he regarded as overly radical measures blocked or diluted by the Council spared the Premier the

[75] Lang's account of the machinations is at Lang (1956) op cit ch 44.

[76] www.parliament.nsw.gov.au/hansard/Documents/1925–26.pdf pp ix–xi. That had never happened in Queensland, where the Council had 60 members (to the Assembly's 72) when it was abolished.

[77] Vol 1 p 110.

[78] Nairn (1995) op cit pp 104–11 provides an insightfully detailed account of the chain of events.

[79] Vol 1 p 327 n 109.

[80] The absentees were Messers Akhurst, Lyons, Smith and Kelly. For brief biographies see Raadi op cit. The four were expelled from the Labour Party at its subsequent Easter conference; Lang (1956) op cit p298. The two voting against were John Percival, nominated by Storey in 1921, and Francis Bryant, nominated by Holman in 1912. Both promptly joined the Nationalists; www.parliament.nsw.gov.au/members/Pages/member-details.aspx?pk=1135); www.parliament.nsw.gov.au/members/Pages/profiles/percival_john-whitehead.aspx.

[81] Lang (1962) op cit p298.

[82] Nairn (1995) op cit ch 5.

consequences of having to administer a law he did not really support and enabled him to consolidate his position among the party's more extreme elements by laying the blame for their legislative disappointments at the hands of an institution which could readily be portrayed not just as an anti-democratic bastion of domestic conservatism, but also as a relic of imperial domination.

Whether Lang promoted his initial bill hoping that it would fail may never be known for sure. His later recollections of the episode certainly offer no support for that analysis. That he succeeded in having 25 new Labour Council appointees so that his government had a notional majority there would suggest his intentions were genuine.

That assumption is reinforced by immediately subsequent events. After the vote, Lang pressed de Chair to appoint a further 10 Labour nominees. Lang's presumption was that de Chair, in refusing, was acting on instructions from the British government, and so he sent his Attorney-General, Edward McTiernan,[83] to London to lobby the then Secretary of State for the Dominions (Sir Leo Amery in Stanley Baldwin's Conservative government) to instruct de Chair to appoint the additional members. Lang was (and remained) convinced that Baldwin's government was pressing de Chair to refuse the appointment request because Baldwin regarded Lang's economic policy programme as unacceptably radical and saw the Council as a means to block its enactment. Lang took one step to temper his supposedly extremist image in London by appointing Lord Chelmsford, Queensland's Governor during the Kidston era and latterly a member of Ramsay Macdonald's first Labour Cabinet,[84] as the New South Wales Agent-General in London. There is likely some force to Lang's suspicions about British interference in the nomination controversy. Certainly the combined effect of Chelmsford's appointment and McTiernan's lobbying did not prompt British intervention favourable to Lang's position.

The 'constitutional' merits of Lang's second 'swamping' request are less obviously compelling than those of the first. The rationale underpinning the first request rested on the premise that primacy of the elected house demanded that the government, having secured an Assembly majority (and as such being the best representative of the electorate's wishes), should not be prevented from implementing the legislative programme put to the electorate by a Council where it lacked a majority.

Labour's Assembly majority over all other parties after the 1925 election was tiny (46–44). The government's capacity to get bills through the Assembly would demand either support from opposition parties or – in the face of united opposition parties – that

[83] McTiernan, then 33, served as Attorney-General in Storey's government when only 28, an appointment due as much to the dearth of lawyers in the parliamentary party as to his own abilities. McTiernan was the son of Irish émigré parents, his father working as a police constable in Sydney. McTiernan initially worked as a Commonwealth civil servant, and completed BA and LLB studies at Sydney University. McTiernan was unfit for military service, and had the good fortune to be selected by Rich as his assistant on the High Court. McTiernan was called to the Bar in 1916. Having been active in the anti-conscription campaign, he won an Assembly seat in 1920 and was immediately appointed Attorney-General. McTiernan cultivated his legal practice in opposition between 1923 and 1925, but achieved no particular distinction as a lawyer before returning to office. Lang (then) regarded him as an able and loyal, if overly cautious, colleague, and records that he sent McTiernan to London partly to advance McTiernan's political education; Lang (1956) op cit pp 297–301; http://adb.anu.edu.au/biography/mctiernan-sir-edward-aloysius-eddie-14854.

[84] Vol 1 p 214 n 17.

no more than one of its own supporters voted against it. de Chair's appointment of 25 Labour nominees reproduced just that scenario in the Council. Thereafter, the government had a (notional) wafer-thin majority in each house, and its success in a vote would rest on opposition support or unswerving loyalty from all its party members.

The government's defeat on the abolition bill was explicable as a result of its inability to persuade all of its nominal supporters to follow the party line: the government had been given, and had then lost, a majority which accurately mirrored the party position in the Assembly. Lang's new request was asking de Chair to give the government a more advantageous position in the Council than it enjoyed in the Assembly. Of course, this was just the position non-Labour governments in New South Wales had enjoyed throughout the 30 years that Labour had been a significant electoral force.

Lang's 'Coups'

Lang had been signally unable – or perhaps unwilling – to broaden his support within the parliamentary party. From late 1925 onwards that support plummeted. This was caused partly by an extraordinary story in the *Labour Daily* – headlined 'A CONTEMPTIBLE AND DEGRADING NATIONALIST PLOT' – likely planted by Willis with Lang's approval, that the Nationalists had set aside £20,000 to bribe four (unnamed) Labour Assembly members to cross the floor and support a no-confidence motion.[85] The suspicion among some members was that the story was floated to discredit members who were not Lang loyalists with their local leagues (where Lang was increasingly popular) and would lead to their deselection as candidates at the next election. The bribery controversy staggered on for some months, before eventually being dismissed by an Assembly select committee – chaired by a young Labour member and barrister, Herbert Evatt – as entirely ill-founded.[86]

Lang's rift with many Assembly members intensified in September 1926, when Loughlin resigned from the Cabinet, raising concerns about Lang's allegedly autocratic leadership and a fear that proposed changes to the party's organisation championed by Lang and Willis would lead to communist infiltration. Loughlin stood for the leadership later that month. The ballot – still limited to the caucus – was 23–23; Lang's last vote was McTiernan's, sent by radio as he sailed from England. Party rules provided that as Lang was not defeated, he remained leader.[87]

Lang had conversely been remarkably effective in consolidating his popularity with party members both in the constituencies and among many of the party's smaller affiliated trade unions, where Willis and – alarmingly for the Loughlin grouping in the caucus – the avowedly communist Garden had great influence. The significance of that popularity was that these groups selected the majority of delegates who attended each year's party conference; and it was conference that wrote the party's rulebook. At the

[85] Nairn (1995) op cit pp 120–22; *LD* 1 December 1925 p1; https://trove.nla.gov.au/newspaper/article/239877594/25632436: 2 December 1925 p1; https://trove.nla.gov.au/newspaper/article/239878622. Such intrigues had been proven to have happened recently in Queensland; vol 1 p 338.

[86] Nairn (1995) op cit p 125.

[87] ibid pp 125–28.

November 1926 conference, Lang won overwhelming support among the delegates to exercise much increased personal control over the parliamentary party. The requirement that the leader be re-elected by the caucus at each parliamentary session was removed, and a motion passed by 274 votes to 4 confirming him as leader until the next Assembly election and empowering him to: "do all things and exercise such powers as he deems necessary in the interests of the movement".[88]

Lang's enhanced powers further alienated the Loughlin faction within the caucus. But the conference exacerbated that fragmentation by approving in principle an overhaul of the party's organisation colloquially – and pejoratively – referred to as 'the Red Rules', which Loughlin and his colleagues feared would provide a covert route for communist infiltration of the party. The new rules would strengthen the influence of the leagues and smaller trade unions (from where Lang and Willis drew high levels of support) within the Executive and at conference, and simultaneously reduce the influence of the caucus and the AWU, where Lang and Willis were much less popular. Conceivably the changes might offer Garden's Trades Hall Reds supporters an ingress into the party's organisation, but, given Lang's long-standing hostility to communism as an ideology, there is no force to suggestions that this was why he supported the changes.

Although adoption of the 'Red Rules' was deferred to a special 1927 conference pending further intra-party discussion, Loughlin resigned the Labour whip in late November, joined by two other Labour members. All three intimated that their votes could not be relied upon to support the government. Lang nevertheless survived (supported by Loughlin's group) a no-confidence motion later that month. But barely 18 months after his 1925 election victory, Lang led a government whose hold on power was feeble.

While much of Lang's political energy was devoted to seeking to push reformist legislation through the Assembly and Council, and some was spent battling his own party colleagues, a little was left over for other enemies.

The Newspaper Tax

Lang quite reasonably assumed that most of the Australian and New South Wales press had little sympathy for his political opinions.[89] Having endured what he regarded as very unfavourable press coverage, Lang and his government in late 1926 retaliated in a fashion that had the added benefit of modestly enhancing state revenues:

> The Sydney newspapers had been most vitriolic in their abuse. So I decided it was high time for them to pay for their fun. So quite guilelessly I slipped into the Budget a proposal that there should be a Newspaper Tax of ½ d per copy.[90]

The measure – enacted as The Finance (Newspapers Taxation) Act 1926 – came before the Assembly on 21 December 1926.[91] It was notionally apolitical in impact,

[88] Cited in ibid p135.

[89] cf ibid p163: "Nearly all the newspapers were anti-Labour, some of them almost rabidly so, so that their exposure of the party was intended to prejudice the public against it, with a main theme being the social and political dangers of its 'redness.'"

[90] Lang (1956) op cit p 340. Lang hoped that the tax would raise (the then significant annual sum of) £600,000.

[91] For his account, see Lang (1956) op cit ch 63.

being applicable to all newspapers other than freesheets, religious papers and those which sold fewer than 15,000 copies. Only five papers would be affected. But only one of those, the *Labour Daily*, could be regarded as sympathetic to Lang's government.

There was an (unhappy) precedent, in terms of motive and method, for the initiative. As noted in volume one,[92] Governor Darling in 1827 had promoted a newspaper tax to suppress critical journalism. That plan fell foul of Forbes CJ, who, as the 'Constitution' then stood, was empowered to veto laws proposed by the Governor. The 1827 episode was invoked by the opposition in the Assembly,[93] and Bavin unsurprisingly condemned the tax as a crudely party political measure. The government effectively guillotined Assembly debate, Lang informing the members that he saw no need to detain them on: "this simple little matter".[94]

Several newspapers immediately issued proceedings before the High Court.[95] Argument in *John Fairfax and Sons Ltd v State of New South Wales*[96] was heard on 21 February 1927 and judgment delivered on 3 March. All seven judges who sat[97] held the statute invalid.

The claimant's case was led by Owen Dixon KC, then a prominent member of the Victoria Bar. Dixon's argument was simple: the tax was an 'excise' on goods per s.90 of the Constitution Act, and thus a matter solely within the competence of the Commonwealth Parliament. Had the question been novel, s.90's obvious meaning per se would offer strong support for Dixon's view. However, he also relied on the recent High Court decision in *Commonwealth and Commonwealth Oil Refineries Ltd v South Australia*,[98] which indicated that an 'excise' would include any state tax levied on goods produced in the state, and that 'goods' included any commodities with a concrete existence.

Attorney-General McTiernan's ingenious (perhaps preposterous) argument was that *Commonwealth Oil Refineries* was not in point because this tax was not levied on the physical manifestation of the newspaper, ie the actual *paper*, but on the information it contained. This, McTiernan suggested, was not a commodity with a concrete existence, but a form of communication which fell outwith s.90. In essence, the value of the newspaper lay not in the *paper*, but in the *news*.

While Isaacs did McTiernan the courtesy of describing that submission as: "very clear and earnest",[99] he – like all his colleagues – saw no merit in it:

> What is the common understanding of a "newspaper" as that word is used by the Legislature of New South Wales? That Legislature speaks of a newspaper just as it is commonly understood, that is, as an article, not only visible, but tangible – the material piece of paper with

[92] At pp 15–16.

[93] *NSWLAD* 22 December 1926 pp 118–19, per Mr Levy.

[94] ibid p111 et seq. More systematic use of the guillotine had been another Lang innovation; see Nelson (1977) op cit pp 76–77.

[95] Exercising an original jurisdiction.

[96] (1927) 38 CLR 139.

[97] Knox CJ, Isaacs, Higgins, Gavan Duffy, Powers, Rich and Starke.

[98] (1926) 38 CLR 408. Both cases are briefly discussed in Sawer (1956) *Australian federal politics and law 1901–1929* pp 297–98.

[99] (1927) 38 CLR 139, 142–43. Birkenhead one imagines might have dismissed it as 'embarrassing and even ridiculous'; vol 1 p 310.

> printed matter upon it. The statutes do not separate, any more than the public mind separates, the printed matter from the material substance of the paper; they treat the "newspaper" as something which is corporeally "issued" and "sold," having pages and copies, and capable of "transmission" to other places.
>
> As used in the New South Wales legislation, therefore, the subject of taxation is unquestionably "goods …".

Lang was unsurprised by this conclusion. Press reports circulated[100] that the day before judgment Lang told the parliamentary party that McTiernan expected to lose, but that he (Lang) wanted to continue the litigation to expose the unacceptably limited nature of the states' fiscal powers. Lang declined to comment on the claim at the time, but reflected on it in his memoirs in comedic terms spliced with a general diatribe about the moral vacuity of lawyers.[101]

Lang's defeat in the *Newspaper Tax* case enabled some newspapers to continue to press the argument that Lang led an extremist government, which – with Lang himself especially culpable – rejected 'traditional forms' of political behaviour. That sentiment was exemplified by the formation in 1926 of a pressure/lobbying group styling itself the New South Wales Constitutional Association. The Association, reported in the *SMH* as professedly a "non-party organisation",[102] issued a five-point plan couched in terms of encouraging parliamentary government, opposing communism, supporting the Empire and encouraging more people to be active in politics at all levels.[103]

The Association's initial Chairman was Sir Thomas Playfair, a wealthy businessman (in the meat trade).[104] Despite its 'non-party' self-identification, the Association's membership and agenda seemed distinctly anti-Lang in tone. Its first engagement with constitutional politics was to denounce Lang's swamping and abolition plan: "… this Association records it emphatic protest against the action of the government in attempting to abolish the Legislative Council without a direct mandate from the electorate".[105] Hughes was announced as the keynote speaker at its first luncheon event in February 1927, although Hughes was ill on the appointed day, and Playfair took the stage in his place.[106] But by then, the Association's notionally non-partisan agenda had already been sidelined. The Association had resolved in November 1926 that: "… while maintaining a non-party character, members would work for the defeat of the Lang government until and during the next general election owing to its continued violation of the principles of the Association".[107] And as matters unfolded over the next six months, it seemed that the pro- and anti-Lang factions in the state Labour Party were doing much of the Association's work for it.

[100] See eg *LD* 2 March 1927, https://trove.nla.gov.au/newspaper/article/239940568; *SMH* 7 March 1927, https://trove.nla.gov.au/newspaper/article/16359491.

[101] Lang (1956) ch 63. Lang's views on lawyers are noted at p 56 n 38 below in another context.

[102] *SMH* 28 January 1926 p11, http://nla.gov.au/nla.news-article16276118. See also http://acms.sl.nsw.gov.au/item/itemDetailPaged.aspx?itemID=447489.

[103] ibid.

[104] http://adb.anu.edu.au/biography/playfair-thomas-alfred-john-jack-8063.

[105] ibid.

[106] *SMH* 22 February 1927 p10, http://nla.gov.au/nla.news-article16356686.

[107] *Barrier Miner* 1 November 1926 p1, http://nla.gov.au/nla.news-articel45952902.

The End of the First Lang Government

Early in 1927, the government finally succeed in having one of its flagship policies enacted. The Child Endowment Act 1927 provided for a flat rate per child payment, paid to mothers. The bill was promoted in 1925, but persistently blocked in the Council. Lang eventually accepted Council amendments, which substantially reduced the payments made. But Lang turned that 'defeat' to his advantage. At the special April 1927 conference, he presented the Act both as a triumph of reform and a testament to the Council's unacceptable power. The Act was: "the best we could squeeze from the magnanimous patriots who control the destinies of this State … the most reactionary, objectionable and insolent nominee House in the Empire".[108]

The conference's timing had, however, prompted further fissure in the party, this time within the Executive, whose majority, reflecting AWU (and so, by extension, pro-Theodore) and anti-Lang/Willis sentiment, denounced the 'Red Rules' as a communist plot, and wanted the conference delayed until June, after the scheduled national party conference, hoping that national Labour criticism of the 'Red Rules' might prevent their adoption. The Executive's Chairman, WH Seale, was, however, a Lang supporter, and called the conference for April to pre-empt that possibility. Seale was expelled by the majority for his pains and then with his supporters purported to establish an alternative Executive.

The special conference went ahead in April, adopted the Red Rules and also authorised Lang to select (and dismiss) members of his Cabinet. With the obvious exception of Willis, most of Lang's Cabinet (including McTiernan) opposed the changes. The tension within the state party then became a clear rupture in May over a by-election (in a safe nationalist seat). The 'AWU Executive' nominated a candidate; and so did the 'Seale Executive'. The extraordinary upshot of this was that Lang and Willis campaigned for the Lang candidate, while most of the Cabinet actively supported the official candidate. Lang's candidate beat his 'official' Labour rival into third place, a success which prompted the national party to adopt a conciliatory stance towards Lang's 'rebellion'. Yet another special state conference was held in July 1927, at which with national party approved the various decisions made at the April conference.

Lang was not magnanimous in victory. Instead, he decided, as the April conference empowered him to do, to dismiss most of his Cabinet and replace them with his own appointees. de Chair had been watching these events with increasing concern. Lang accepted that the proposed mass sacking would require the government's resignation. Since there was no obvious basis to think that a new Lang government could command an Assembly majority, de Chair accepted the resignation and formation of a new Cabinet on condition that a dissolution would promptly follow. The election was scheduled for October 1927.

In the interim, Lang subsequently recalled: "I had the congenial task of appointing a new Cabinet … It was a chance to reward those who had been loyal to the Easter

[108] Quoted in Nairn (1995) op cit p146. On Lang's motivation for the policy and his account of the difficulties of enacting it, see Lang (1956) op cit chs 42–43. A more dispassionate account is offered in Jelly (1977) 'Child endowment' in Radi and Spearitt op cit.

conference. The problem of selection was not very difficult. They just about selected themselves."[109] Lang did not add that one reason that 'they just about selected themselves' was that he had so few 'loyal' members to choose from. Lang sought to broaden that choice, anticipating winning the election by securing the deselection of several 'disloyal' members as Labour candidates. Herbert Evatt, the young barrister who led the inquiry into the *Labour Daily* bribery allegations, was among them. McTiernan decided to retire from state politics, and returned to legal practice. The Labour Party's position within New South Wales looked increasingly fragile as the election approached, but Lang's position within the party had never been stronger.

[109] Lang (1956) op cit p326.

2

The Immediate Legal Roots of the *Trethowan* Controversy

> Mr. GOSLING: … This bill is so much waste paper, because when the Labour Party comes into office it will exercise the powers of the government of a sovereign State. The Premier may have his last word but the public will possibly change the government; and if it does as soon as we obtain control of this Chamber, and the Upper House, no legal verbiage can stop Parliament from repealing the bill which we are now considering. No lawyer can deny that.
>
> Mr. BAVIN: That is quite true. But we do not seek to bind future Parliaments. We could not do that, even if we wanted to do it. We are not trying to do it. As long as you go to the country and the public support you, you are entitled to do what you like!
>
> An exchange between a Labour MLA and the Premier, Sir Thomas Bavin, at second reading of the Constitution (Legislative Council) Amendment Bill in the Assembly on 12 March 1929.

I. Lang in Opposition(s) 1927–30

In one sense, Lang's Labour Party 'won' the 1927 Assembly election. Labour received a larger share of the vote and more Assembly seats than any other party, albeit gaining less on both counts than in 1925 (43% rather than 47% of the vote, and 40 rather than 46 seats). Unhappily for Lang, the New South Wales Nationalist and Country parties had followed the national lead and campaigned as partners in a prospective coalition. Between them (and joined by two Independent nationalists) they secured 48 of the 90 seats. Sir Thomas Rainsford Bavin, leader of the state's Nationalists, was the new Premier.

Table 2.1 New South Wales Legislative Assembly election, 1927 (8 October 1927)

Party	% vote	Seats won	Change
Nationalist	38.0	33	−1
Independent Nationalist	2.6	2	+1
Country Party[a]	8.8	13	+4
Australian Labour Party	43.0	40	−6
Independent Labour	2.8	2	+1

[a] I have equated the Country Party with the 1925 Progressives in the 'change' column.

To Bavin in New South Wales

The Nationalists' political platform does not lend itself to easy characterisation. In terms of economic policy, for example, Bavin became increasingly hostile to minimum wage and maximum working hours legislation and to trade unionism more generally, but successfully promoted legislation increasing taxation on the more affluent. His tactical acumen was sufficient for him to engineer a pre-electoral pact with the Country Party for the 1927 election, from which he emerged as Premier, leading a coalition administration. Given the Labour Party's strife-ridden state, it is perhaps surprising that Bavin's majority was not greater.

In addition to promoting bills reversing some of the Lang government's social welfare legislation, Bavin's administration took a markedly anti-union position on industrial relations matters. These were obvious and expected areas of dispute between the parties. But it was Bavin's alteration of the state's position on an initiative championed by the Bruce/Page national government to which Lang was perhaps most vigorously opposed.

To the Bruce/Page Commonwealth Governments

Following the November 1925 Commonwealth election,[1] Bruce remained as Prime Minister with Earle Page as Treasurer. Bruce had encapsulated his coalition government's policy agenda in the slogan 'Men, Money and Markets': encouraging immigration (primarily from Britain), facilitating loans (rather than raising taxes) for investment in industrial enterprises and infrastructure development, and boosting exports of agricultural and manufactured products.

Page's dominant concern after the 1925 election was to lend not simply just a statutory but a constitutional basis to the Loan Council arrangements[2] and to a broader rebalancing of Commonwealth–state financial relations. State governments of various political hues[3] expressed little support for reforms which would likely undermine their financial autonomy (as Lang liked to style it, their 'sovereignty') until, in 1926, Page's unsubtle threat to revoke the per capita payments[4] on which the states' respective fiscal viability effectively depended eventually overcame state resistance. The negotiation process culminated in December 1927 in a 'Financial Agreement' being reached between the Commonwealth government and the states.[5] The core of the Agreement was that the Commonwealth would assume responsibility for repaying all existing and future state loans, per capita payments would be discontinued other than as a contribution to meeting states' loan interest obligations and the Loan Council arrangements would be given a legal basis.[6]

[1] P 12 table 1.4 above.

[2] Vol 1 pp 334–36.

[3] As Ward notes: "During the 1920s, the same voters who returned conservative governments to power in the federal sphere often voted Labour quite happily in State elections" (1978) op cit pp 154–55.

[4] Vol 1 p 171.

[5] The Agreement is reproduced as sch.1 to the Financial Agreement Act 1928.

[6] Page's account is at Page (1963) *Truant surgeon* pp 126–34.

It seems unlikely that a Lang government would have approved the Agreement, given that Lang had not participated in the Loan Council. But immediately after the October 1927 state election, Bavin's government had taken New South Wales back into the Loan Council, approved the 'Financial Agreement' and supported the Bruce/Page administration's proposals to give the Agreement a constitutional basis. Those proposals were a key aspect of the Nationalist and Country Party's joint programme at the (November) 1928 Commonwealth election. The coalition retained sufficient electoral popularity to achieve a workable House majority, albeit reduced from 27 seats to nine, and remained dominant in the Senate.

Table 2.2 The 1928 Commonwealth election (17 November 1928)

House of Representatives	% vote	Seats won	Change
Nationalists	39.0	29	-8
Country	10.5	13	-1
Labour	44.6	31	+8
Country Progressive	1.6	1	+1
Independent	4.2	1	–
Senate[a]			
Nationalists	39.2	24	-1
Labour	48.9	7	-1
Country	11.1	5	+2

[a] 19 seats contested.

The election was held alongside a constitutional amendment referendum on Bruce/Page's Financial Agreement reform. The proposal was to insert a new s.105A into the Constitution. Lang's opposition to the policy was not widely shared. The national Labour Party did not campaign against the initiative. Some 74% of voters nationally supported the change, and a majority was secured in all the states. Few voters, it seemed, appreciated the significance of what was being done. Ward's characterisation of the episode is acute: "Thus, with remarkably little fuss, was carried through the greatest constitutional change in the history of the Commonwealth."[7] The lack of 'fuss' is perhaps attributable to the rather misleading way in which s.105A headlined the reform as one concerned with 'agreements' between the Commonwealth and the states. On more careful reading, however, the 'agreement' envisaged by s.105A appears to be one granting the Commonwealth Parliament authority to impose terms on the states.

S.105A(2) empowered the Commonwealth Parliament retrospectively to validate the financial agreement reached in 1927 (which it promptly did),[8] while s.105A(3)

[7] Ward (1978) op cit p157.

[8] Financial Agreement Act 1928. The Act contains only five short sections and the Agreement itself in a schedule. S.2 announced simply that: "The Agreement … is approved." The Act, to Page's evident surprise, was opposed by the Labour opposition notwithstanding the party's support for the preceding constitutional amendment; Page op cit pp 131–33.

empowered it to: "make laws for the carrying out by the parties thereto of any such agreement". Per s.105A(4), the terms of any agreement could only be varied with the consent of 'the parties' to it – which, of course, meant that the Commonwealth had a veto power over any alteration. There seemed to be little understanding on the part of voters (and little acknowledgement by politicians) that s.105A(3)–(4) might empower the Commonwealth Parliament to impose enforcement mechanisms on the states.[9]

Despite Bruce's success in steering through the constitutional amendment, his coalition's hold on power proved short-lived, primarily because of its inept handling of several major industrial disputes. Reform to industrial relations – by which was meant curtailing the power of the trade unions – had been a recurrent concern of the Bruce/Page administrations since the 1922 election.[10] The promotion of (mostly British) immigration[11] – the 'Men' element of the government's economic programme – was largely driven by a supposition that increasing the labour supply would, while promoting economic growth more generally, exert downward pressure on wages. For that reason, the national and state Labour parties had consistently opposed any significant immigration while there was unemployment among the existing population.

Bruce's governments were consistently concerned that the balance of power in industrial matters unduly favoured the trade unions. The national government's capacity to address such problems was obviously constrained (albeit to a lesser extent than before 1920 as a consequence of the *Engineers* decision)[12] by the Constitution's division of power between the states and the Commonwealth, the latter's authority being restricted to (crudely put) matters with an international or interstate dimension. The concern also had a more avowedly party political dimension, in that Bruce's administration attributed much industrial unrest – especially strikes by shipping and dockworkers in 1925 – to the activities of 'communist' agitators. Bruce and Page had rooted their 1925 election campaign strategy very much in 'Red Scare' tactics, with evident success.[13]

More specifically, the Bruce government promoted legislation which ostensibly enhanced its capacity to deal with industrial disputes within its jurisdiction, in particular by promoting legislation which empowered it to deport 'immigrants' who had engaged in such activities. On that issue, the Bruce government suffered some substantial embarrassment when seeking to deport two Seamen's Union activists, long resident in Australia but of Dutch and Irish nationality. The subsequent litigation before the High Court – *Re Yates; Ex parte Walsh*[14] – provided the young Labour Assembly member Herbert Evatt with the opportunity to consolidate his political credentials among Labour voters and trade unions in a fashion that (electorally) served him well when he subsequently broke with Lang.[15] Evatt persuaded the High Court that the Constitution's grant of power (per s.51(xvii)) to the Commonwealth Parliament over immigration did not extend to the deportation of non-British nationals who (like Yates and Walsh) had made Australia their permanent home, since such people were not 'immigrants'.

[9] Edwards (1965) *Bruce of Melbourne* pp 133–34.
[10] See generally Ward (1978) op cit pp 158–62.
[11] 'White Australia' remained a cross-party tenet of political faith.
[12] Vol 1 pp 330–33.
[13] Sawer (1956) *Australian federal politics and law 1901–1929* pp 256–58: Ward (1978) op cit pp 158–62.
[14] [1925] HCA 53, (1925) 37 CLR 36.
[15] P 24 above.

The Bruce government also promoted legislation making it a criminal offence for unions or employers to engage in strikes or lockouts during the currency of a binding arbitration award. The Crimes Act 1926 was notionally even-handed between employers and workers/trade unions.[16] During the currency of an arbitration court award, it was as much an offence for employers to lock out their employees as it was for employees to go on strike. In practice, the government acted with some alacrity in bringing such legal proceedings against trade unions and their members, but not against employers. Its bona fides were put to the test by a major dispute in the New South Wales coal mines in 1928, when a cartel of employers announced that its members would no longer honour an arbitration award and would close the mines if employees did not accept reductions in wages and extension of hours. When the mines were subsequently shut, the Bruce government initially indicated it would bring legal proceedings against the John Brown company, but shortly afterwards (with Bavin's support and approval) changed its position. The decision enabled the Labour opposition – and Theodore in particular – to conduct a scathingly effective parliamentary and press campaign attacking the government for its apparent class-based hypocrisy.[17] Hughes, still 'a Labour man' on economic policy issues and still seeking revenge against Bruce and Page for his unceremonious ejection from power in 1922,[18] was persuaded to vote against the government on a Labour motion condemning its behaviour.

The Yates and John Brown incidents spoke to a broader incoherence in the Bruce/Page government industrial relations policies. In 1926, the government proposed a constitutional amendment to increase the Commonwealth's powers in industrial relations matters, but this was heavily rejected by voters. Two years later, in an extraordinary volte face, Bruce promoted a bill (the misleadingly named Maritime Industries Bill) which would largely eliminate the Commonwealth's industrial relations powers in many areas and enhance those of the states (not coincidentally, five of the six,[19] including New South Wales, were then controlled by Nationalist/Country Party governments). The initiative was firmly opposed by the national Labour Party, and by Hughes (likely acting in secret concert with Theodore)[20] and a handful of Nationalist members. Hughes moved a motion that the bill's passage be adjourned pending a referendum or general election, and when Bruce rashly made the issue one of confidence, Hughes carried several other Nationalist members with him in the ensuing division,[21] in which the government was defeated by one vote and promptly resigned to fight a new election.

[16] S.17 inserting a new s.30(j) into the Crimes Act 1914.

[17] See especially Theodore's speech in the House on a no-confidence motion at *HRD* 15 August 1929 p7. Hughes's speech is at ibid p39. A biographer describes Bruce's decision to revoke the prosecution as: "an act of political lunacy"; Edwards op cit p159; on the Brown case generally, see ibid ch 16.

[18] Sawer convincingly suggests that the projected prosecution was fraught with both jurisdictional and evidential issues, and that its withdrawal was readily justifiable on purely 'legal' grounds; Sawer (1956) op cit pp 313–16. Lang's less measured critique is at Lang (1956) op cit ch 47.

[19] Queensland was then the only Labour-governed state.

[20] Fitzgerald op cit pp 222–23.

[21] Hughes's motion is at *HRD* 10 September 1929 p841; Bruce's confidence concession is at p849; and the vote is at p866.

To the Labour Commonwealth Government

The October 1929 national election produced a resounding success for the Labour Party, which took 45 House seats. The Nationalists retained just 14, and the Country Party 10. Labour was led into the election by James Scullin[22] – the mover of the socialisation objective at the 1921 Brisbane national party conference[23] – who formed a ministry in which he was Prime Minister and Foreign Secretary, with Theodore, now deputy leader of the national party, as Treasurer.

Table 2.3 The 1929 Commonwealth election (12 October 1929)

House of Representatives	**% vote**	**Seats won**	**Change**
Nationalist	33.9	14	−15
Country Party	10.2	10	−3
Australian Labour Party	48.8	46	+15
Independent	2.1	1	–
Independent Nationalist	3.9	3	+3
Country Progressives	1.0	1	+1
Senate[a]			
Nationalist		24	
Country Party		5	
Australian Labour Party		7	

[a] There was no Senate election in 1929. The Senate figures reproduced here are from the 1928 election.

The new government immediately faced two substantial difficulties. None of the parties had evidently grasped during the campaign that the international economy was approaching an acute crisis. The Wall Street Crash occurred within a week of the election, presenting Scullin's government with the twin prospects of accelerated collapse in demand for Australia's two main exports – wool and wheat – and a decline in the availability of international loan funds to plug the fiscal gap caused by a shrinkage in tax revenues.

The government's capacity to adopt radical responses to this situation was constrained in part by constitutional circumstances. Because the 1929 election came less than a year after the 1928 poll, there was no Senate election.[24] Consequently, the Nationalists retained a large Senate majority and with it the capacity to block any government bills.

Whether Scullin was in principle attracted to any other economic recipe than the wage retrenchment and escalating tariffs favoured by Bruce and Page seems unlikely.

[22] Scullin became party leader in 1928. Born in Victoria in 1876, Scullin had virtually no formal education. He ran a grocer's shop during his twenties, and became involved in Labour politics and trade union activities at an early age. He unsuccessfully ran against Deakin for a House seat in 1906, was elected to the House in 1910, but lost his seat in 1913. For the next decade, he edited a Victoria Newspaper, the *Ballarat Evening Echo*, espousing an anti-conscription position during the war. He was re-elected to the House in 1922, becoming deputy party leader in 1925; http://adb.anu.edu.au/biography/scullin-james-henry-8375; Ward (1978) op cit pp 173–75. For a generally approbatory biography, see Robertson (1974) *J H Scullin: a political biography.*

[23] Vol 1 pp 324–25.

[24] Senators serve fixed terms unless there is a double dissolution; vol 1 p 158.

Although Scullin had moved the 1921 socialisation objective, an initiative Theodore – then Premier of Queensland – had done much to water down, he had no particular expertise on economic policy matters. Theodore was perhaps the only member of the government – indeed, the only politician in any party – who had even begun to grasp the possibilities of Keynesian economic theory, and especially the use of reflationary note issues, as a tool to counter economic depression. Such ideas were anathema to Gibson[25] qua Chairman of the Bank Board and to the Senate majority. Theodore's scope to give them administrative or legislative effect was thus very limited.

It would perhaps credit Page with an unwarranted degree of foresight to suggest that the 1924 Commonwealth Bank reforms[26] were a pre-emptive strike against the prospect of a future Labour government being seized with a Keynesian enthusiasm for inflationary economic policies 'paid for' by a substantial note issue not backed by gold reserves, but that was the effect that the reforms had when the Scullin government came to power. There was no prospect that the 1924 Act could be amended to restore government control over the note issue because Labour was in a Senate minority. The Bank Board could not be replaced en masse, because members sat for statutory seven-year terms. Even the modest reflation Theodore was contemplating demanded that the Scullin government persuade Gibson and the Board to approve the necessary note issue. And the prospects of that happening seemed beyond remote.[27]

However, in July 1930, Theodore was forced from office. In May 1929, Queensland electors had returned a Country Party and Nationalist coalition government to power,[28] a government for which discrediting Theodore (albeit not resurrecting the Legislative Council) seemed a primary concern. The new government promptly established a Royal Commission to investigate allegations that Theodore, while Premier, had engineered the sale of a mine (Mungana) in which he had an undeclared interest to the state for a grossly inflated price. The Commission reported in July 1930, and concluded that Theodore had engaged in dishonest dealing. Theodore resigned as Treasurer to devote his energies to clearing his name, and challenged the Queensland government to prosecute him.[29]

The resignation deprived Scullin of his most economically literate colleague. The gap was partly filled by Gibson, who prompted Scullin to request the Bank of England to offer advice on future economic policy. The Bank of England's emissary was an economist named Sir Otto Niemayer, whose prescription to cure Australia's economic ills was a swingeing reduction of national and state government expenditure, cuts in wage levels and extensions of the working week. It was a programme with which Gibson was fully in agreement. And while Scullin had appointed himself Treasurer on Theodore's resignation, it appeared to be Gibson and Niemayer whose ideas held sway.[30]

[25] Vol 1 pp 335–36.

[26] Vol 1 pp 334–36.

[27] The position was nicely stated by Frank Anstey, a left-inclined cabinet minister: "We had no power. From the first moment of our existence we were only the stuffed effigy of a government", cited in Hart (1970) 'Lyons: Labor minister – leader of the UAP' p37 in Cooksey (ed) (1970a) *The great depression in Australia.*

[28] With 43 of the 72 seats.

[29] Fitzgerald op cit ch 7: Robertson op cit pp 249–51.

[30] See variously Attard (1992) 'The Bank of England and the origins of the Niemayer mission, 1921–1930' *Australian Economic History Review* 66: Cain (2005) *Jack Lang and the great depression* ch 6: Robertson (1970) 'Scullin as Prime Minister: seven critical decisions' in Cooksey op cit.

Niemayer's proposals were formally adopted by the national and state governments (that being Bavin's administration in New South Wales) in the so-called 'Melbourne agreement' in August 1930. Lang fiercely and very visibly opposed both the agreement and the overall thrust of the government's economic policy. It may overstate the case to suggest Lang was informedly championing an expressly Keynesian response to the depression, but his position clearly favoured reflationary rather than deflationary initiatives,[31] in terms both of public employment projects and welfare benefit provision, and opposition to wages reduction in both the private and public sectors. The 'Lang Plan', as it was subsequently styled, went through various incarnations in 1930, but its consistent key component was that reflation (or, perhaps more accurately, the rejection of deflation) could be financed by renegotiating the terms (by significantly reducing interest rates) of Australia's (state and national) war loans from Britain. Lang was particularly exercised by the fact that Britain had done just that in respect of its wartime loans from the United States, but would not extend the same benefit to Australia. The underlying threat, initially implicit, was that Australian governments should and would, if necessary, 'repudiate'[32] their loan obligations and divert the moneys saved to bolstering the domestic economy. Lang also proposed capping the interest payable on all Australian government loans, irrespective of the terms of the original agreements, and also advocated a reflationary issue of currency.

Lang also adopted a trenchantly critical position towards the Scullin government's unwillingness and/or inability to intervene effectively in the New South Wales mining dispute. During the 1929 election campaign, Theodore had promised that a Labour government would end the strike by restarting the prosecution of the John Brown company: "if Labour were returned, the mines in the northern coalfields would be open in a fortnight".[33] The promise was not pursued. Scullin instead adopted more conciliatory tactics, and expressly disavowed responsibility for Theodore's campaign statements.[34] Scullin's attempts to broker a settlement were unsuccessful, and the strike eventually ended with the miners returning to work on reduced wages. From Lang's perspective, the episode amounted to a betrayal by Scullin and Theodore of both the miners and the wider labour movement.[35]

II. The Constitution (Legislative Council) Amendment Act 1929

The New South Wales coal strike had proved even more damaging to Bavin's Nationalist state administration than to Scullin's national government. Bavin adopted bluntly confrontational tactics towards the unions, culminating in providing armed police protection for non-union workers to cross picket lines. This provoked persistent public disorder,

[31] cf Clark (1977) 'Was Lang right?' in Radi and Spearritt op cit; (1976) 'The battle of the plans' *Economics* (August).

[32] This being the term used by opposition parties to characterise Theodore's Judges Retirement Bill; vol 1 pp 321–22.

[33] Fitzgerald op cit p227. The speech is contemporaneously reported in *SMH* 7 October 1929, https://trove.nla.gov.au/newspaper/article/16590404: *Musswellbrook Chronicle* 8 October 1929 p1, https://trove.nla.gov.au/newspaper/article/107927290. See also Nairn (1995) op cit pp 184–86; Robertson (1974) op cit pp 220–26.

[34] ibid p225.

[35] Lang recounts events in depth in Lang (1962) op cit pp 163–72.

culminating on 16 December 1929 in the (fatal) shooting of one striker.[36] Bavin blamed the death squarely on the strikers.[37] Lang, in response, moved a motion in the Assembly that:

> [T]his House deplores the loss of life which occurred at Rothbury yesterday, and censures the government for permitting the use of the state police to further the efforts of the mine-owners in their attitude of open defiance of the law.[38]

The motion was defeated; but in such circumstances, the frequently raised spectre of a 'communist' Lang-led party acquiring political power had diminished electoral traction. As the 1930 Assembly election approached, the prospect of Bavin's administration remaining in office seemed increasingly remote.

That prospect had prompted the Bavin government to secure the passage of legislation designed to protect the Council against a Theodore-style and Lang-led abolition. In 1921, as a backbencher, Bavin – conveniently overlooking Holman's 1917 initiative – denounced Storey's efforts to add 16 Labour members to the Council.[39] His objections were professedly rooted in grand constitutional rather than party political concerns:

> These appointments, good or bad, were made on some principle hitherto unknown to the constitutional law of this State. And what that principle is, I do not know. Up to the present, appointments to the Council have been made on grounds that, although no part of our written Constitution, are fairly well defined and understood. Speaking generally, those grounds are that new appointments are necessary to bring the number of members up to the conventional standard, or to secure reasonable representation for interests that are unrepresented, or to enable a government to pass legislation for which there is a proved public demand. This statement, though not intended to be perfectly precise, substantially covers the ground hitherto recognised. These sixteen appointments cannot be, and in fact are hardly sought to be. Justified on any of these grounds. There was no deficiency in the number of members. There was no evidence of any inadequate representation of any interests in the community, and certainly not any evidence of inadequate representation of those interests which the government claims to represent.

Bavin's suggestion that the Labour Party was adequately represented in the Council even after Storey's appointments was risible. That ludicrous assertion rather colours the notionally bipartisan nature of his criticism. Bavin was much concerned that Storey's initiative set a precedent for downgrading the Council from an autonomous body to being a mere reflex of the government. More generally, Bavin deprecated the assumption that he saw as implicit in the episode that a Governor should invariably follow the advice of his ministers rather than exercise his own judgement on contentious political questions. As noted above, Bavin developed this critique more fully in the 1926 episode. Bavin had signed off his 1921 critique with a rhetorical flourish: "If our Constitution is

[36] Nairn (1995) op cit pp 185–86: Dixson (1970) 'Rothbury' in Cooksey (1970a) op cit. Lang responded to the shooting with a spectacularly polemical speech to a party conference, urging Scullin to seize the mines and worry afterwards about the constitutional inconvenience of not having the necessary legal power; Nairn (1995) op cit pp 187–88; Lang (1962) op cit pp 171–72. For (unsurprisingly) divergent contemporaneous coverage of the death, see *LD* 17 December 1929 p1, https://trove.nla.gov.au/newspaper/article/239311475; *SMH* 18 December 1929 p19, https://trove.nla.gov.au/newspaper/article/16611039.

[37] *NSWLAD* 17 December 1929 p2514.

[38] ibid p2517.

[39] The denunciation came in a newspaper letter; *SMH* 21 September 1921, http://nla.gov.au/nla.news-article239705078.

to be altered it should be done with the full knowledge and assent of the people of this State. – Yours etc T R BAVIN."

Eight years later, the mechanism Bavin as Premier chose to increase the likelihood that the Council could not be abolished without 'the full knowledge and assent of the people' was enacted as the Constitution (Legislative Council) Amendment Act 1929.

The Text of the Act

Bavin's legislation was brief in terms and limited in scope:

> **CONSTITUTION (LEGISLATIVE COUNCIL) AMENDMENT ACT. Act No. 28, 1929**
>
> An Act to provide that the Legislative Council shall not be abolished nor certain provisions with respect to its constitution or powers be altered until a bill for the purpose has been approved by the electors on a referendum; to amend the Constitution Act, 1902, and certain other Acts; and for purposes connected therewith. [Reserved, 26th March, 1929.]
>
> BE it enacted by the King's Most Excellent Majesty, by and with the advice and consent of the Legislative Council and Legislative Assembly of New South Wales in Parliament assembled, and by the authority of the same, as follows:–
>
> 1. This Act may be cited as the "Constitution (Legislative Council) Amendment Act, 1929," and shall commence on a date to be appointed by the Governor and notified by proclamation published in the Gazette.
>
> 2. The Constitution Act, 1902, as amended by subsequent Acts is amended by inserting next after section seven the following new section:–
>
> 7A. (1) The Legislative Council shall not be abolished nor, subject to the provisions of subsection six of this section, shall its constitution or powers be altered except in the manner provided in this section.
>
> (2) A Bill for any purpose within subsection one of this section shall not be presented to the Governor for His Majesty's assent until the Bill has been approved by the electors in accordance with this section.
>
> (3) On a day not sooner than two months after the passage of the Bill through both Houses of the Legislature the Bill shall be submitted to the electors qualified to vote for the election of members of the Legislative Assembly. Such day shall be appointed by the Legislature.
>
> (4) When the Bill is submitted to the electors the vote shall be taken in such manner as the Legislature prescribes.
>
> (5) If a majority of the electors voting approve the Bill, it shall be presented to the Governor for His Majesty's assent.
>
> (6) The provisions of this section shall extend to any Bill for the repeal or amendment of this section …

The Act's drafting was largely the work of Sir John Peden.[40] Peden had been an outstanding student of both classics and law at Sydney University. After a brief career at the

[40] There is a friendly biography in Griffith (2006) 'Sir John Peden: representing the public interest' in Hogan and Turner (eds) *The worldly art of politics*. See also the obituary in *SMH* 1 June 1946, http://nla/gov/au/nla.news-article17981941; http://adb.anu.edu.au/biography/peden-sir-john-beverley-8008; www.parliament.nsw.gov.au/members/Pages/member-details.aspx?pk=1228.

Bar, Peden returned to the university's law school, becoming Challis Professor of Law and Dean in 1910, a position he retained for 30 years, having also been appointed a KC in 1924. As an academic, he specialised in constitutional law. He was appointed to the Council in 1917 by Holman, whom Peden had taught when Holman was a student. Peden was initially – at least nominally – an independent member of the Council. In party political terms, he sat in the middle of the conservative spectrum. (His first 'governmental' role had been as a major force behind a rationalisation of the state court system, including introducing a mandatory retirement age for Supreme Court judges, which Theodore and John Mullan had invoked during the passage of the Retirement Bill as a means to counter accusations of political vindictiveness.[41]) Peden was a close friend of Bavin (the two met as students), and was appointed as Council President during Bavin's 1927–30 administration. One biographer describes Peden as: "undoubtedly a man of the right, but he was still his own man".[42] Lang's view was more acerbic; he regarded Peden as: "one of a coterie of the state's most crusted Tories. They believed that their mission was to stop Labour from governing."[43] Lang's view was perhaps unfairly hyperbolic; Peden first came to public prominence as member of the Council when, almost immediately after his appointment, he led an effective rearguard action to wreck a bill proposed by Holman (echoing for New South Wales the authoritarian intolerance of dissent displayed by Hughes on the national stage)[44] which sought to impose political disqualification sanctions on any person convicted of 'sedition'; a concept defined sufficiently widely to embrace any opposition to the war.[45]

It might be thought that the clear purpose of Peden's 1929 text was to safeguard both the Council's existence and its (then) current powers and composition against alteration by 'normal' simple majority legislation. The primary threat the new s.7A of the Constitution Act was intended to counter was Lang's Labour Party following Theodore's Queensland lead and securing an Assembly majority in the 1930 election, while simultaneously acquiring an appointive majority – building on the 1917 Holman, 1921 Storey and 1926 Lang swamping precedents[46] – in the Council; such majorities that would then vote for a bill to abolish the Council entirely. The events of February 1926 suggested that Lang might not be able to rely on Labour Council members actually voting for abolition, but Peden's work was perhaps[47] directed at providing a legal rather than just political barrier to abolition. That presumption is obviously inferable from s.7A's text, inasmuch as all of its various procedural steps are configured as matters which *shall* or *shall not* occur, a choice of words which might be thought to denote mandatory and so legally enforceable requirements.

[41] Vol 1 pp 321–22.

[42] Griffith op cit p159.

[43] Lang J (1962) *The great bust* p295.

[44] See in particular the account at vol 1 pp 264–66 of Hughes's attempts to prosecute Ryan and Theodore for 'sedition'.

[45] Clune and Griffith (2006) *Decision and deliberation: the Parliament of New South Wales 1856–2003* pp 273–74.

[46] Respectively pp 5, 5 and 16–17 above.

[47] As suggested below, the easy assumption that Bavin and Peden thought that they were creating a legal as opposed to moral impediment to abolition may not be well founded.

S.7A was apparently designed to effect a double change to the 'manner' (the term used in s.7A(1)) of lawmaking within New South Wales with respect to the existence, powers and composition of the Council. At first sight, the use of the term 'manner' might be thought a reference to s.4 [BAA] of the New South Wales Constitution Act 1855,[48] which, it may be recalled, stated that:

> It shall be lawful for the Legislature of New South Wales to make laws altering or repealing all or any of the provisions of the said reserved Bill in the same manner as any other laws for the good government of the said Colony subject however to the conditions imposed by the said reserved Bill on the alteration of the provisions thereof in certain particulars until and unless the said conditions shall be repealed or altered by the authority of the said legislature.

As noted in chapter one of volume one, that use of the term 'manner' in s.4 [BAA][49] was apparently intended by its promoter – Lord John Russell – to denote bicameral, bare majority, express (and likely also implied) repeal lawmaking.[50]

The word 'manner' in s.7A(1) might alternatively or additionally be thought to refer to CLVA 1865 s.5,[51] which provided inter alia that colonial legislation passed by a representative legislature which altered its own 'constitution, powers and procedures' would have to comply with the 'manner and form' then required by colonial law.[52] A further possible source for the word 'manner' – without the 'and form' addendum – was s.128 of the Commonwealth Constitution, which permits constitutional reform through a complex referendum process.[53]

The Law Officers' (Palmer and Collier's) 1864 Report had seemingly supported the proposition that colonial legislatures should be able to create 'special majority' lawmaking processes for 'particular subjects', and used the term 'form' (without the 'manner and' prefix) to refer to such 'special' procedures.[54] The history of constitutional dispute in Queensland (per Lutwyche) and South Australia (per Boothby and Gwynne) in the early 1860s which had prompted a stream of validatory Imperial legislation to rescue colonial statutes from legal invalidity and led to the 1864 report also indicates that devices such as reservation and laying before were also regarded as legally enforceable 'special procedures'.[55] It can certainly be sensibly – if not irrebuttably – suggested that insofar as Peden's proposed law was designed to attach a 'special procedure' to a 'particular subject', it fell within the 1864 Law Officers' understanding of the legal effect the proposed s.5 would have.

However, if Peden's text was directly inspired by s.5, it is strange that s.7A did not fully reproduce verbatim either s.5's 'manner and form' phraseology or the 'constitution, powers and procedures' formula. Rather, s.7A(1) referred to the 'constitution and powers' of the Council, after having already begun by dealing with the question of the 'abolition' of the Council. As discussed in chapter four of volume one, the drafting

48 S.4 [BAA] is discussed at pp 46–47 above.
49 British Act Addendum; see vol 1 p 45 n 46.
50 Vol 1 pp 48–49.
51 Vol 1 pp 108–09.
52 ibid.
53 Vol 1 pp 164–65.
54 Vol 1 pp 103–04.
55 Vol 1 ch 3.

of s.5 was not a model of clarity. Read literally, s.5 did not grant representative legislatures any express power of 'abolition' with respect to themselves or their component parts. The express power of 'abolition' in s.5 arose only in respect of courts, and could be exercised by any colonial legislature, whether representative or not. It would seem credible, however, that abolishing one part of a bicameral representative legislature would be a law 'respecting the constitution' of that legislature: abolition of the Council would reconstitute the legislature as a unicameral (plus royal assent) body. This proposition had, of course, been accepted by several members of the High Court in *Taylor*[56] and would seem to be what occurred in Queensland when the Council was subsequently abolished.[57]

With perhaps unintended irony, Peden chose as the barrier to creation of a unicameral legislature not a 'special majority' in the 1864 Report narrow sense but a device which could be characterised as lending the legislature a tricameral nature (prior to the giving of the royal assent). The initial barrier to simple majority legislation was the requirement in s.7A(2) that a bill could not be presented to the Governor for the purposes of giving the royal assent unless the bill was previously 'approved by the electors in accordance with this section': namely, by a referendum.[58] The Act did not impose enhanced majorities in either house, or require repeat votes or place temporal restrictions on a bill's passage as it went through its various intra-parliamentary stages (beyond the proviso in s.7A(3), which made it clear that the referendum would have to take place no sooner than two months from the bill having been passed in the Assembly and the Council).[59] Again ironically, whether intended or not, Peden chose an entrenchment device regularly included by Australian state Labour parties in their policy agendas.[60] The choice of that device, rather than, for example, resuscitating the two-thirds majority requirement in one or both houses which, by reason of its association with Wentworth in the reactionary stage of his political life, would have been difficult to defend in moral terms, was presumably intended in part to enable the Nationalists to portray any Labour opposition to the proposed law as hypocritical. Such criticism would likely be more telling, given that the referendum was the accepted process for amendment of the national constitution: the powers or existence of the Senate could not be altered other than by the process laid out in s.128 of the Constitution Act.[61] The referendum had also been used in New South Wales in 1903 as a precursor to an 'ordinary' Act reducing the size of the Assembly.[62]

S.7A(6) was arguably the crucial provision in the new legislation. The requirement in s.7A(2) that the abolition of the Council required the addition of approval in a referendum to the 'normal' lawmaking process per se could at best be seen as an entrenching

[56] *Taylor v Attorney-General* (1917) 23 CLR 457; vol 1 pp 262–64.

[57] Vol 1 pp 325–328.

[58] Palmer and Collier's Report did not address the question of referendums being 'special majorities', most likely because the referendum was then a largely unknown creature in British (and British colonial) constitutional practice.

[59] The two-month minimum was presumably simply taken from s.128 in the national Constitution.

[60] Ross (1947) 'The philosophy of the Australian Labor Party' *The Antioch Review* 109.

[61] Vol 1 pp 164–65.

[62] Vol 1 pp 206–08.

device only in the very limited sense of Pope Cooper's 'Two Act' entrenchment thesis, ie that s.7A would have to be repealed by one Act passed in the normal way and thereafter the Council could be abolished by a second Act passed in the normal way. But even that degree of entrenchment might be thought prima facie hard to reconcile with the Privy Council's decision in *McCawley*.[63] *McCawley* appeared to endorse wholeheartedly the notion that the (albeit rebuttable) presumption applying to the lawmaking competence of Australia's state legislatures was that applying to the British Parliament: namely, that repeal of existing statutory provisions could be effected by bicameral bare majority legislation that either expressly repealed the earlier provision or did so impliedly. For s.7A to be effective in a legal sense, it would have to be differentiated in some meaningful way from the implicit entrenchment device ridiculed by the Privy Council in *McCawley*.[64]

That differentiation might be found in the suggestion that s.7A(6) could be read as having the intended (or hoped for) effect of *entrenching the s.7A(2) entrenchment*; or, in other words, as being an example of '*double entrenchment*'. Such a device had been canvassed by Professor Berriedale Keith in (1916) *Imperial unity and the dominions* in a passage referring to Kidston's successful effort[65] to remove the two-thirds majority proviso from s.9 of the Queensland Constitution Act 1867:

> If a Dominion Parliament enact to-morrow that any Act which it passes must be passed by a two-thirds majority to take effect as an alteration of the constitution, then this condition becomes one which, so long as the Act in question stands, cannot be undone by the Parliament save in the prescribed manner, that is to say, if the Act has been careful to make it clear that this provision itself is to be protected in this way. In Queensland indeed, in 1908, it was found possible to evade a difficulty that no alteration of the constitution of the Legislative Council could be made except by a two-thirds majority in the Council by repealing the proviso in the Constitution Act of 1867, which made this necessary, as the proviso itself was not covered by the requirement, *but the really effective method of requiring that the majority should apply also to any alteration of the law affecting the principle would secure the effectiveness of the rule*. The limit thus put on the powers of Dominion Parliaments is at first sight rather curious, but it follows inevitably from the express provision in [s.5 of] the Colonial Laws Validity Act, 1865.[66]

S.5, Berriedale Keith suggested, offered 'representative legislatures'[67] hitherto unappreciated possibilities to remove a small range of political questions from the ordinary lawmaking process. Given Berriedale Keith's eminence as a constitutional commentator and scholar, it seems likely that Peden was familiar with and influenced by this suggestion. Berriedale Keith's view in 1916 was also foreshadowed eight years earlier in his (1908) *Responsible government in the Dominions*, wherein (at p88) he remarked briefly in general terms that s.5 empowered colonial legislatures to 'restrict' themselves in relation to altering certain aspects of their respective colony's constitution.

Berriedale Keith, in turn – although he does not acknowledge the point in his book – was surely familiar with Charles Lilley's analysis of the repeal by simple majority in 1871

[63] [1920] AC 691; vol 1 pp 308–314.
[64] ibid.
[65] Vol 1 pp 229–33.
[66] Pp 389–90, emphasis added. The text is available at https://archive.org/stream/imperialunitydom00keit-uoft/imperialunitydom00keituoft_djvu.txt.
[67] But not presumably s.1 'colonial legislatures' that were not 'representative'; vol 1 pp 112–13.

of the two-thirds majority clause in s.10 of the Queensland Constitution Act 1867.[68] S.7A(6) can readily be seen as supplying the 'omission' which Lilley had identified in the 1867 Act's provisions.[69]

One of Peden's successors as the Challis Professor of Law, WL Morrison, has suggested that Peden was led to the s.7A formulation – and especially s.7A(6) – by Dicey's *(Introduction to the study of the) Law of the Constitution*, describing it as "the authoritative work on general constitutional matters" up to 1939 for all law students at Sydney, and as a work for which Peden had: "particular reverence".[70] Morrison makes no suggestion that Peden was influenced by Berriedale Keith. That Dicey's book was a prominent text in Sydney's law faculty in the 1920s seems entirely likely. But Morrison's observation is more by way of anecdote than evidenced assertion, and he offers no detailed explanation of how Dicey's book might have led Peden to 'latch on'[71] to s.5's 'manner and form' proviso s.5 as a means to frustrate Lang's future efforts to abolish the Council.

Sources closer to home might be thought a more obvious inspiration. Ryan had acknowledged in his submissions before the Queensland Supreme Court in *Taylor*[72] that s.5 might be used to create an entrenching device, and one would certainly expect Peden, if not Berriedale Keith, to have been aware of that. More pertinently still, the High Court's judgment in *Taylor*[73] had indicated perfectly clearly that s.5 could be invoked to replace a Legislature previously composed of an Assembly and a Council with one composed of an Assembly and a referendum. If s.5 could sustain that change, it is not a large step to assert that s.5 could also be invoked to replace a Legislature previously composed of an Assembly and a Council with one composed of an Assembly *and* a Council *and* a referendum.

Passages in *McCawley* also support that presumption. Lord Birkenhead had concluded that the court system *was not* entrenched in any form in Queensland; he had not concluded that the court system *could not* be entrenched. S.7(A) arguably met one of the weaknesses Birkenhead had identified in Feez and Stumm's case:

> … [T]hey would have no difficulty in pointing to specific articles in the legislative instrument or instruments which created the constitution, prescribing with meticulous precision the methods by which, and by which alone, it could be altered.[74]

S.7A was meticulously precise. It might also be a new example of the 'one special and individual case' idea referred to in *McCawley*.[75]

Peden's personal papers deposited in the State Library of New South Wales do not offer much insight into his inspiration. There is no reference to Lilley's 'omission' analysis,

[68] Vol 1 pp 128–29.
[69] There is no indication that Peden was inspired by the double entrenchment provisions in the South Africa Act 1909 (vol 1 p 231 n 111); nor is there any reference to that Act in the ensuing legislative debates on the Peden/Bavin bill.
[70] Morrison (1991) 'The future scope of Australian common law' 13 *Sydney LR* 335, 338.
[71] ibid 340.
[72] [1917] St R Qd 208, 218; vol 1 pp 250–51.
[73] Vol 1 pp 262–64.
[74] [1920] AC 691, 711; vol 1 p 310.
[75] [1920] AC 691, 712; vol 1 p 310.

to Berridedale Keith's 1908 suggestion or to the obviously similar double entrenchment device found in the South Africa Act 1909.[76] The most intriguing source is a single page of typescript misfiled between two pages of a copy of a 1926 memorandum by members of the Council to the British government protesting Lang's swamping initiative. The page, which is not dated and which does not identify its author, says inter alia:

> These provisions are legal restrictions, and not merely political restrictions on the power of the state Parliament … The legal basis of these restraints is the Colonial Laws Validity Act 1865 s.5 … The effect of this proviso [s.5] is discussed in the judgment of Isaacs and Rich in the McCauley [*sic*] v The King (26 CLR 9 at pp 54,57) where it is pointed out that if no special provision as to the manner and form of passing a particular class of law exists, then the ordinary method may be followed: but if as to given classes of law a specific method is prescribed it must be followed.[77]

It seems perfectly plausible that Peden authored the note.[78] He – and presumably Bavin wearing his KC hat – must have been very familiar with *McCawley*, and both were surely sufficiently adept as lawyers to appreciate that the case was decided on a 'had not entrenched' but not a 'could not entrench' basis. But if that surmise is correct, it is not one given much support by the relevant parliamentary debates.

Debate in the Council

Conventional practice in New South Wales required that any bill affecting the Council should begin its legislative passage there rather than in the Assembly.[79] The bill came on for second reading on 10 May 1928,[80] when the government's case was opened by the then Attorney-General, Francis Boyce.[81]

[76] Vol 1 p 231 fn 111.

[77] Peden Family Collection (Legal Papers – Legislative Council Bill) ML MSS 1663 1 (p2 of the box). Peden's lecture notes from 1940 on the subject of New South Wales constitutional law make no reference to the origins of s.7A; ibid ML MSS 1663 9, p268. The various boxes of letters do not contain any correspondence on the issue.

[78] There is also, in Peden's handwriting, an undated note with no page number taking the form of a proposed amendment to s.16 of the Constitution Act 1902 (the provision authorising the Governor to appoint members of the Legislative Council), which was presumably intended to provide a statutory basis for the Governor to refuse to accede to a swamping request (and, as such, to provide an additional or alternative basis to s.7A to safeguard the Legislative Council's existence): "It is hereby declared that in the exercise of the authority conferred upon the Governor by or in pursuance of this section the Governor may at his own discretion refuse to be guided by the advice of the Executive Council"; Peden Family Collection (Legal Papers – Legislative Council Bill) ML MSS 1663.

[79] The convention was evidently not accepted in Queensland, where the abolition Act had begun life in the Assembly; vol 1 p 325.

[80] *NSWLCD* 10 May 1928 p502. There were 93 members of the Council (three more than in the Assembly) in 1928; www.parliament.nsw.gov.au/hansard/Documents/1928-29.pdf.

[81] Born in New South Wales in 1872, Boyce came from a wealthy background. He took BA and LLB degrees at the University of Sydney before qualifying at the Bar. He was a protégé of Barton's, and stood unsuccessfully as a Liberal in the 1905 Assembly elections. He did not again contest an election, but drifted into the fringes of Nationalist politics and was appointed to the Council by Fuller in 1923, then served as Minister in Fuller's government before being chosen as Attorney-General by Bavin in 1927. Boyce was subsequently appointed to the State Supreme Court in 1932; http://adb.anu.edu.au/biography/boyce-francis-stewart-5320.

Boyce's speech is notable for his apparent assumption at various points that s.7A simply could not have any *legal* effect, ie it could be repealed in its entirety at any time in the normal bicameral simple majority plus royal assent manner:

> I will admit at once that this bill could be repealed by another Parliament. I do not suppose anyone needs authority for that because authorities as old as Lord Bacon have pointed it out, but I read from Dicey on the "Law of the Constitution," where that gentleman says:
>
> "That Parliaments have more than once intended and endeavoured to pass Acts which should tie the hands of their successors is certain, but the endeavour has always ended in failure. Of statutes intended to ·arrest the possible course of future legislation the most noteworthy are the Acts which embody the treaties of union with Scotland and Ireland."
>
> These Acts are the classic examples to show that an Act of Parliament cannot be passed which will bind another equally sovereign body which comes afterwards.[82]

But Boyce then suggested that the bill when enacted would place a legal constraint *on the Governor*. The original formulation of s.7A(2) contained the words in italics:

> (2) A Bill for any purpose within subsection one of this section shall not be presented to the Governor for His Majesty's assent until the Bill has been approved by the electors in accordance with this section *and any such bill shall contain a provision to that effect*.

The assertion is peculiar, since the text of the proposed s.7A was directed at whoever might be responsible for passing any bill to the Governor, not to the Governor himself. The effect Boyce was suggesting would surely have to have been drafted quite differently; ie

> (2) A Bill for any purpose within subsection one of this section shall not be accepted by the Governor for His Majesty's assent until the Bill has been approved by the electors in accordance with this section *and any such bill shall contain a provision to that effect*.

As noted below, such linguistic and/or conceptual imprecision was not uncommon among participants in the legislative debates. If Boyce's assertion accurately describes the government's intention, however, it is perhaps surprising that no provision was made in the bill to specify by what legal method the Governor would be prevented from assenting to the 'bill'.[83] A legal impediment of this sort on the Governor's discretion would be so radical a departure from previous practice that the need for an explicit remedial mechanism is obvious. Its absence might indicate that Boyce's ambition was limited to the hope that the Governor *would not* as a matter of politics assent to a bill to abolish the Council which did not make such provision, rather than to the expectation that as a matter of law the Governor *could not* do so.

However, we are then pointed back towards s.7A being intended to have legal rather than political effects by Boyce's apparent recognition that that legal effect would subsist

[82] *NSWLCD* 10 May 1928 p502. Although Boyce does not make the point in terms, his speech does rather suggest that he did believe – contra *McCawley* – that any such repeal would have to be express.

[83] See eg Sawer G (1944) 'Injunction, parliamentary process, and the restriction of parliamentary competence' *LQR* 83. The Equity Act 1901 s.16(1) contained a broad grant of jurisdiction to the Supreme Court to grant injunctions, in terms which did not expressly exclude (and equally did not expressly include) such a grant in respect of parliamentary proceedings. It may be that Boyce – and the drafters of the Bill – had this provision in mind; but there is no reference to it in the debates.

only while s.7A(2) remained on the statute book. And he then directed the Council's attention to s.7A(6), describing it as a "very important" provision which would apparently ensure that s.7A itself could not be repealed unless the repeal was approved in a referendum.

The overall incoherence of Boyce's argument, which seemed to assert both that Parliament could and could not repeal s.7A in the usual way, also seemed to puzzle both some of Boyce's Council colleagues and the Attorney-General himself:

> The Hon. Sir JOSEPH CARRUTHERS: The Minister has me confused. He quoted from "Dicey" that Parliament cannot tie the hands of another Parliament; but this is an answer to "Dicey." This is a way of tying the hands!
>
> The Hon. F. S. BOYCE: It is the best we can do.[84]

The Council adjourned shortly after this exchange, and the second reading resumed on 15 May 1928. The overwhelming bulk of the resumed debate was devoted to consideration of the history of the Council and the merits (or lack thereof) of retaining it, whether in its current or an amended form. The entrenchment issue received little attention. Willis, opening for the opposition, seemed to replicate Boyce's earlier confusion as to both the intended and the likely legal effects of the measure, and especially of the proposed s.7A(6):

> But the bill in its entirety is a cunningly drawn bill. It looks very innocent at first glance, but it is one of the most cunning bills that has come before this chamber since I have been a member … I refer to the power of any government to tie the hands of its successors. I think it is accepted that no government has a right to tie the hands of its successors …
>
> The answer of the Minister is that this does not tie the hands of succeeding governments, but merely provides machinery with which they may operate. I fail to find the distinction between having your hands tied and being told you may do things, but in a way prescribed, especially when it has been shown that the way prescribed would make it exceedingly difficult to do things at all.[85]

The second reading vote was 42–6 in favour,[86] whereupon the bill went immediately into committee. Little progress was made that evening; proceedings adjourned at 10.40 pm on a more prosaic note:

> The Hon. Sir JOSEPH CARRUTHERS: I would like to call your attention to the fact that some hon. members object to being kept in cold storage. This is a freezing chamber in the early part of the day and if, Mr. President, you can do anything to add a little warmth to the atmosphere, some of us will be very pleased.

[84] *NSWLCD* 10 May 1928 p506.

[85] *NSWLCD* 15 May 1928 pp 573–74. The only other member to engage with the question was James Concannon (one of Lang's 1925 appointees – and who had voted for abolition in 1926) at p593, and he seemed as confused (or uncertain) as Boyce and Willis: "Clause 6 of this particular bill seems to me to strike a fundamental blow at the principle of Parliament, or the right of the representatives of the people in the Legislative Assembly to determine what the policy and the legislation of the future shall be. It appears me that if it is possible for this government to introduce a bill to provide for an amendment of the Constitution in certain directions it is also competent for any incoming Administration to introduce a bill to repeal this present one." Willis, like many of his legislative contemporaries, repeatedly used the term 'Government' when he must have meant – even if he did not realise it – 'the Legislature'. Concannon was more rigorous in limiting his use of the term to the introduction rather than enactment of a bill.

[86] So barely half of the Council's 93 members participated in the vote.

> The Hon. F. S. BOYCE: I may inform the honourable member that arrangements have been made to install radiators to-morrow.[87]

The committee stage continued the next day. Attention focused on the proposed s.7A(2)'s last clause – "*and any such bill shall contain a provision to that effect*" – to which Boyce had briefly alluded in his second reading speech. Carruthers led the debate on this point. He seemingly considered that even without those words – which Boyce had so oddly characterised as placing a legal impediment on the Governor granting the royal assent – s.7A would, as he termed it: "intercept the royal assent"[88] if no referendum had actually been held. Why, then, was there any need for such a clause: "I do not think the words in the bill help us one iota. They are merely reiteration. They will not carry us any further."[89]

In response, Boyce gave some insight into the intentions of: "the gentlemen responsible for drafting the bill", even though he did not identify the 'gentlemen' by name: "Although one padlock is put on I see no objection to there being two if the second will make the door tighter."[90] The committee stage then ended with Boyce repeating the ambiguity as to the bill's intended legal effect in which he was mired at second reading:

> I do not put it forward as being something to tie the hands of Parliament. That is hardly the way to describe it. I do not want to tie the hands of Parliament; all I want is to ensure that the people – the other parties to the Constitution – shall have a full voice, and the fullest possible voice, on this question.[91]

Perhaps the most notable aspect of the bill's passage in the Council is that not one member at any point made any reference to CLVA 1865 s.5, nor to any other provision of the 1865 Act. Nor was any considered reference made to the High Court's decision in *Taylor* or the Privy Council's judgment in *McCawley*. There was not a single suggestion that the effect of s.7A might be to reconstitute the Legislature into a differently composed body for the (single) purpose of abolishing the Council, nor that adding a referendum to the normal lawmaking process might be a 'manner and form' proviso per s.5 or a 'special majority' for a 'particular purpose', as the Law Officers used those terms in the 1864 Report. Nor was any explicit consideration given to whether an entrenchment device might be rooted in s.4 [BAA] of the 1855 Act – or, conversely, whether s.4 [BAA] precluded any such device from being effective, notwithstanding subsequent enactment of the CLVA 1865. Whatever weight the 'gentlemen' drafters of s.7A to whom Boyce had referred might have attached to s.4 [BAA] and/or s.5 respectively was not a subject of discussion.[92]

Assuming Peden to have been one of the 'gentlemen', it is intriguing that he took no significant part in the Council debate. His single contribution came at the end of the committee stage,[93] when he moved an amendment to modify the bill's initial title, which

[87] *NSWLCD* 15 May 1928 p601.
[88] *NSWLCD* 16 May 1928 p659.
[89] ibid.
[90] ibid p660.
[91] ibid p662.
[92] No member of the Council made any reference to Berriedale Keith's analysis, to Lilley's 'omission' speech or to the similar provisions of the South Africa Act 1909.
[93] *NSWLCD* 16 May 1928 p663.

he thought too widely cast. In his very brief speech, he shed no light at all on the sources that inspired s.7A and offered no view on whether the referendum requirement would be legally enforceable.[94]

There was no further debate at third reading, which occurred on 17 May. And then, for 10 months, the bill sat on the table of the Assembly.[95]

Debate in the Assembly

The bill was put forward by Bavin for second reading on 12 March 1929.[96] The apparent urgency underlying the election commitment ("in the first working session") had evidently receded. The day's activities had begun with a bitter debate over several government-sponsored motions (all eventually approved by a majority of members) to suspend several Labour members for contempt. The fractious atmosphere abated somewhat as the Assembly proceeded through several uncontentious questions to ministers and the final stages of bills relating to public hospitals and the regulation of surveyors, before debate on the bill commenced.

Bavin led for the government. He began by reiterating the Nationalists' manifesto promise in the 1927 election. Bavin's advocacy of the bill professedly lay less in a desire to preserve the Council per se, or in a concern to safeguard the state against 'socialism', than in an appeal to sentiments of democratic morality:

> We are determined that there should be no repetition of what we saw in the last Parliament when there was an effort to destroy the Legislative Council and to make a fundamental alteration in the Constitution of the state without consulting the people.[97]

Bavin also asserted that the New South Wales Constitution recognised a 'fundamental distinction' between laws: "which involve a change of the machinery by which the laws are made, and the ordinary laws which govern the lives and interests of members of the community".[98] The bill's purpose, Bavin asserted, was to give effect to that principle.

In one, formalistic, sense, that observation is manifestly correct: the origins of s.4 [BAA] of the 1855 Act lay in Russell's assumption – approved without challenge or debate by the Commons and Lords despite being opposed by William Wentworth and Edward Deas Thomson[99] – that s.4 [BAA] was needed to effect amendment to sch.1

[94] In a lecture to the New South Wales Constitutional Association in March 1930, Peden expressed uncertainty as to whether s.7A would be upheld in a legal challenge to an abolition bill undertaken through the normal lawmaking process: "That was a point of law which remained to be decided, and some eminent lawyers believed that the Courts would decide that the Act could be repealed in the ordinary way"; *SMH* 1 April 1930 p10, https://trove.nla.gov.au/newspaper/article/16638297.

[95] *NSWLCD* 17 May 1928 p717.

[96] *NSWLAD* 12 March 1929 p 3619 et seq.

[97] ibid p3621. Bavin was not willing to acknowledge that the Council had since its inception been a body that acted without in any sense 'consulting the people', an omission which sparked increasingly fierce exchanges as the debate progressed.

[98] ibid p3620.

[99] Vol 1 p 48 n 58.

of the Act because the general legislative power given in s.1 of the schedule could not achieve that objective.[100] In another, substantive, sense, the observation is absurd, since Russell's purpose in promoting s.4 was to place all matters within the competence of the Legislature on an equal procedural footing; bare bicameral majorities with either express or implied amending/repealing effects would suffice. In a third sense, the observation is problematic, because of the point that any court would likely accept, namely that whatever the effect of s.4 [BAA] may have been, to the extent of any inconsistency between s.4 [BAA] and s.5 of the CLVA 1865, the latter provision should surely prevail.

But while Bavin seemed clear about the purpose of his government's bill, he seemed (at best) uncertain (or confused, or perhaps disingenuous) about its legal effect. Echoing Boyce's analysis in the Council, he made this comment in response to Lang's suggestion that the next Parliament would repeal the measure in the ordinary way if Labour won the next election:

> The next Parliament may repeal this bill, if it is able to get the Legislative Council to assent to its repeal, and if the leader of the Opposition, supposing him to be in control of that Parliament, passes a law to take away from the people the right to express an opinion on a fundamental alteration of the Constitution.[101]

One might have thought that the presumed legal point of cl.7A(6) was to ensure that the bill – if enacted – could not be repealed by the next 'Parliament' in the form of the Assembly and the Council (and royal assent) even if the Assembly and Council's members voted unanimously for its repeal, but that approval in a referendum would be required as well. Bavin appears here not to recognise that possibility. This could be attributable to the remark being made off the cuff in the heat of debate, rather than as an indication that Bavin did not really understand (or, more cynically, would not admit) what Peden's proposal was intended to do.

However, Bavin made similar comments on several occasions during the debate. In response to a Labour member's assertion that the bill was an attempt to bind future parliaments, Bavin interjected "Nobody is trying to do that here".[102] The exchange then proceeded:

> Mr. GOSLING: … This bill is so much waste paper, because when the Labour Party comes into office it will exercise the powers of the government of a sovereign State. The Premier may have his last word but the public will possibly change the government; and if it does as soon as we obtain control of this Chamber, and the Upper House, no legal verbiage can stop Parliament from repealing the bill which we are now considering. No lawyer can deny that.
>
> Mr. BAVIN: That is quite true. But we do not seek to bind future Parliaments. We could not do that, even if we wanted to do it. We are not trying to do it. As long as you go to the country and the public support you, you are entitled to do what you like!
>
> Mr. GOSLING: I had an impression that hon. members supporting the government thought that this bill if it is passed will prevent a victorious Labour government from abolishing the Upper House.

[100] Vol 1 pp 46–48.
[101] *NSWLAD* 12 March 1929 p3624.
[102] ibid p3695.

> Mr. BAVIN: That was never suggested. But it will put difficulties in the way of your doing it without consulting the people. That is all. I only want to insist on your consulting the people – you might try to dodge it – before you attempt to abolish the Upper House! ….
>
> MR GOSLING: If that is so, this bill is so much "poppycock" and the Premier is trying to make his supporters in this House and outside think that he is doing something. In my opinion on the face of it subclause (6) reads as if this legislation was going to bind future Parliaments. I am sure it cannot.[103]

Mr Gosling was followed by several other members who shared his 'poppycock' view of cl.7A(6).[104]

The subtle – or perhaps semantically technical – point to be made here, which point evidently did not occur to Bavin or any other member of either house who spoke in the debate, was that s.7A might be taken to have *redefined* the Legislature for the one special purpose of reforming or abolishing the Council. If one accepts that characterisation of the effect of s.7A, then the 'Legislature' was not bound, because the 'Legislature' now consisted of Assembly, Council and referendum plus royal assent.

Despite the evident lack of clarity as to the bill's intended legal effect, it passed second reading the next day by 44 votes to 32. It was then immediately taken into committee. Bavin again led for the government, and again suggested that he doubted the bill when enacted would or should have a legal, entrenching effect. In a curious episode, Bavin moved an amendment to the original text to remove the above-mentioned italicised words from cl.7A(2). Boyce, we may recall, had placed great weight on these words, seeing them as a means to control the Governor's capacity to assent to an abolition bill; 'make the door tighter', as he put it. Bavin had now decided to remove them: "This amendment is made in pursuance of the opinion I have already expressed that it is not desirable to attempt to tie the hands of future Parliaments."[105]

Bavin then told the Assembly clearly that in his view the bill, if enacted, would have no legal effect at all, but would operate only as a source of political pressure on a future Labour-controlled Legislature. His comment was prompted by an intervention from a Labour backbencher (who, in equating the Assembly with the Legislature, displayed an unhappy misunderstanding of basic constitutional principle):

> Mr. TULLY: If this bill is passed, will this House have the right to repeal it.
>
> Mr. BAVIN: Of course, it will. I am not trying to tie the hands of a future Parliament.
>
> Mr LANG: You cannot!

[103] ibid pp 3696–97.

[104] Sir Thomas Henley, ibid pp 3698–99: "I think that this bill has no value, and will not be worth the paper it is written on." Mr McKell at p3704: "The peculiar part of this particular piece of legislation is that not only does it propose that before any alteration of the Constitution is made there shall be a referendum, but it goes further and says that this piece of legislation itself shall not be altered unless a referendum is taken. I submit that is an absolute absurdity. The bill in this respect is of no value whatever. If in six months' time. Parliament says that this piece of legislation is repealed, that is the end of it, and it is repealed. For this Parliament to purport to bind future Parliaments in this way is simply futile." Henley was elected to the Assembly in 1904 as a Liberal, and served briefly as a minister in Fuller's Nationalist administrations. By 1929, he had become (according to his entry in the *Australian dictionary of biography*) increasingly irascible personally and politically, an assertion borne out by his criticism of his party's line on this issue; http://adb.anu.edu.au/biography/henley-sir-thomas-6637. McKell, a Labour member, was elected to the Assembly in 1917 and had been a minister in Lang's first government.

[105] *NSWLAD* 13 March 1929 p 3710. To adapt Boyce's metaphor, leaving the door closed rather than locked.

> Mr. BAVIN: I am aware of that. I have not reached the age I have reached without realising that. I have spent some little time in the study of constitutional problems and I know that we cannot prevent any subsequent Parliament from repealing this measure. If members of the Opposition like to go to the country and tell the people that they are going to take away from them the right of expressing an opinion on an important constitutional alteration and the people give them authority to take that right away I have not the slightest objection. All I want to do is to preserve, as far as I am able, the right of the people to say whether the Constitution shall be altered in regard to the abolition of the Legislative Council or not.

Given that the bill was arguably effecting a significant change to the Constitution, it was propelled through its parliamentary passage with remarkable speed.[106] The report stage was the briefest of formalities at the conclusion of the committee stage, and third reading was set for the next day.

The third reading debate occupies barely three pages – which includes the lists of Ayes (41) and Noes (35) – of the records of the Assembly debates. The session was dominated by a denunciatory speech from Lang, which began with an attack on the Bavin government's apparent duplicity and with the claim that the bill was in legal terms a futile measure:

> Mr. LANG: I protest against the third reading of this measure. After considering all that was said during the debates on the second readings and Committee stages, and after further examining the bill, I am even more strongly of the opinion that the measure does what the government says it does not do. It attempts to tie the hands of future Parliaments, and because it does that it is a measure which this House should not pass. In any case, I look upon the bill as so much waste paper, for what an Act of Parliament can do an Act of Parliament can undo. The Constitution cannot be amended in the way in which the government pretends to be amending it by this bill. If this bill becomes law it will be an Act of Parliament, and nothing else, and an Act of Parliament can always be repealed.

As in the debates in the Council, the CLVA 1865, Lilley's 'omission' observations, Berriedale Keith's *Cooper* analysis, the High Court judgments in *Taylor*, the Privy Council's decision in *McCawley* and the double entrenchment provisions of the South Africa Act 1909 were not referred to by any speakers in the Assembly. S.4 [BAA] of the 1855 Act received only the briefest of mentions.

The bill was reserved for assent on 29 March, which was granted – evidently without any attempt by Lang to forestall it – shortly thereafter.

The Constitution Further Amendment (Referendum) Act 1930

It is, given the content of the legislative debates on the bill, difficult to conclude with any confidence that Bavin and his ministers expected, even if they hoped (and there is not even much evidence to support the latter), that s.7A could and would function as a legal rather than political impediment to the Council's abolition. However, s.7A was one element of the Bavin government's two-part strategy to secure the Council's long-term

[106] Perhaps not so remarkable, given that Theodore's government had pressed its abolition bill through both houses with similar haste; vol 1 pp 325–27.

viability. The second element was laid out in the Constitution Further Amendment (Referendum) Act 1930. The Act made provision for the holding of any referendum for s.7A purposes, but it also contained several schedules, the first of which was a draft Act which would significantly alter the Council's composition and powers, in a manner much influenced by the terms of the British Parliament Act 1911, which had curbed the powers of the House of Lords and the subsequent Bryce Commission – which reported in 1917 – as to the role that house should play in Britain's (then) modern Constitution.[107]

The scheduled Act (s.2) provided that the Council would in future have a fixed composition of 60 members. Those members would – after a curious fashion – be 'elected':

> Such Members shall be elected at elections at which the electors shall be the Members of the Legislative Council and the Members of the Legislative Assembly voting as one electoral body and recording their votes at sittings of the respective Houses of the Parliament.

The first electorate would comprise the Assembly and the Council members in the unreformed Council. Per s.3, 'elections' would be at three-year intervals, but with only one-quarter of the 60 seats contested on each occasion. The proposed Act also made provision to limit the reformed Council's powers of legislative veto. If the Council rejected or 'failed to pass' an appropriations bill, that bill could, once a month had expired, be sent straight to the Governor for assent.

Whether Bavin sincerely regarded this mooted reform as desirable is unclear. He was certainly in no hurry to present the proposal to a s.7A referendum. Although an enabling bill to set up the machinery for a referendum was enacted, the machinery was not put into place before the next Assembly election, in October 1930. To the extent, however, that Bavin had envisaged s.7A as a measure to protect the Council against a future Labour administration, his foresight proved well founded.

[107] For a supportive view, see Pratt (1929) 'Proposed reform of Legislative Council in New South Wales' *The Australian Quarterly* 80. On Bryce and the House of Lords, see Loveland (2015) *Constitutional law, administrative law and human rights: a critical introduction* pp 165–67; Shell (1992) *The House of Lords* ch 1.

3

Trethowan in the New South Wales Courts

> Parliament in its wisdom might well think that there were possible changes of so important and so far reaching a character that a special procedure ought to be followed before they could become law … [A] proposal of so far reaching and so momentous a character as that for the substitution of a unicameral system for a bicameral system … is one which Parliament might not unreasonably consider of such importance that it should not be left to be determined by the passage of an Act in the ordinary way through both Houses.
>
> Street CJ in *Trethowan v Peden and Others* (1930) 31 SR NSW 183, 202–03.

I. The 'Big Fella' Returns: The 1930 Election

The 1930 election was the finest hour of Jack Lang's political career. Lang ran the Labour campaign against what he perceived to be a host of enemies, in the form both of people and policy. Bavin's Nationalists topped the list; but Lang's relations with Scullin's national government were at best strained, there was a pro-Scullin faction within the New South Wales party, a new Governor was in post and the worldwide depression, with its obviously deleterious implications for state finances, showed no signs of abating.

But Labour had taken 55 of the Assembly's 90 seats, giving Lang in principle an overwhelming lower house majority if – and a very big if – he could maintain discipline in party ranks. He also enjoyed the novel prospect of a Cabinet containing no obvious enemies, and at least initially a broadly supportive parliamentary party.[1] Lang's administration did not have such a majority in the Council, and could not to be sure even as to how many of the Council's nominally Labour members would regularly support the government. But the Council provided Lang with two enemies on which the state Labour Party could train its unusually (if only temporarily) unified sights: the Council itself and the legislative provisions Bavin had promoted to protect it against the Labour government now in power.

[1] Nairn (1995) op cit pp 210–11.

Table 3.1 New South Wales Legislative Assembly election, 1930 (25 October 1930)[a]

Party	% vote	Seats won	Change
Nationalist	30.5	23	−12
Country Party	9.5	12	−1
Australian Labour Party	55.0	55	+13

[a] I have included the two independent Nationalists who won seats in 1925 with the Nationalists and the two independent Labour members from 1925 with the Labour members for the purposes of the 'change' column.

The New Government's Plans for the Legislative Council

In reaction to the criticisms levelled at his 1926 attempt to abolish the Council that he had not signalled the Labour Party's intention to do so in the 1925 election, Lang placed abolition high on Labour's list of policy objectives in its 1930 election campaign. Lang rooted the policy in the long-standing Labour hostility to second chambers per se, but also suggested that the Council was an unnecessary burden on the public purse. For good measure, building on the second theme, Lang also indicated that a Labour government would seek to reduce the size of the Assembly and press for abolition of the office of State Governor throughout the country.[2]

de Chair had been succeeded as Governor by Sir Phillip Game in May 1930. Game was a career soldier, rising to the rank of major during World War I before joining the newly created Royal Flying Corps in 1916 and becoming Air Vice Marshall before retiring in 1929.[3] That a man with no experience either of Australia or of political governance could be appointed as Governor is perhaps a strong indication of the then British government's rather patronising attitude towards New South Wales; although – and here one enters the realm of speculation – the appointment of so obviously inexperienced and so quintessentially British a candidate might be seen as installing a Governor who would adopt an appropriately conservative position towards a future Lang administration.

Arriving in Australia in May 1930, Game promptly formed a friendly relationship with Bavin, to the extent of sending Bavin private commiserations at the result of the October election. Game's first dealing of substance with Lang, barely a week after the election, was to consider Lang's request for a mass appointment to the Council, with reports of the numbers sought varying between 40 and 80. Lang did not conceal the fact that he hoped this time to succeed where he failed in 1926 to fill the Council with Labour members who would vote for abolition. Game indicated a willingness to accept 30 nominations, which likely would not have secured Lang a working majority, but equivocated over approving a larger number, which might be deployed to abolish the Council. In Lang's recollection, Game was deliberately obstructive to Lang's request, and had acted improperly by seeking advice from Peden and the state's then Chief Justice,

[2] The relevant parts of the 'policy speech' are at Lang (1962) op cit pp 296–97.

[3] http://adb.anu.edu.au/biography/game-sir-philip-woolcott-6272. de Chair was 66 in 1930, and on leaving New South Wales returned – in retirement – to London.

Sir Phillip Street,[4] about s.7A's likely legal efficacy should Lang's government seek to repeal it and abolish the Council through the ordinary simple majority process.[5]

The Council as then constituted offered no immediate obstacles to the new government's initial legislative programme, much of which was designed to ameliorate the economic hardships caused by the depression. Measures were promoted and promptly passed to abolish the use of distress by landlords as a remedy against tenants in rent arrears, to enhance the court's powers to prevent evictions and to empower courts to postpone foreclosure proceedings in respect of residential mortgages. Lang's government also imposed a new tax on gambling winnings, and successfully promoted (as Theodore had previously done in Queensland) a bill establishing a state lottery.[6]

Amidst this hectic legislative programme, and while Lang pressed Game on nominating new members to the Council, his government also took steps to remove the referendum requirement in respect of the Council's abolition introduced by the 1929 Act. (Indeed, on Lang's account, those steps were a direct response to Game's refusal to appoint all the additional members to the Council that Lang had requested.[7]) The government scheme to achieve this objective had two elements, contained in two separate bills.

The terms of the first bill, introduced into the Council on 3 December 1930 as The Constitution (Amendment) Bill 1930,[8] were simple:

S.1. This Act may be cited as the "Constitution Amendment Act, 1930".
S.2. The Constitution (Legislative Council) Amendment Act, 1929, and s. 7A of the Constitution Act, 1902, as amended by subsequent Acts, and the Constitution Further Amendment Act (Referendum) Act, 1930, are repealed.

The measure was given a first reading in the Council session on 3 December 1930, and was scheduled for second reading later that day.

The second bill, entitled the Constitution Further Amendment Act (Legislative Council Abolition) Bill 1930, also received its first reading on 3 December, and was set for second reading on 4 December. Its proposed terms were:

S.1. This Act may be cited as the "Constitution Further Amendment Act (Legislative Council Abolition) Act, 1930" and shall be read with the Constitution Act 1902, as amended by subsequent Acts.
S.2. (1) The Legislative Council of N.S.W. is abolished.
(2) The seat of every member of the said Legislative Council shall, on and after the commencement of the Act, be vacant, and the office of member of the Legislative Council is abolished.

The apparent logic of the Lang government's scheme was that once s.7A had been repealed through the usual simple majority in both houses plus royal assent process, the Legislature could abolish the Council in the same way.

[4] Of whom more is said below.
[5] Lang (1970) op cit pp 107–09, 112–14.
[6] Vol 1 p 318: Nairn (1995) op cit pp 211–14.
[7] Lang (1962) op cit pp 297–99.
[8] *SMH* 3 December 1930, https://trove.nla.gov.au/newspaper/article/16735518/1164661.

The 'logic' is, however, puzzling. If s.7A(6) was of no special legal effect – in the sense that it was repealable in the simple majority fashion – then, per *McCawley*, there would be no need either for a *Cooper*-esque 'Two Act' repeal process or even for the explicit repeal of any part of s.7A. An Act passed by the simple majority process which abolished the Council without making any reference at all to s.7A would be valid. In other words, the first of the two envisaged Acts was entirely redundant.

The strategy has obvious echoes of the way in which the two-thirds clauses of the 1855 Act were removed in the late 1850s,[9] of the repeal of the two-thirds clause in s.10 of the Queensland Constitution Act 1867 in 1871[10] and of Kidston's tactic to remove the remaining two-thirds clause (s.9) in Queensland's Constitution.[11] Lang's government perhaps had this history in mind as a legitimising – for the purposes of public opinion – precedent, with the two-thirds provisos used as an analogy for the s.7A referendum (although neither precedent had involved a two-thirds clause protecting the two-thirds clause in the way that s.7A(6) perhaps protected s.7A(2)). If s.7A was indeed entrenched, a Two Act by simple majority repeal would be ineffective; and if it was not entrenched, a Two Act by simple majority repeal would be unnecessary. The middle point Lang's government adopted is a curiosity.

Little light is shed by the bills' (brief) parliamentary history. Willis – reappointed to Lang's Cabinet and party leader in the Council – led for the government at second reading for the first bill on 3 December.[12] Willis quoted at length from Boyce's second reading speech in 1929 to suggest that s.7A was amenable to repeal in the ordinary way. Willis appeared to accept that the matter would have to be resolved in the courts, but nonetheless offered his own – and presumably the government's – view of the legal position. Relying largely on Dicey's *Law of the Constitution*, Willis suggested that s.7A(6) was 'bad in law'. Debate in either house was not extensive; the opposition now apparently proceeded on the basis that the issue would better be fought as a legal rather than a political one. Given the apparent uncertainty evinced by both Bavin and Boyce as to the 1929 Act's legal effect, that choice is perhaps a surprising one. Nonetheless, both bills completed their passages through the Assembly and Council early in December 1930. A week later, the matter was before the courts.

II. The *Trethowan* Hearing in the New South Wales Supreme Court

Trethowan was in some respects a 'friendly' action, insofar as Lang's bills to repeal s.7A and to abolish the Council were not opposed by the Nationalist and Country parties either in the Council or in the Assembly. One of the small ironies of the litigation was that the Assembly and Council's standing orders placed responsibility for sending a bill which originated in the Council for the royal assent with the President of the Council.

[9] Vol 1 pp 56–58.
[10] Vol 1 pp 127–128.
[11] Vol 1 pp 228–230.
[12] *NSWLAD* 3 December 1930 p98.

This was, of course, Sir John Peden, the author of s.7A. The initial substance of the claim was therefore a request for an injunction against Peden to prevent both the s.7A repeal bill and the Council abolition bill being sent for the royal assent until a referendum had been held in which each was approved.

The primary titular plaintiff was Arthur Trethowan.[13] Trethowan was a successful farmer and a (by then) relatively minor figure in the Country Party. He was nominated to the Council in December 1916 by Holman immediately after Holman's move to the Nationalists, largely, it seems, to attract Country Party support for the new government,[14] and was still sitting in the early 1930s. Trethowan's role was essentially that of figurehead for the Nationalist/Country Party opposition coalition. Trethowan was joined in bringing the case by the – in the circumstances aptly named – Thomas Playfair,[15] who first came to political prominence as Chairman of the New South Wales Constitutional Association,[16] before being appointed to the Council by Bavin in 1927.

The case began life in the New South Wales Courts as *Trethowan and another v Peden and others*. Peden, having made it known that he intended to present either or both of the bills for the royal assent, unsurprisingly offered no defence. Whether Peden actually intended to present the bills might be doubted; had his expressed intention been sincere, one assumes he might have done so before proceedings were issued. The more credible interpretation is that Peden was fully involved with formulating the claim. Behind the legal façade, it was Lang's administration that stood in the constitutional dock: the '*others*' were Lang and his ministers. The government had evidently not sought to compel Peden to send the bill for assent.[17] It seems likely that Lang, given the force of his own (and apparently Bavin's) belief that the entrenching clause was a futile legal gesture, was content to let the legal proceedings run their course, expecting that his view would eventually be held legally correct.[18]

The case initially came before Long Innes J in the Supreme Court on 11 December 1930 as an application for an interim injunction, pending hearing of the claim for the grant of a permanent injunction on the basis that Peden had no power to present either bill. Long Innes had been appointed to the Court in 1925. Born in Sydney in 1869, he was schooled in England and took undergraduate and graduate law degrees at Oxford. He practised briefly at the English Bar, before returning to Sydney and building a practice

[13] http://adb.anu.edu.au/biography/trethowan-sir-arthur-king-8849.

[14] P 5 above.

[15] http://adb.anu.edu.au/biography/playfair-thomas-alfred-john-jack-8063.

[16] P 22 above.

[17] There was some press speculation that Lang had threatened to advise the Governor to dismiss Peden if Peden did not present the bills; see the *SMH* 8 December 1930 p9 article dramatically entitled 'UPPER HOUSE. Drastic schemes suggested', https://trove.nla.gov.au/newspaper/page/1164742. See also *LD* 5 December 1930, which ran a lengthy article entitled 'PEDEN AGAINST THE PEOPLE?', which began: "THWARTING DEMOCRACY OUT of the labyrinth of Tory tactics, whereby the enemies of democracy hope to save the Legislative Council and thwart forever the will of the people, emerges the/knightly figure of Sir John/Beverley Peden, LLB., K.C. – inter alia President of the Council", https://trove.nla.gov.au/newspaper/article/236944303.

[18] Nairn suggests Lang was content to let Trethowan's suit (slowly) make its way through the courts: "That legal action would obviously take a long time. So there remains at least a whiff of suspicion that Lang as in 1925–1926, proposed to use the inevitable strife over abolition to deflect and confuse any possible criticism from the Labour Party and the labour movement should he encounter any intractable problems in Parliament"; Nairn (1995) op cit p213.

in equity and commercial law, becoming a silk in 1916. He had no obvious party political affiliations, and appears never to have run for elective office.[19]

Long Innes J had the power under the relevant legislation, the Equity Act 1901,[20] to hear the application for a permanent injunction sitting alone. Mindful, no doubt, of the case's political significance, per s.6 of the Act he referred the matter directly to the full court. He was evidently surprised that Lang and his ministers refused to undertake at the initial hearing that they would refrain from any attempt to have the bills presented to the Governor until the matter was heard.[21] He thus granted the interim injunction pending the hearing, which was – with understandable promptness – set down for four days later. *Trethowan and others v Peden and others*[22] was then argued in the New South Wales Supreme Court for four days shortly before Christmas 1930.[23]

The Court

Long Innes was one of five judges who heard the claim. He was joined by Street CJ and Ferguson, Owen and James Chief Justice, Phillip Street, born in 1864, was raised and educated in Sydney.[24] After a brief career in practice, Street accepted a junior judicial appointment in 1907. He made steady progress through the judicial ranks, and was appointed Chief Justice by Fuller's Nationalist/Progressive (in effect, by Bavin qua Attorney-General) coalition government in January 1925. Street had no obviously partisan political affiliations, but it is likely that his political sympathies did not predispose him favourably towards Lang's administration. The appointment was reported in the *SMH* of 21 January 1925 without any allusion being made to Street's likely political views.[25] An article in *The Sun* a week earlier had hinted at a more proximate relationship between Bavin and Street: although, since *The Sun* also predicted – erroneously, as it turned out – that Bavin favoured Street's appointment so that he (Bavin) could promptly take Street's Supreme Court seat, it is perhaps a hint to which one should not attach great weight.[26]

[19] http://adb.anu.edu.au/biography/innes-reginald-heath-6793.

[20] www.austlii.edu.au/au/legis/nsw/num_act/ea1901n24139.pdf. The claim seems to have been brought under the aforementioned s.16 of the Act.

[21] There is no obvious evidence that Lang planned such steps.

[22] [1930] 31 SR (NSW) 183, www.austlii.edu.au/au/cases/nsw/NSWStRp/1930/90.pdf.

[23] Before turning to the submissions and judgments in the litigation, it should be noted that it evidently did not occur to any of the judges or counsel involved in the case that the New South Wales legislature which enacted the 1929 Act might not have been 'representative' per ss. 1 and 5 of the CLVA 1865. On the most strictly literal reading of s.1 (ie that exactly 'half' of the total membership had to be elective), the legislature failed the test. Moreover, following Lang's determined – if only partially successful – swamping exercises, the Council actually contained more members in 1929 than the Assembly, so that fewer than half of the legislature's members were then elected; p17 above. The prevailing assumption seemed simply that ss. 1 and 5 were satisfied because one of the two houses was elected. A further point – which also seemed to have passed everyone by – was that if Bavin's reforms were to be held valid and if the referendum process was a part of the Legislature, then the Legislature thus created could not be representative per s.1 because two of its three parts (excluding the Governor in giving the royal assent) would not be elected!

[24] http://adb.anu.edu.au/biography/street-sir-philip-whistler-8696.

[25] At p14, https://trove.nla.gov.au/newspaper/article/16187309. *The Herald* limited its views as to Street's suitability to the comment that he: "possessed the logical, well-balanced, and judicial mind necessary for the efficient carrying out of the functions of a Judge".

[26] 14 January 1925 p7, https://trove.nla.gov.au/newspaper/article/222942145.

David Ferguson, also born and educated in Sydney, was appointed to the Court in 1912 by McGowen's Labour government, after a legal career combining practice and academia. Like Street, Ferguson had never pursued an active political career. He was to retire from the court in 1931 and was knighted three years later.[27] Ferguson had been thrust sensationally into the public eye in 1921, when he presided over an extraordinary claim for false imprisonment brought by a catholic nun, Sister Mary Ligouri, against the Bishop of Wagga Wagga, Joseph Dwyer. The nun had been born a Protestant (her birth name was Bridget Partridge) and had embraced Catholicism in her teens; press coverage of the trial – which ended in judgment for the bishop – had painted luridly sectarian tales of the Catholic Church using force to prevent Miss Partridge escaping its clutches.[28]

Langer Owen, though Sydney born, was educated in England, attending Charterhouse and then Oxford.[29] He returned to Sydney to practise at the Bar, specialising in equity and bankruptcy, and became King's Counsel in 1916. Owen served in several governmental roles during the war, and he was appointed to the Court in 1922 during Fuller's Nationalist administration, where he served for 10 years. He, too, had never pursued political office.[30]

The court's final member, Augustus James, had a twin-track political and legal career. He was born in Sydney in 1866, attended Sydney University and built a practice at the common law Bar. He had also been a Nationalist Assembly member from 1907 to 1920, and a minister in Holman's post-1917 government. Despite his political sympathies, he was appointed to the Court by Storey's Labour government in 1921.[31]

Counsel

Herbert Evatt KC led for the government. Evatt,[32] then only 36, graduated from Sydney University, where he was taught constitutional law by Peden.[33] Evatt had been appointed silk in 1929. He was widely considered one of the most brilliant practitioners

[27] http://adb.anu.edu.au/biography/ferguson-sir-david-gilbert-6156. The appointment was received approvingly in the *SMH* 6 March 1912 p7, https://trove.nla.gov.au/newspaper/article/15315177.

[28] The proceedings are reported extensively in the *(Sydney) Daily Telegraph* in July 1921. Lang saw the episode as one ingredient in a successful sectarian-inspired Nationalist effort in the 1922 election to paint the (Dooley-led) Labour Party as secretive proponents of an extremist (and Irish) Catholic ideology (1956) op cit ch 36. The – in Lang's view – prime mover in the Nationalist campaign, Fuller's Minister of Justice Thomas Ley, subsequently retired to England, where he was convicted of murder in 1946, sentenced to death and reprieved on being found insane, only to die soon afterwards in Broadmoor; http://adb.anu.edu.au/biography/ley-thomas-john-7191.

[29] http://adb.anu.edu.au/biography/owen-sir-langer-meade-loftus-8499.

[30] *SM* 13 October 1922 p8, https://trove.nla.gov.au/newspaper/article/16046463.

[31] www.records.nsw.gov.au/person/86. This source suggests, in a nice illustration of the way in which some Labour politicians saw electoral politics as more important than judicial influence, that James was initially appointed as a temporary judge, with the lure of a permanent appointment to follow, to trigger a by-election in James's seat, which Labour hoped to win.

[32] A flattering portrait id offered by Tennant (1970) *Evatt: politics and justice*. For a truncated view, see http://adb.anu.edu.au/biography/evatt-herbert-vere-bert-10131.

[33] Tennant suggests Peden was so impressed by Evatt – "my most brilliant student" – that he kept Evatt's LLB essays and offered them to Evatt's fiancée for her to read before the wedding; op cit p32. Evatt's university accomplishments are recounted in Dalziel (1967) *Evatt the enigma* pp 5–6.

at the Australian Bar.[34] Evatt was junior counsel for New South Wales in *Engineers*, and achieved public prominence – and much goodwill within the labour movement – by appearing in various high-profile cases for trade union activists against the Bruce government.[35] By 1930, Evatt was also a disaffected ex-member of the state Labour Party. Evatt was elected to the Assembly in 1925, coming to prominence in heading the investigation into the *Labour Daily*'s sensational bribery allegations,[36] but rapidly found himself unable to support Lang's style of party governance (he voted against the newspaper tax in the caucus)[37] and had been Dixon's junior counsel against the New South Wales government in the *Smith's Weekly* newspaper tax case.[38] Evatt had voted for Loughlin in the 1926 leadership election.[39]

It has been suggested (including by one of Evatt's several biographers)[40] that Evatt designed Lang's strategy to abolish the Council. This seems unlikely. The claim is not made in Tennant's assiduous account of Evatt's career, and Lang does not grant Evatt any credit.[41] More significantly, the path initially followed by the Lang government was a carbon copy of the scheme successfully pressed by Theodore in Queensland eight years earlier: it was imitation, not innovation. By the time *Trethowan* reached the New South Wales courts, Evatt and Lang had broken on rancorous political and personal terms.[42] Evatt was subsequently deselected by the party as a candidate for the next election. He nonetheless retained his seat, standing as an independent Labour candidate. Evatt ran his political career alongside his legal practice for the next few years, but did not contest the 1930 election. That Lang should have chosen to instruct Evatt is perhaps a good illustration of Lang's readiness to put aside personal and political animosities to secure the most competent assistance.

[34] See the adulatory biography in the *SMH* 19 December 1930 p11, https://trove.nla.gov.au/ndp/del/article/16739864.

[35] Tenannt op cit pp 38–44, 52–58.

[36] P 19 above.

[37] Lang (1956) op cit p341.

[38] Lang took a dim view of lawyer/politicians as a group: "The lawyer in politics invariably finds himself up against the problem of a split personality. When is he the lawyer? When is he the politician? The trouble is that most lawyer politicians are usually much more inclined to act as lawyers than as politicians. That is why very early in my career I supported a move to make lawyers ineligible to join the Labour Party. I believed they couldn't serve two masters – the law and the Labour Party …"; Lang (1956) op cit p38. 'Early in his career' Lang would, of course, have seen the lawyer politicians Hughes and Holman rat on the party to spectacular effect both nationally and in New South Wales. Lang does not make any mention of Tom Ryan – an exception perhaps to prove the rule – in this critique.

[39] Nairn (1995) op cit p128 records Lang dismissing Evatt as part of a dissatisfied Labour 'intelligentsia', a term Lang used in a pejorative sense. Lang was here tapping into rather than creating a long-standing antipathy to 'intellectuals' among some Labour activists; Tennant's biography of Evatt (op cit) captures the point nicely in ch 3, which is entitled: 'The labour party detested "Bloody BAs"'.

[40] The assertion is made in Crocket (1993) *Evatt, a life* p111; Buckley, Dale and Reynolds (1994) *Doc Evatt* p58. My thanks to Jeffrey Goldsworthy's article for identifying those sources; Goldsworthy (2007) 'Trethowan's case' in Winterton (ed) *State constitutional landmarks*.

[41] Tennant (op cit ch 5) discusses the case and its immediate background, but makes no suggestion that Evatt was a major player in the episode.

[42] Tennant (ibid p 62) quotes Evatt referring to Lang in June 1927 as: "the biggest crook in the labour movement" and accusing him of taking unwarranted personal credit for his government's reformist legislation. Lang had previously responded to Evatt's criticism of him by describing Evatt as: "an insignificant politician" engaged in a campaign of "personal abuse and falsehood"; ibid p563. Evatt's accusation about Lang's exaggeration of his role as a policymaker is echoed in later studies of the period; see especially Nairn (1995) op cit pp 155–59; Nelson op cit; Clune and Griffith op cit pp 229–32.

Trethowan and Playfair's case was presented by three King's Counsel. The lead KC was David Maughan, an Oxford-educated, Sydney-born Australian. Maughan's career at the Bar had been primarily in the field of equity, but he had developed a strong professional personal interest in constitutional issues, largely in opposition to Lang's manoeuvrings. Such was his commitment on this particular matter that he apparently agreed to act on a pro bono basis.[43] The two other silks were George Flannery KC and EM Mitchell KC. Flannery had been born and educated in Sydney.[44] Flannery dabbled in politics when young, but thereafter devoted his energies to the Bar. Although he initially practised in commercial law areas, he developed a public law practice in both the New South Wales and federal courts. He took silk in 1920 and resisted any temptation to take an appointment to the bench. Mitchell could draw on the experience of having been Ryan's 'junior' before the High Court in *McCawley*. His having been briefed by Ryan was not dependent on his political sympathies. As noted above, Mitchell had unsuccessfully sought selection as a National Party candidate for the House in 1918,[45] and in the late 1920s his political inclinations led him to devote some of his intellectual and political energies to vigorous criticism of Lang's government.[46]

Submissions

When argument began on 15 December 1930, the court's public gallery was packed; many potential observers could not gain admission. Evatt's initial submissions, wrapped around the lunchbreak, lasted over four hours.[47] The *SMH* report suggested Evatt had faced a challenging judicial audience:

> For four hours and a half Dr. Evatt elaborated the ministry's defence. There were not half a dozen interruptions from the opposing counsel, but the Bench was more animated. Dr. Evatt had to contend with many penetrating questions, most of them on obscure constitutional points. The table was littered with legal books, the reports of cases from which he was quoting. At one stage the young barrister read for 10 minutes, while the five Judges wrote furiously at his dictation.[48]

Evatt advanced an argument based on several distinct points. The core of Evatt's submission – invoking Birkenhead's language in *McCawley* – was that New South Wales had a 'flexible' or 'uncontrolled' Constitution, within which the legislature was a sovereign body except insofar as the state's powers were restricted by the Commonwealth Constitution (and s.2 of the CLVA 1865).[49] Evatt's notion of 'sovereign' was an essentially

[43] http://adb.anu.edu.au/biography/maughan-sir-david-7530.
[44] http://adb.anu.edu.au/biography/flannery-george-ernest-6187.
[45] Vol 1 p 280 n 3.
[46] http://adb.anu.edu.au/biography/mitchell-sir-edward-fancourt-7603.
[47] I draw here on *SMH* reports: 16 December 1930 pp 11–12, https://trove.nla.gov.au/ndp/del/article/16739211; 17 December 1930 pp 12–13, https://trove.nla.gov.au/ndp/del/article/16739279; 18 December 1930 pp 11–12, https://trove.nla.gov.au/ndp/del/article/16739743; 19 December 1930 p12, https://trove.nla.gov.au/newspaper/article/16740075. I also draw on the summary of counsel's submissions in *Trethowan* (1930) 31 NSW SR 183, 188–96.
[48] *SMH* 16 December 1930 p11, https://trove.nla.gov.au/ndp/del/article/16739211.
[49] Evatt referred to the provisions (ss. 106 and 107; see vol 1 pp 161–62) in the Commonwealth Constitution which expressly preserved the autonomy of the states with regard to their respective constitutions.

procedural one: namely, that laws that fell within the legislature's substantive competence could always be enacted through the ordinary bicameral simple majority process.[50] Evatt invoked academic rather than judicial authority to support this assertion, drawing in particular on Blackstone's *Commentaries* and Dicey's *Law of the Constitution*.

Rather than suggest that this 'sovereign' power was inherent in the Legislature, as was the position with the British Parliament, Evatt submitted that it was rooted in s.4 [BAA] of the Constitution Act 1855. The submission had obvious attractions, given the way in which s.4 [BAA] had been invoked in 1857 to overcome the ostensibly 'entrenched' two-thirds majority provisions in the initial 1855 Constitution.[51]

The government's case was that the s.4 [BAA] power had not been affected by CLVA 1865 s.5. Evatt referred to the 1865 Act as a 'confirmatory' rather than 'restrictive' statute, and what it 'confirmed' was the Legislature's perpetual capacity to alter any law by the ordinary process. Evatt sought support for this proposition both in *Taylor* and in *McCawley*.[52] Evatt was correct in suggesting that s.5 was confirmatory in nature, but he entirely misrepresented (it seems hard to believe he misunderstood) what s.5 was confirming. The constitutional disputes in Queensland and South Australia in the early 1860s and the steady stream of retrospective validating legislation passed by the Imperial Parliament to resolve those disputes, a stream culminating in the 1865 Act, indicated that the moral propriety and legal enforceability of what s.5 termed 'manner and form' departures from the 'ordinary way' of legislating in colonial legislatures was not seriously contested, whether those departures derived from Imperial or colonial legislation.

At its heart, Evatt's primary argument was not that the Legislature lacked the power to enact whatever 'manner and form' requirements it pleased, but that any such law could at any future point be amended or repealed by the ordinary lawmaking process. Any attempt to entrench a particular substantive law or lawmaking procedure might have some political or moral force, but would in legal terms be futile. Although Evatt did not note the point, this is just what Bavin had told the Assembly – with Lang's concurrence – during the bill's passage: a purported legal entrenchment mechanism might stiffen the political barriers facing a government wishing to promote its repeal, but it actually had no legal effect at all.[53] The (unarticulated) paradox at play here in Evatt's argument was that the Legislature could not use the ordinary lawmaking process to entrench 'particular subjects' by creating an extraordinary lawmaking process because that ordinary lawmaking process was itself entrenched (and would remain so until s.4 [BAA] was itself amended or repealed by the Imperial Parliament).

[50] In any context, the procedural/substantive dichotomy is simplistic. In this context, it is particularly simplistic on the obvious basis that one can credibly contend that part of a lawmaker's substantive powers might extend to altering its own lawmaking procedures.

[51] The two-thirds clause was removed by an Act which was not the subject of a division in either house, so the legality of a bare majority repeal never arose for legal dispute in New South Wales; vol 1 pp 56–57. It had apparently not occurred to Evatt – or, if it had, he did not share the point with the court – that s.4 [BAA] might also be used to reintroduce enhanced majorities or other special procedures; vol 1 pp 52–53.

[52] Vol 1 pp 262–64 and 308–314 respectively.

[53] Pp 44–47 above. Reference to parliamentary debates as an aid to statutory interpretation would not have been regarded as appropriate in that era.

The second (and alternative) line of argument was more prosaic, and echoed Feez and Stumm's unsuccessful assertions before the High Court in *Taylor*.[54] Evatt contended that the referendum device was not a 'manner and form' provision per CLVA 1865 s.5. That concept embraced only innovations regulating the procedures of the original components of the Legislature, for example by requiring enhanced majorities or repeat votes, or reserving bills for the Monarch's personal assent. Creation of an additional and external component to the lawmaking process fell outside the provision. (It apparently did not occur to the government's legal team that the addition of a further unelected – and of course the electorate was not elected – component to the legislature would arguably deprive it of its 'representative character' per CLVA 1865 s.1.) There is obvious support for that proposition in the narrow sense in the 'special majority' sections of Palmer and Collier's 1864 Report.[55] But, as already remarked, one would hardly have expected the Law Officers to address the question of whether referendums were akin to 'special majorities' because referendums were not a feature of the British constitutional landscape in 1864.

Evatt's third submission was that s.7A was invalid because it interfered with parliamentary privilege, in that it prevented ministers (in their legislative capacity) from approaching the Monarch to seek the royal assent and/or because it interfered with the Monarch's power to assent to a bill when asked to do so. For the purposes of the second limb of this argument, Evatt submitted that in giving assent the Monarch was part of the Legislature and was performing a legislative function.

The fourth argument, which Evatt did not pursue at length, was that Trethowan and Playfair lacked locus standi to seek an injunction because they did not have any private legal right that would be affected by repeal of s.7A and the Council's consequent abolition.

Maughan led the claimants' case. The fundamental premise of his argument was that the unquestioned power of the British Parliament always to be able to enact any law by the 'ordinary process' had no relevance to colonial constitutions. That New South Wales's legislature had been granted such an (internal) power by s.4 [BAA] of the 1855 Act was also no longer relevant, as CLVA 1865 s.5 had empowered the Legislature, if it so desired: "to convert a flexible and uncontrolled constitution into a rigid and controlled constitution".[56] This was the proposition made clear by Lord Birkenhead in *McCawley*, which proposition (that s.5 impliedly overrode s.4 [BAA] to the extent of any inconsistency) is simply an application to statutes dealing with colonial law of the doctrine of implied repeal.[57]

Maughan also spoke to the standing question. He submitted that Trethowan and Playfair each had the requisite legal right at stake in the form of the various financial benefits they derived from Council membership, and additionally suggested that their mere status as Council members would suffice for standing purposes.

Flannery reiterated Maughan's submissions concerning the 1865 Act. He also dealt with the suggestion that adding an 'external' component to the lawmaking process was

[54] Vol 1 pp 259–262.
[55] Vol 1 pp 103–04.
[56] (1930) 31 SR NSW 183, 191.
[57] Maughan did not suggest that s.4 [BAA] might give the same power as CLVA 1865 s.5.

not a 'manner and form' amendment per s.5. This could not be restrictively viewed as limited to the internal proceedings of the Legislature's original parts, but would encompass: "any essential condition prescribed by statute for observance in the enactment of a bill between its introduction and the time when it becomes law". In Flannery's submission, s.7A created a new legislative body, modelled on the constitutional amendment procedure in s.128 of the Commonwealth Constitution, and had for the particular purpose of abolishing the Council lent the state Constitution a 'controlled' rather than 'flexible' character. Like Evatt, Flannery overlooked the point that this might compromise the Legislature's representative character if it entailed the introduction of a further, non-elected body into the lawmaking process.

III. The Judgment

The Court did not tarry in deciding the matter. Argument ended on 18 December. Judgment was handed down five days later:

> The Banco Court, in which the judgments were read, was crowded to the point of discomfort, seeing the state of the weather. Legal men, politicians and the general public occupied every available inch of sitting and standing room.[58]

Street CJ's Judgment

Street gave the first and most expansive judgment. The crucial question was:

> Can one Parliament, by providing that a proposal to remove a restriction which it has imposed shall not be carried into effect without complying with conditions which it lays down, bind a succeeding Parliament so as to prevent it from removing the restriction by an Act passed in the ordinary way.[59]

The Chief Justice acknowledged that the question: "is not free from difficulty, and my mind has fluctuated during the course of the argument …".[60] In respect of the British Parliament, the answer to that question was clearly 'No'. He was, however, clear that little assistance could be found by considering the Imperial Parliament's position. However powerful New South Wales's Legislature might be, it was a subordinate Legislature deriving its authority solely from Imperial statutes.[61]

Although Street indicated that he accepted that s.4 [BAA] had empowered the Legislature to remove the two-thirds majority provisions of s.17 [s.15] and s.42 [s.36] of sch.1 of the 1855 Act by a simple majority process, he rejected Evatt's submission that this power had not been affected by the CLVA 1865. Following and quoting extensively from Isaacs and Rich's analysis of s.5 in *McCawley*, Street was unimpressed with Evatt's

[58] *LD* 24 December 1930 p5, https://trove.nla.gov.au/newspaper/article/236937838.
[59] *Trethowan* (1930) 31 NSW SR 183, 201.
[60] ibid.
[61] ibid 198.

submission that 'manner and form' per s.5 permitted alterations to the Legislature's existing procedures but did not include adding further components to the lawmaking process. He saw no distinction between enhanced majorities in either house and using a referendum: "I can see no difference in principle between a condition of that kind and a condition requiring a direct reference to the people by a recognized method of ascertaining their opinion on questions of great public importance."[62] Indeed, in an early passage he emphasised the legitimacy of the referendum device: "it is a well-recognised method of ascertaining the will of the people on any question that may be submitted to them".[63] Such a measure was undoubtedly a 'manner and form' proviso within s.5.

Street was also not swayed by Evatt's submissions concerning parliamentary privilege and locus standi.[64] Street held that injuncting Peden would not interfere with privilege because it would be done to uphold a 'statutory mandate' enacted in s.7A. A better explanation might be that s.7A impliedly abrogated parliamentary privileges – which, of course, in New South Wales had a statutory base rather than being an inherent characteristic of each house[65] – to the extent required to safeguard application of s.7A itself. Street also accepted that the benefits Trethowan and Playfair derived from Council membership gave them locus standi.

However close Street was to Bavin in personal and political terms, and however antagonistic ideologically he may have been to Lang's government, there is no obvious basis to attribute these aspects of his judgment to such factors. The conclusion reached and the reasons for it are entirely credible.

Street did, however, step into less obviously defensible legal territory by also repeatedly observing that one could see sound 'political' reasons for providing entrenched legal protection to the Council:

> Parliament in its wisdom might well think that there were possible changes of so important and so far reaching a character that a special procedure ought to be followed before they could become law … [A] proposal of so far reaching and so momentous a character as that for the substitution of a unicameral system for a bicameral system … is one which Parliament might not unreasonably consider of such importance that it should not be left to be determined by the passage of an Act in the ordinary way through both Houses.[66]

As a statement of political principle, the observation is unobjectionable. The 'Parliament' to which Street is referring here, however, is the New South Wales Legislature, not the Imperial Parliament. Whether some, most or all of the New South Wales Legislature's members might consider entrenchment of some values a sensible idea is beside the

[62] ibid 203–04. It is not clear if Street regarded the referendum as a component part of a redefined legislature or as an additional, external element. The above-quoted passage points towards the latter conclusion, although at p203 he talked several times of a 'special form of procedure' within Parliament, which points towards the former. The term 'condition' is the one used in s.4 [BAA] in respect (impliedly) of the two-thirds provisions and by Palmer and Collier's 1864 Report (at para A-3) in referring to special majority provisions; vol 1 p 103–04.

[63] ibid 197. He recognised this most obviously as the amendment mechanism for the Australian Constitution; pp 164–65 above.

[64] *Trethowan* (1930) 31 NSW SR 183, 205–06.

[65] I have suggested elsewhere (Loveland (2015) *Constitutional law, administrative law and human rights* ch 8) that an argument might be made that Art 9 of the Bill of Rights has placed all parliamentary privilege in Britain on a statutory basis.

[66] *Trethowan* (1930) 31 NSW SR 183, 202–03.

point. The point before the court was whether the Imperial Parliament had empowered the New South Wales Legislature to achieve that end. It might be suggested that considered exploration of the 'wisdom' of the Imperial Parliament in passing the CLVA 1865 could have led to a similar conclusion without raising the inference that Street was influenced by domestic party political factors. As noted in chapter four of volume one, there was no debate at all in either the Commons or the Lords on any part of the 1865 Act.[67] However, insofar as we might equate Parliament's unarticulated wisdom with the intentions of Palmerston's government or, pre-dating that, of the policy ideas floated in the Law Officers' Report,[68] it is correct to say that one can find support for the suggestion that s.5 might be used to reinstate the kinds of unusual lawmaking processes that s.4 [BAA] of the 1855 Act had been introduced to remove. What we cannot find in the Report, however, is any explanation as to why in political terms such 'special majorities' for 'particular subjects' might be desirable.[69]

James limited himself to a single sentence concurrence with Street's opinion. Two other members of the Court offered their own reasons for supporting the Chief Justice's conclusion.

Ferguson's judgment was less an inquiry into the 'Legislature's' power as one into its identity or composition. In his oral submissions, Evatt had apparently[70] invoked a *reductio ad absurdum* argument that if the Legislature could introduce a referendum requirement, it could also: "provide that the repealing bill should be submitted to Tattersall's Club, or that three years should elapse after its introduction before it should finally become law".[71] Street had suggested briefly that such examples were unhelpful; Ferguson took the point further, observing that the Legislature (by which he meant the Assembly, Council and royal assent) could do many extraordinary things:

> All that means is that there is nothing in the constitution forbidding the legislature to do insane things. One would not expect to find such a provision there. The constitution of every free civilised community is based on the assumption that the body to which it commits the power of making its laws may be trusted to bring to the exercise of that power a reasonable degree of sanity. If at any time that trust should prove to be misplaced, then the state would be in very evil case, and would be hard put to it to find a way of escaping disaster.[72]

Stressing that New South Wales's Legislature was not sovereign, but a creation of the British Parliament, and after quoting s.4 [BAA] and CLVA 1865 s.5, Ferguson focused attention squarely on s.5's effect on the Legislature's powers:

> The effect of the Act was that that law-making machinery was put in the hands of the Legislature, with the fullest power of remodelling it, by altering either its own structure or its mode of operation. Either, or both, might be changed, and changed, and changed again. But at any moment the change could be made in one way, and one way only, that is, by passing a new law, a law which must be enacted by the Legislature as then constituted, and in the method prescribed by the law at that moment in force.[73]

[67] Vol 1 pp 105–06.
[68] Vol 1 pp 101–05.
[69] ibid.
[70] The point is not noted in the summary of submissions in the NSW SR, nor in the *SMH* accounts cited at n 47 above.
[71] [1930] 31 NSW SR 183, 208.
[72] ibid 209.
[73] ibid 210.

Seen in that context, the effect of the legislation promoted by Bavin's government was that the Legislature had redefined itself for the particular purposes identified in s.7A to include the referendum. Unlike Street, Ferguson did not comment on the political desirability of entrenchment.[74] His judgment was rooted in s.5. In enacting s.7A, the Legislature:

> … did what the Colonial Laws Validity Act expressly authorised it to do. It altered the powers or the procedure of the Legislature. It did it in the manner and form required by the law for the time being in force in the state. From that moment that provision has been part of the Constitution, and is the law of New South Wales to-day.
>
> It may be altered, the Legislature has full power to alter it by repealing sub-so (6). But that repeal to be effective, can, in my opinion, be brought about only in the manner prescribed by the law in force to-day, that is, by a bill which, after passing through both Houses, is approved by the electors before being presented for the Royal assent.[75]

Owen also concurred as to the result and much of the reasoning, although he too eschewed any reference to the political merits of entrenchment. He was, however, more explicit than his colleagues in meeting Evatt's submissions about the 'entrenched' nature of the power given by s.4 [BAA]:

> It is said that s. 4 of the Act 18 & 19 Vict. c. 54, and s. 5 of the Colonial Laws (Validity) Act are in some way repugnant to or inconsistent with one another. Both sections are still in force and must be taken together and construed as existing portions of the written constitution, but one must bear in mind that the Colonial Laws (Validity) Act with its s. 5 is the later Act, and if there be any repugnancy or inconsistency, to use the words of Isaacs J. and Rich J. in *McCawley* v. *The King* … the later Act completely passed is fatal to the earlier one.[76]

Owen suggested that Evatt was seeking to seduce the court into adopting an inappropriate approach to the task of statutory interpretation: namely, to assume that the British Parliament's intention in enacting s.4 [BAA] was to ensure that New South Wales's Legislature would always be able to enact any law through the ordinary bicameral bare majority process, and that CLVA 1865 s.5 should be read in a way consistent with that intention. Although Owen accepted that such unusual interpretive techniques might be permissible when a statute's words had no clear meaning, they were not legitimate when the relevant statute was – like s.5 – entirely unambiguous.[77]

Like Street and Ferguson, Owen found Isaacs and Rich's analysis in *McCawley* authoritative. S.5 had clearly created: "an absolute charter, no matter what the British legislature had previously said".[78] That 'absolute charter' empowered the Legislature to alter the manner and form of the lawmaking process required to enact laws affecting its own 'constitution, powers and procedure'. S.7A affected both the powers and

[74] He concurred with Street CJ on the parliamentary privilege and standing issues; ibid 211.

[75] ibid.

[76] *Trethowan* (1930) 31 NSW SR 183, 217.

[77] He made the point with a lengthy quotation from Lord Halsbury's judgment in *Leader v Duffey* (1888) 3 AC 301 (HL). *Leader* might be thought of tenuous relevance to the issue in *Trethowan*, as it concerned the interpretation of a family trust, not a statute, and certainly not a statute creating or modifying a 'constitution'. The passage echoes Griffith and Barton's ill-founded reliance on company law cases in *McCawley*; vol 1 pp 284 and 286.

[78] *Trethowan* (1930) 31 NSW SR 183, 217–18.

constitution of the legislature – "it introduces an element (the vote of the people) into the Constitution itself"[79] – and so clearly fell within s.5.

Long Innes was the only dissentient. His lengthy judgment[80] on the central entrenchment point is quite bewildering, resting – to put it kindly – on a melange of partial endorsement of Evatt's submissions, mixed with novel assertions of his own invention and some evident misunderstandings or misrepresentations of High Court and Privy Council authority.

Long Innes began with the ostensibly remarkable proposition that the CLVA 1865 (whether per s.5 or any other provision) was not relevant to resolving the question before the court. The important statute was the 1855 Act, which Long Innes referred to as a: "*special* Act passed for the purpose of conferring a constitution on New South Wales".[81] He then quoted s.4 [BAA] in full and referred to the definition of 'the Legislature' in s.9 [BAA].[82] In Long Innes's view, the 1865 Act did not in any sense alter the powers given to the Legislature by the 1855 legislation; such powers were: "co-extensive with and equal to those previously conferred …".[83] He reached this result – ie that the 1865 Act did not impact upon the 1855 Act – in part by engaging in some tortuous linguistic pedantry in relation to the analysis offered by Isaacs and Rich in *McCawley* of the relationship between the two statutes:

> It is also true that in the case in question Isaacs and Rich JJ. (at p. 51) said: "At the moment, therefore, of the passing of the Colonial Laws Validity Act, 1865, s. 5 was, so far as its language extends, an absolute Charter, no matter what the British Legislature had previously said." But they did not say it was" *the* absolute Charter," nor "an exhaustive Charter," but only "so far as its language extends, an absolute Charter.[84]

Since Long Innes could see nothing in the 'language' of the 1865 Act affecting the powers given to the New South Wales Legislature in 1855, if the Bavin/Peden inspired amendments to s.7 of the Constitution Act 1902 were valid, their validity would have to be found in the 1855 legislation.

Long Innes sought to bolster this view by noting that no suggestion was made in *Powell v Apollo Candle*[85] – decided in 1885 – that s.4 [BAA] had been in any way affected by the 1865 Act. That observation is correct. But since *Apollo* was concerned only with the question of whether s.4 [BAA] empowered the Legislature to give the Governor the capacity to impose import duties – and so did not raise a CLVA 1865 point at all (indeed, the 1865 Act is not even referred to in Collier's[86] judgment or cited by counsel) – its relevance to the question before the court in *Trethowan* is hard to discern.

The judgment appeared at one point to accept Evatt's submission that the 'Legislature' per s.4 [BAA] could not add an 'external' element to itself, but promptly limited the

[79] ibid 218–19.
[80] ibid 222–35.
[81] ibid 222; emphasis added.
[82] Vol 1 p 46 n 48.
[83] *Trethowan* (1930) 31 NSW SR 183, 208.
[84] ibid 224.
[85] (1885) 10 AC 232; discussed at vol 1 pp 150–52.
[86] Collier qua Law Officer was one of the two 'authors' of the 1865 Act (vol 1 p 67) and would surely have invoked it in *Powell* had it been relevant.

application of that proposition to 'ad hoc' additions.[87] Long Innes picked up Evatt's 'Tattersall's Club' submission in reaching the conclusion that:

> I do not think, for instance, that, if the Legislature had enacted ... that the control of racing should be entrusted to the Australian Jockey Club, and had further enacted that a Bill to repeal that legislation should not be introduced or presented for Royal assent without the consent of the ... Jockey Club ... the Jockey Club ... could properly be regarded as part of the Legislature mentioned in s. 4 of 18 & 19 Vict. c. 54 [the 1855 Act].[88]

However, Long Innes also concluded that 'the Legislature' *could* add such an 'external' element, for example a referendum, to itself for *all* legislative purposes. To do so would: "Constitute the general body of electors a constituent part of the Legislature for the future; in that event the Legislature so altered would by virtue of s.9 of that Act be the Legislature referred to in s.4."[89]

Given that s.5 makes provision for 'manner and form' innovation for one (or perhaps two)[90] specific (or, if one prefers, 'ad hoc') purpose, Long Innes's reasoning and conclusion on this are distinctly unpersuasive. Long Innes did not have to meet this point, however, since he had already decided – and perhaps one wonders for that reason – that the 1865 Act was irrelevant to the question before him.

That conclusion is reinforced by Long Innes's puzzling invocation of the High Court's decision in *Cooper*.[91] Since the reasoning that underlay *Cooper* was characterised as 'embarrassing and even ridiculous' by the Privy Council in *McCawley*,[92] *Cooper* seems an unlikely source of authority to support the Lang government's argument. The Privy Council's denunciation of Pope Cooper's 'Two Act entrenchment' thesis in *McCawley* lay in Cooper's inability to identify any textual source to root a justification for departure from the default manner of legislating (ie bare bicameral majoritarianism plus the royal assent, producing implied as well as express repeal). The Privy Council clearly accepted that CLVA 1865 s.5 (and perhaps also cl.22 of the 1859 Order in Council) empowered the Queensland Legislature to alter its lawmaking processes regarding any matter identified in s.5[1] and [2] – including the appointment and tenure of Supreme Court judges. The claim against McCawley had failed because the Queensland Legislature *had not* done so, not because it *could not* do so. It is difficult to find in *McCawley* any indication that the New South Wales Legislature did not have just the same power under s.5.[93]

Long Innes seemingly sought to circumvent that obvious conclusion by selectively (mis-) quoting from Birkenhead's judgment. At 229–30 Long Innes extracts the phrase

[87] *Trethowan* (1930) 31 NSW SR 183, 230.

[88] ibid. The quoted passage ended: "see *Russell* v. *The Queen* (7 A.C. 829, 835); *Hodge* v. *The Queen* (9 A.C.117, 132)". The relevance of these two Canadian-rooted judgments is obscure. *Russell* held that the Canadian Parliament could enact temperance legislation through its general legislative power to promote 'peace, order and good government' in Canada, and could empower statutory bodies to apply the law, while *Hodge* came to the same conclusion in respect of Provincial power. Neither case remotely concerned alterations to a legislature's institutional identity.

[89] *Trethowan* (1930) 31 NSW SR 183, 231.

[90] Depending on whether the 'manner and form' proviso in s.5[3] applies both to the courts (s.5[1]) and to the legislatures (s.5[2]); pp 113–14 above.

[91] Vol 1 pp 222–23. Long Innes refers to *Cooper* (1930) 31 NSW SR 183 at 225 and 228.

[92] [1920] AC 691, 705 (Lord Birkenhead); vol 1 p 310.

[93] Although for the reasons outlined at vol 1 pp 64–65 it is not obvious that the New South Wales Legislature had power equivalent to that provided to its Queensland counterpart by c 22.

'Master of its own household' from Birkenhead's opinion (the 'its' being the Queensland Legislature), equating being 'Master' with always being able to enact any measures by the bicameral bare majority process. The (short) sentence from which the 'Master' quote is taken reads: "The Legislature of Queensland is the master of its own household, *except in so far as its powers have in special cases been restricted*".[94] The second clause, which Long Innes must have seen and deliberately omitted, wholly contradicts the assertion he makes in drawing on the first.

Long Innes ended his judgment on the central point by returning – with a rhetorical flourish – to the 'full power' concept articulated in s.4 [BAA] of the 1855 Act and its effect on CLVA 1865 s.5:[95]

> Nor does "full power to make laws respecting the constitution, powers and procedure of such Legislature" involve a power to act in excess of those powers. "Full power to make laws" necessarily involves equally full power to unmake or repeal them; and sub-so 6 of S. 7A purports to shackle or control that full power, because it makes the exercise of that power dependent upon the approval of an outside body which does not form part of the Legislature itself. By whatever road, therefore, I arrive at the same conclusion.

Conclusion

None of the judges – nor, it seems, of the counsel – made any reference to the Assembly or Council debates conducted during the bill's passage. That omission is no doubt attributable to the dominant assumption then prevailing in British (and, by extension, British colonial) law that it was not permissible for courts to refer to Hansard and legislators' speeches therein as a guide to the meaning of statutory provisions.[96]

A more surprising omission given s.7A's specific content was any reference to a recent, post-*Taylor* (1919) Privy Council decision relating to the constitutional propriety of a Canadian province introducing the referendum as an element of its legislative process. In *Re the Initiative and Referendum Act*,[97] the Privy Council had invalidated such a law promoted in Manitoba, on the narrow ground that the law contravened a clear requirement in s.92(1) of the British North America Act 1867 which prevented provinces from altering their respective constitutions in a fashion that affected the powers of the Lieutenant-Governor. However, the judgment (delivered by Haldane) had concluded with an observation that certainly implied – albeit without making reference to CLVA 1865 s.5 – that using a referendum as an additional or alternative element of a colonial legislature might not be lawful:

> … No doubt a body, with a power of legislation on the subjects entrusted to it so ample as that enjoyed by a Provincial Legislature in Canada, could, while preserving its own capacity intact, seek the assistance of subordinate agencies, as had been done when in *Hodge v. The Queen*, the Legislature of Ontario was held entitled to entrust to a Board of Commissioners authority to enact

[94] [1920] AC 691, 714; emphasis added.

[95] *Trethowan* (1930) 31 NSW SR 183, 232.

[96] For an overview of that orthodoxy and its subsequent erosion in Britain, see Loveland (2015) op cit pp 249–54.

[97] [1919] AC 935.

> regulations relating to taverns; *but it does not follow that it can create and endow with its own capacity a new legislative power not created by the Act to which it owes its own existence.* Their Lordships do no more than draw attention to the gravity of the constitutional questions which thus arise.[98]

Taylor would have provided the Privy Council with an opportunity to explore that issue further, but, as noted above, the Privy Council – with Haldane taking the lead – had refused permission for further appeal.[99] The New South Wales State Reports record that the Canadian case was mentioned only by Flannery, in brief and rather confusing terms.[100] Flannery appeared to invoke it as a clear authority that a colonial legislature could redefine itself in a fashion that added a referendum to its existing composition. Prima facie, such a submission would seem ill-judged. But it was perhaps tailored to make the point that such redefinition would not amount to 'creating a *new* legislative power'. However the submission was put, the case was not addressed in any of the judgments.

IV. Reaction to the Judgment

The judgment was widely and extensively reported. The anti-Lang position was succinctly stated in a leader in the *Riverina Recorder* on 27 December 1930 (albeit with selective recall of the prominence the abolition issue enjoyed in the 1930 election campaign):

> The decision of the Court is a signal defeat of the shameless attempt of Mr. Lang to ride roughshod over the electors. Whether or not the Legislative Council should be abolished was never a vital issue at the general election; when the Second Chamber was mentioned it was referred to only incidentally. Yet, although he obtained no mandate, Mr Lang set out to destroy the Legislative Council by a legislative act.[101]

A more cynically inclined (or perhaps insightful) editorial in the *(Grafton) Daily Examiner* on 29 December 1930 speculated that Lang was in no hurry to see the Council abolished, as it provided him with a helpful – if unacknowledged – buffer against the more radically inclined members of the party caucus and Executive:

> There remains the question of what the government will do in the event of interference by the Council with any of its legislative plans. The general impression is that in such circumstances Mr. Lang will go to the Governor with a request, for more appointments to the Council to enable him to give effect to his policy. If the necessary consent is forthcoming the government will have a second Chamber to its own liking and it will no longer have any Parliamentary obstacle to Labor policy – a condition which might not be altogether an unmixed blessing to Mr. Lang.[102]

[98] ibid 943; emphasis added. The *Hodge* point is essentially the Canadian equivalent of the decision in *Appollo Candle*; pp 150–151 above. The British North America Act 1867 post-dated the CLVA 1865, and so – although the point was not pursued in the case – it would be arguable that any power regarding referendums that might be derived from the CLVA 1865 s.5 would have been overridden to the extent of any inconsistency between them by s.92 of the British North America Act.

[99] Vol 1 pp 278–79. The referendum device was not in issue in *McCawley*, but one could credibly imagine it could be presented – to adapt Birkenhead's terminology – as a 'special case restriction' on the ordinary way of legislating.

[100] *Trethowan* (1930) 31 NSW SR 183, 193.

[101] https://trove.nla.gov.au/newspaper/article/143818642.

[102] https://trove.nla.gov.au/newspaper/article/195620059. This was the point made by Nairn's substantial biography of Lang (1995) op cit ch 5.

There was also public sympathy for the notion that the Council should certainly be reformed, if not abolished. This view was most clearly put in a long editorial in the *Lithgow Mercury* on 29 December 1930, which, after castigating Bavin for not putting his supposed reform agenda to a referendum vote before 1930 state election,[103] saw little merit in the status quo:

> Speaking quite frankly, we do not think the people as a whole are very interested in the fate of the Council – that, as a matter of fact, they are in different whether it goes or stays. Of one thing we are quite certain, in its present form it has outlived its usefulness as a revisory chamber, and therefore there is no justification for its continued existence. It was instituted, as also was the Senate, as a non-party body, a buffer as it were between the people and ill-considered and hasty legislation. To-day it does not function as such.
>
> Take away a few level-headed and clear-thinking members, men who are worthy of a place in any legislature in the world, and there remain men who are not of this generation, septuagenarians, and even octogenarians, who still live in the past, and others whose appointments' were for party purposes, and whose only claim to a free railway pass and the right to enter the best club in Sydney, is that they have been faithful members of a party.[104]

Evatt and McTiernan to the High Court; and Isaacs as Governor-General

The *Mercury*'s disdainful allusion to 'appointment for party purposes' given to 'faithful members of party' had now acquired another dimension. A new feature had appeared on the judicial landscape after argument in *Trethowan* concluded. Both Evatt and McTiernan were appointed to the High Court in December 1930.

The appointments were another example of the chaotic, faction-ridden nature of Labour government decision-making, this time in the national arena. Per s.72(i) of the Constitution, High Court judges were formally appointed by the Governor-General in Council. In substance, the appointment power in the normal course of events during the tenure of a Nationalist government would be the Prime Minister's, acting with the support of his Cabinet colleagues. The reality of the appointment process under a Labour government was more complicated, in that party expectations were that Cabinet would act on instructions from the parliamentary caucus. Placing both Evatt and McTiernan on the Court had been mooted in Cabinet early in 1930, but Scullin was evidently reluctant to proceed, as such appointments might prompt criticism as indulging party political bias.[105] This was most obvious in respect of McTiernan, who, after breaking with Lang and leaving New South Wales politics, was returned as a Labour member of the House in 1929 election. Evatt did not hold elective office in 1930, but was a member of the Labour Party whose attachment to (centrist) Labour ideology was entirely candid.

Given that Australian history both pre- and post-confederation was littered with examples of Conservative and Liberal Premiers and Prime Ministers appointing their

[103] Pp 47–48 above.
[104] https://trove.nla.gov.au/newspaper/article/219580427.
[105] Robertson (1974) op cit p283.

party political allies to the bench, Scullin's hesitancy over Evatt and McTiernan might be seen either as an unusually principled embrace of the notion that judicial independence should involve a judge's ideological inclinations as well as his tenure of office or as a feeble pre-emptive acquiescence to Labour's political opponents. However, in late 1930, Scullin (along with his Attorney-General, Frank Brennan) was in London attending an Imperial Conference and as such, given the then limited nature of inter-continental communication technology, unable to exercise much influence over caucus views on the Evatt/McTiernan appointment issue.

Scullin's primary concern while in London was to overcome the evident hostility of King George V and the British government (then Ramsay MacDonald's second ministry, governing as a minority administration with Liberal support) to Isaacs's appointment as Australia's first *Australian* Governor-General. Isaacs's accomplishments as a politician and lawyer might readily be thought far greater than any previous incumbent of the office, but it seems that the King felt that these attributes were outweighed by Isaacs not being British (and, one might suspect, because Isaacs was Jewish). Scullin stood firm, making it clear that he would, if necessary, press the matter to a referendum in Australia. With ill grace, complaining that Scullin had 'put a gun to his head', George V eventually acquiesced.[106] That controversy, alongside discussion relating to the expected enactment of the Statute of Westminster to grant independent 'Dominion status' to Britain's white colonies and the increasing economic problems threatened by the onset of the Great Depression, consumed much of Scullin's attention, pushing the question of new High Court judges from the front of his mind.

The prime mover in the Evatt/McTiernan appointments was the acting Attorney-General, a South Australian Senator named John Daly.[107] Daly, born to working-class parents in South Australia in 1891, had left school at 13 to work as a pie seller. He later became an office junior in a law firm, and successively a conveyancer, solicitor and finally – in 1919 – a barrister. Much of his practice was in trade union matters, often on a pro bono basis. He was first elected as a Senator in 1928, while Labour was in opposition, and was almost immediately appointed as party leader in the Senate. Daly's personal politics were 'flexible' even by contemporary Labour standards. He had publicly sided with Lang in opposing the Niemayer plan and was ousted from the Cabinet for so doing in March 1931, only to recant his apostasy three months later and return to office.

Daly's enthusiasm for appointing Labour men to the Court was reportedly nourished by his own desire shortly to join them.[108] Scullin was evidently unwilling to defy the majority of the Labour caucus on the issue, and sought lamely to distance himself from the appointments by suggesting subsequently that the matter had been resolved while the ship on which he was returning to Australia was out of radio contact.[109]

[106] ibid pp 285–88: Cowen (1967) *Isaac Isaacs* ch 8, especially pp 191–204.

[107] http://adb.anu.edu.au/biography/daly-john-joseph-5874.

[108] *SMH* 29 December 1930 p 8, https://trove.nla.gov.au/newspaper/article/16741684.

[109] Robertson op cit p288. Scullin's unhappiness and acquiescence are recorded in telegrams from him leaked to and published by the *SMH* 16 March 1931 p9, https://trove.nla.gov.au/newspaper/article/16762121.

The appointments attracted considerable criticism from conservative political circles and parts of the legal profession.[110] The council of the South Australian Law Society adopted the following resolution:

> The council expresses its strongest disapproval of the action of the Federal government in appointing and threatening to appoint men to the High Court regardless of the qualifications generally considered necessary, and solely on account of their political views, In the opinion of the council, vacancies on the High Court bench should be filled only by persons of the highest standing in the profession and of proved professional ability.[111]

McTiernan's appointment was generally seen as the more problematic, in part because he was a member of the House and in part because he lacked Evatt's distinction at the Bar.[112] *The Sydney Morning Herald*[113] greeted the appointments with an article that recited at length the Labour caucus's desire to appoint sympathetic judges. It nonetheless observed that: "Dr. Evatt's appointment is the culmination of a brilliant career at the Bar, where he has been one of the foremost advocates for several years". McTiernan, in contrast, was described as being regarded as merely: "learned and sound". The *Herald* also repeated quite widespread speculation that Evatt would be appointed Chief Justice when Isaacs became Governor-General. The government did not subsequently press that issue, apparently in the face of opposition from existing members of the Court.[114]

Immediately judgment in *Trethowan* was issued, Lang considered whether the appropriate course to follow was an appeal to the High Court or an attempt to bypass that court and go straight to the Privy Council.[115] Given Lang's repeatedly professed antipathy towards British interference in domestic Australian affairs, the latter course might have been thought rather ill-advised from a domestic political perspective. Nor, given the Privy Council's lucid support (just ten years earlier) in *McCawley* of the proposition that Australian state legislatures could enact effective entrenching legislation, was it particularly credible to assume that the Privy Council would afford the government's arguments a friendly welcome. But neither was it obvious that the High Court would offer a more helpful forum. Even if one were to attach any credence to the simplistic political reductionism expressed by the South Australian Law Society, Lang could hardly count either Evatt or McTiernan among his personal friends or ideological bedfellows, although both might be thought potentially sympathetic to the government's *Trethowan* case. Lang subsequently decided not to seek to go directly to the Privy Council. Instead, the government applied to the High Court (which sat without Evatt, who recused himself) for permission to appeal, which was granted on 9 January 1931.

[110] http://adb.anu.edu.au/biography/mctiernan-sir-edward-aloysius-eddie-14854.

[111] *SMH* December 1930 p8, https://trove.nla.gov.au/newspaper/article/16741684.

[112] cf Sawer (1967) *Australian federalism in the courts* p65, noting that when Scullin's government: "looked around for men with Labour sympathies to appoint to the High Court in 1930, they could find only one – Dr HV Evatt KC – who beyond question had the professional standing which would make his appointment seem justifiable to the legal profession and which would enable him to compete on equal terms with his High Court colleagues". The Law Society criticism echoed that made of the Powers and Piddington appointments by Fisher's Labour government in 1913 (vol 1 pp 256–57). Unlike Piddington, McTiernan was not deterred from taking the post.

[113] 19 December 1930 p11, https://trove.nla.gov.au/ndp/del/article/16739864.

[114] Tennant op cit p 72.

[115] *LD* 24 December 1930 p5, https://trove.nla.gov.au/newspaper/article/236937838.

4

Trethowan before the High Court

> There is no reason why a Parliament representing the people should be powerless to determine whether the constitutional salvation of the state is to be reached by cautious and well considered steps rather than by rash and ill-considered measures.
>
> Rich J in *Attorney-General for New South Wales v Trethowan* (1931) 44 CLR 394, 420.

While Scullin apparently did not want to associate himself with the Evatt and McTiernan appointments,[1] he dived into fierce controversy on returning from the Imperial Conference by reappointing Theodore as Treasurer on 26 January 1931.[2] Scullin thereby exacerbated the split with Lang and his supporters – for Lang's personal antipathy to Theodore evidently outweighed the fact that Theodore's increasing attraction to Keynes' economic ideas meant that he was likely the most receptive of national Labour politicians to the reflationary economic policy that Lang favoured.[3] But Scullin's initiative also opened a new party fissure to the right. Two senior ministers resigned from office, protesting Theodore's reinstatement, ostensibly because an unacceptable moral cloud still hung over Theodore's head.

Joseph Lyons entered Scullin's Cabinet as Postmaster-General. Elected to Tasmania's Assembly in 1909, he served as a minister from 1914 to 1916, and became Labour leader in opposition in 1917 when the state party split over conscription; Lyons held firmly anti-conscriptionist views. He became Premier in 1923 upon the collapse of the Nationalist/Country Party coalition, led the party to victory in the 1925 election, was Premier of a moderate social democratic administration until 1928 and then,

[1] Robertson suggests Scullin sacked Daly from the Cabinet because of Daly's role in the episode; op cit p 314.

[2] The conference led to enactment of the Statute of Westminster 1931, which inter alia (s.2) released the named Dominions (including Australia) from the controls of s.2 of the CLVA 1865 (p 107 above) and (s.4) announced that British legislation would only in future apply to a Dominion if the Dominion's consent to such application was recorded in the text of the relevant Act (per s.10, ss.2–6 of the Act would apply to Australia only consequent upon its adoption by Commonwealth legislation). The Statute of Westminster did not, however, affect the position of the Australian states vis-à-vis the CLVA 1865, and made explicit provision to the effect that (s.8) the Act did not affect the s.128 entrenchment mechanism in the national constitution nor (s.9) empower the Commonwealth to alter the states' legal powers. See generally Wheare (1953) *The Statute of Westminster and Dominion status*. On the argument that the Act's evident grant of legal autonomy was not taken at face value in Australia, see Clark (2016) 'Cautious constitutionalism: Commonwealth legislative independence and the Statute of Westminster 1931–1942' *Macquarie LJ* 41. For further explanation of Australia's belated (1942) decision to adopt the Act, see Lee (2016) 'States' rights and Australia's adoption of the Statute of Westminster 1931–1942' *History Australia* 258.

[3] See especially the tracing of Theodore's ideas in Fitzgerald op cit ch 8.

Labour having lost the 1928 state election to the Nationalists, at Scullin's request he contested (successfully) a House seat in 1929.[4] As Premier, Lyons's economic instincts were conservative; he had supported the 1926–27 permanent Loan Council reforms.[5] Appointed by Scullin as acting Treasurer while Scullin attended the Imperial Conference, Lyons diligently implemented Niemeyer and Gibson's economic plans in the Melbourne Agreement and clashed publicly with Theodore over his backbench efforts to shift the party in a Keynesian direction. To Lyons, Theodore's return was both a personal and policy-based affront.

James Fenton was a Victorian who began working life as a printer and journalist. Initially a Liberal, he joined Labour in 1908 and won a House seat. Like Lyons and Scullin, he had opposed conscription. Fenton became a whip in the early 1920s, and Scullin, who counted him a friend, appointed him Minister of Trade in the 1929 Cabinet and acting Prime Minister during the Imperial Conference. Fenton, however, shared Lyons's views both on policy and Theodore's personal qualities, and resigned accordingly.[6]

Rumors immediately surfaced that Lyons and Fenton were being courted by the Nationalists and a shadowy group of Melbourne-based financiers, seeking a repeat of Hughes's ratting during the war, to lead a coalition government composed primarily of Nationalists.[7] Scullin had had to persuade the House caucus to approve Theodore's reinstatement. The vote was just 24–19 in favour.[8] Lyons and Fenton remained as party members. Should they follow Hughes's lead, other Labour members would likely join them. Scullin's difficulties were exacerbated by the loss to the Nationalists of McTiernan's former House seat. And as the national Labour Party seemingly stood again on the brink of fragmentation, *Trethowan* reached the High Court.

I. The Hearing

Trethowan was argued on 20–21 January 1931, a week after permission was granted. The permission had been conditional. The High Court indicated that it would hear the matter in somewhat abstract terms as to whether non-compliance with the referendum requirement would make any 'Act' invalid, and would not decide whether that issue could be pre-empted by issuing an injunction to prevent a bill being presented for assent.

The Court

The Scullin government's unwillingness to press Evatt's appointment as Chief Justice had an immediately beneficial effect for Gavan Duffy, who stepped into that role.[9] Of the

[4] Ward (1978) op cit pp 185–86; http://adb.anu.edu.au/biography/lyons-joseph-aloysius-joe-7278.
[5] Cain op cit pp 72–74.
[6] http://adb.anu.edu.au/biography/fenton-james-edward-6155.
[7] Hart (1970) 'Lyons – Labour Minister – leader of the UAP' in Cooksey (ed) *The great depression in Australia.*
[8] Fitzgerald op cit p285.
[9] On Gavan Duffy as Chief Justice see inter alia Appleby (2015) 'The Gavan Duffy court' in Dixon and Williams (eds) *The High Court, the constitution and Australian politics.*

McCawley bench, only Gavan Duffy and Rich remained. They were joined in *Trethowan* by Starke, McTiernan and Owen Dixon.

Dixon was to become perhaps the most influential of twentieth-century Australian judges. Called to the Bar in Melbourne in 1910, Dixon rapidly developed a formidable reputation for advocacy before the higher courts, particularly in constitutional matters,[10] and served temporarily on the Victorian Supreme Court. He had never held or sought elected political office. He was appointed by Bruce's government to the High Court in January 1929, replacing Higgins, who died on 13 January.[11]

McTiernan's participation might be thought distinctly problematic. McTiernan certainly had an intimate insider's knowledge of the case, and good reason to regard Lang with political disapprobation and personal hostility. He did not appear to think that either matter required him to recuse himself.

Counsel and Submissions

Lang's cause was now led by Edward Loxton KC, an intriguing choice for Lang to make. Loxton's politics were distinctly conservative: he had campaigned actively for conscription and sat as an 'Independent Nationalist' in the Assembly between 1920 and 1925.[12] Maughan again led for Trethowan, assisted by Mitchell.

The hearing began on 20 January, with Loxton making the first submissions.[13] Loxton did not pursue the peripheral standing or privilege arguments Evatt had unsuccessfully run below. His energies were directed solely to establishing s.7A(6)'s invalidity: "The crux of the matter is this: can the state Legislature deprive itself of the right to alter its mind?" Loxton insisted the answer was 'No'.

Loxton characterised the referendum as a 'third party', to which the 1929 Act sought to give the Legislature's powers. Surprisingly, the reports do not record Loxton dwelling on the sceptical views expressed by the Privy Council in *In re Initiative and Referendum*[14] as to the lawfulness of the referendum as a lawmaking device. Answering interventions from Starke, Loxton accepted that the Legislature's powers could be and were limited by Imperial Acts. But – drawing presumably on *Apollo Candle*[15] – those powers were nonetheless 'plenary' and, crucially: "The Imperial Legislature had never conferred on

[10] He led for the claimants in the *Newspaper Tax* case; pp 20–21 above.

[11] http://adb.anu.edu.au/biography/dixon-sir-owen-10024. Dixon became Chief Justice in 1952 until his retirement in 1964, having interrupted his judicial career to serve as Australia's ambassador to Washington during the Second World War.

[12] www.parliament.nsw.gov.au/members/Pages/member-details.aspx?pk=1143; Smith (2006) *Against the machines: minor parties and independents in New South Wales* p35.

[13] References to submissions and questions are taken from the CLR report ([1931] CLR 394) report and (if quoted without a footnote reference) from coverage in the *LD* and *SMH* 21 and 22 January 1931 (*LD*: https://trove.nla.gov.au/newspaper/article/236948457, https://trove.nla.gov.au/newspaper/article/236949814; *SMH*: https://trove.nla.gov.au/newspaper/article/16747437, https://trove.nla.gov.au/newspaper/article/16747969). There is sufficient difference between the two papers' reports and the CLR report in terms both of material included and its ordering to suggest that many potentially important submissions and questions went unrecorded. The CLR report of Loxton's submissions is distinctly skimpy.

[14] Pp 66–67 above.

[15] Vol 1 pp 150–152.

the state Legislature the right to destroy its independence." Then, apparently referring to the insertion and subsequent removal of the two-thirds clauses in the 1855 Act, Loxton submitted:

> The Imperial Parliament provided for certain conditions to be complied with before drastic legislation could be passed, but it also saw fit to create a creature of such vitality that it could wipe out every safeguard that the Imperial Parliament had imposed.

The 'such vitality' presumably alluded to s.4 [BAA], and the power it gave (according to Russell's despatch) to the Legislature to alter sch.1 of the 1855 Act in the same 'manner' (ie bicameral bare majoritarianism plus royal assent) as it might alter any other (ie non-sch.1) New South Wales laws. To that historical juncture, Loxton's submission had some force.[16] Birkenhead had not unambiguously held in *McCawley* that colonial legislatures had entrenching powers prior to the CLVA being passed, even though Isaacs and Rich clearly held that view.

In the afternoon, however, when Loxton moved to CLVA 1865 s.5's effect, upon which Trethowan and Playfair primarily relied, that force rather ebbed away.[17] As to what s.5 did and did not do, Loxton made three submissions, with varying levels of credibility.

The first was a fanciful (mis-)use of the accepted principle that an Act cast in general terms should not be taken impliedly to repeal or amend an earlier Act dealing with a specific issue, ie here CLVA 1865 s.5 (generally applicable to all representative legislatures) should not override s.4 [BAA] (applicable only to the New South Wales Legislature). The weakness of this proposition is obvious: all representative legislatures were the creation of (very) specific Imperial Acts. If Loxton's submission were correct, then s.5 could not apply to any representative legislature – a plainly implausible proposition, given its text and the context of its enactment.

The second was the (less crude) suggestion that if Trethowan's argument was correct, then the Legislature could by a bare majority entrench in *any fashion any laws on any subject matter*: "The present Parliament, with equal force might declare that a future Parliament could not pass any law with respect to industry, arbitration or the basic wage without the consent of the Australian Labour Party ..."[18]

This proposition requires a segmented reading of s.5's 'constitution, powers and procedure' proviso. It demands that 'constitution' and 'procedure' each be read as dealing with the Legislature's institutional identity, while 'powers' refers to its substantive competence(s). An objection to that argument is that the Imperial Parliament is unlikely

[16] There is a peculiar passage in [1931] CLR 394 at 402 which states that Loxton submitted that s.4 [BAA] was repealed by the 1857 New South Wales Act (vol 1 pp 56–57); but even though 'repealed', s.4 remained 'operative'. The submission does not feature in the *SMH* or *LD* accounts. It is difficult to accept the CLR account as accurate, given that the 1857 New South Wales Act could not have repealed s.4 [BAA] (see at vol 1 pp 64–65 the discussion of the normative distinction between s.4 [BAA] and its Queensland equivalent in cl. 22 of the 1859 Order in Council) and a repealed provision cannot in any event be 'operative'. A 'better' argument might be that the CA 1902 – in repealing sch.1 of the 1855 Act (vol 1 pp 202–05) – had not 'repealed' s.4 [BAA] but had made it redundant as there was no longer a sch.1 for it apply to.

[17] Again, nobody noted that both in 1929 and 1931 the Legislature might not be 'representative' per CLVA 1865 s.1 and s.5 because there were more members of the Council than of the Assembly.

[18] *LD* 21 January 1931 p5. By 'declare' Loxton presumably meant 'enact'.

to have separated two 'identity' issues with a 'competence' issue. That objection is readily rebuttable. Neither the Commons nor the Lords discussed s.5 or any other part of the bill that became the CLVA 1865, and there is no sound basis for assuming that the Act's final form was arrived at through a process involving any forensic parliamentary exactitude. A better objection is that the context of the Act's enactment – and especially the Law Officers' Report – was grounded in 'identity' rather than 'competence issues', and so s.5's allusion to 'powers' should be seen as an unnecessary duplication of the sentiments encapsulated in 'constitution' and 'procedure'.[19]

Loxton's third proposition, echoing Evatt's submission below, was that s.5 'manner and form' embraced only alterations to the existing elements of the Legislature. In other words, s.5 might permit enforceable enactments of provisions demanding enhanced majorities in either or both houses, imposing particular time restraints or requiring assent to be given by the Monarch rather than a Governor, but did not extend to making a new, external body part of the Legislature. There is no indication that Loxton returned to Palmer and Collier's Report to buttress this submission. (Loxton seemingly did not address the point – and evidently was not pressed on the issue – of whether s.5 therefore precluded the abolition of one of the two houses of the Legislature. Presumably that issue was regarded as settled by *Taylor* and the subsequent abolition of Queensland's Council.) According to the CLR report, Loxton reinforced this point by taking the court to s.9 [BAA] and submitting: "The legislature referred to in sec.9 consists of three component parts, the Upper House, the Lower House and the Crown."[20]

The submission prima facie seems quite powerful. However s.9 [BAA] actually says that 'the Legislature':

> … shall include as well as the Legislature to be constituted under the said reserved Bill [ie sch.1] and this Act, as *any future Legislature* which may be established in the said Colony under the Powers in the said reserved Bill and this Act contained.[21]

Loxton's use of s.9 [BAA] might therefore seem poorly conceived, since the Assembly plus Council plus referendum plus Crown lawmaker created by s.7A might be thought a 'future' Legislature per s.9 [BAA]. But s.9 [BAA] does not refer to *any* future legislature; it refers only to such a legislature created through the 1855 Act.[22] And it is not immediately obvious where one might find within either the [BAA] element of the 1855 Act or sch.1 any 'future Legislature' envisaged other than the one alluded to in s.15 [s.17] and s.36 [s.42], ie one in which the Assembly has more members representing different constituencies and/or one which contains 'another' Council with elected and/or appointed members. There is certainly no 'third party' addendum to the original legislature adverted to anywhere in the 1855 Act. (Loxton did not make it clear that s.3 of the Constitution Act 1902 (CA 1902) had modified s.9 [BAA], removing the

[19] Vol 1 pp 111–12. More precisely, 'powers' would extend only to matters of 'competence' concerning the legislature's identity.

[20] *Trethowan* (1931) 44 CLR 394, 403.

[21] Emphasis added. The 'as' before 'any future' makes no grammatical sense, and is another example of the sloppy drafting pervading Imperial legislation on colonial issues.

[22] Vol 1 p 46 n 48.

'any future Legislature' caveat and replacing it with the "unless the context or subject-matter otherwise indicates or requires" formula,[23] fearing perhaps that those words might be taken to include a referendum device.)

To frame the argument somewhat differently, Loxton – and Evatt below – apparently submitted that CLVA 1865 s.5's effect in New South Wales was constrained by the particularistic meaning of the notion of 'the Legislature' in that territory. The purported lawmaker created by s.7A(6) was not – because of s.9 [BAA] (and CA 1902 s.3) – a 'Legislature' at all; therefore it could not exercise any powers per CLVA 1865 s.5 because those powers were granted only to representative *legislatures*.

Loxton concluded the state's case in a more contemporaneously specific way, tied into the more expansive theoretical proposition that the state 'Legislature' could only ever be a bicameral, bare majoritarian lawmaker, but did so in terms which seemed to undermine his (most powerful) 'manner and form' provision argument:

> Although the 1929 Bill purported only to prescribe the manner and form in which the Legislative Council could be abolished, it actually struck a blow at the fundamental powers of Parliament. It attempted to deprive Parliament of sovereign power. Before a particular party left the House to face an antagonistic electorate at the hustings it could enumerate a list of matters upon which its successors could not legislate if the state Court's decision held good. If you can limit legislation for a month you can limit it for a hundred years.[24]

Maughan was asked by Gavan Duffy CJ during Loxton's submission if Trethowan contended that the *Legislature* could not repeal the 1929 Act. The answer was short: "No, Your Honour." Maughan expanded on that answer on day two.

Maughan began by invoking *McCawley* to support the proposition that the consequence of the CLVA 1865's enactment was that colonial parliaments were to become: "their own constitution makers". Maughan submitted that the representative legislatures' constitution-making power had only two limits: that it could not deprive the legislature of its representative character; and that it had to comply with s.5's 'manner and form' requirements. Per *McCawley*, colonial constitutions might be either 'flexible' or 'rigid', and s.5 enabled colonial legislatures to move their colonies' respective constitutions from the flexible to the rigid or vice versa.

Maughan can hardly be criticised for using Birkenhead's terminology, but, as already suggested, the terminology suggesting that there is a binary divide between 'rigid' and 'flexible' is inapposite.[25] So, if in New South Wales a law affecting subject A could only be enacted if approved by a bare majority (of members voting) of the Assembly and – after a delay of at least one month – by a bare Council majority, then the New South Wales Constitution is a little less flexible (or a little more rigid) than before, but it is not 'rigid' in any absolute sense. Relatedly, the 'flexible' status quo could become *more flexible* if – as in Queensland – the Council was abolished so that only a bare Assembly majority was required prior to the royal assent being given. If.7A(6) was valid, its consequence was that on one specific issue changing the law had become a little more difficult.

[23] Vol 1 pp 203–04.

[24] *LD* 21 January 1931 p5. The submission again assumes that 'powers' in s.5 betokens a 'competence' rather than 'identity' issue.

[25] Vol 1 pp 308–09.

Maughan nonetheless pitched his submissions more broadly, since if s.7A(6)'s modest entrenchment was valid it could only be because less modest devices would also be valid, as s.5 placed no obvious textual limits on permissible 'manner and form' provisions. *In extremis*, Maughan's logic had to accept that s.5 allowed a 'manner and form' that would effectively preclude change: "If one [New South Wales] Parliament says that parliament cannot alter a law except by a unanimous vote that goes on for ever, unless you can get a unanimous vote to repeal it. I stand or fall by that."[26]

Maughan dug into the CLVA 1865's underlying history, drawing expressly on Palmer and Collier's Report to sustain the proposition that Parliament intended in 1865 both to cure such failures of legislative 'form' (wherever they occurred) that had prompted some of Boothby's judgments[27] and to empower colonial legislatures to *introduce* such restraints. He met Loxton's s.9 [BAA] point in a two-stage submission: firstly, that s.5 had either "replaced or expounded" the provisions in the 1855 Act; and secondly, that the s.7A(6) lawmaker was properly seen as a 'legislature' within s.5:

> The particular machinery that we desire to embody in the Constitution of New South Wales by the Act of 1929 is a compulsory referendum. It is not any new-fangled nor theoretical machine. It is well known to anyone who has studied constitutional law and we have lived in the atmosphere of a constitution controlled by a referendum for the last 31 years. It has actually been employed in Queensland …
>
> … I submit that the Parliament of New South Wales can add any units which it thinks fit to the Legislature and having added them it can destroy them provided always that it observes the rule laid down for the time being for the law of destruction. I submit that it can set up a referendum for all purposes and it becomes a part of the Legislature … In this case four persons had to approve of the law – the Legislative Assembly, the Legislative Council, the electors, and the King. There is no reason why the colonial legislature should not have different branches. There is nothing inconsistent with Section 5 in finding that a representative legislature has two separate sets of units dealing with two separate kinds of laws …[28]

In short terms, Maughan submitted that a colony's 'Legislature' could have different (even multiple) identities for different (even multiple) purposes.

Loxton declined the opportunity to reply. The High Court informed the parties that judgment would be reserved. As Lang and Bavin awaited the decision, the contexts of both national and New South Wales politics became yet more fractious and uncertain.

[26] *LD* 22 January 1931 p5.

[27] Vol 1 pp 101–05 above. Maughan evidently did not also refer to Lutwyche's judgments, which had (before 1865) prompted enactment of Imperial legislation similar to the CLVA but applicable only to Queensland; vol 1 pp 68–79.

[28] *SMH* 22 January 1931 p10. Maughan also missed (or deliberately omitted) the inconvenient point for his argument that such a four-part legislature (or three-part if we discount the Crown) could not be representative per CLVA 1865 s.1 and s.5. He was not pressed on the issue from the bench. It is not clear if Maughan accepted or rejected Loxton's argument that the 'powers' element of s.5 went beyond 'identity' issues and embraced *all matters of substantive competence*. The 'competence' question raised by s.7A relates to an 'identity' issue, ie 'Can the Legislature be given a new identity for the purpose of regulating future changes to its identity?', rather than 'Can the Legislature be given a new identity for the purpose of regulating future changes to the level of income tax, or of public employees' wages?'. Given his detailed engagement with the history of the CLVA 1865's enactment, it seems more likely that he was rejecting Loxton's broad construction of 'powers'.

II. To the Right and to the Left: The Incipient Collapse of Scullin's Government

Within weeks of resuming office, Theodore made his increasing attachment to Keynesian economic theory very clear, and also managed to carry Scullin with him. What became known as 'the Theodore Plan' emerged in February 1931. It involved a modest reflationary programme, including issuing currency not fully backed by gold reserves, but firmly rejected any suggestion that Australia would not honour its international and internal debts.

Scullin called a Premiers' conference in Canberra in early February to seek state support for the Theodore Plan. The conference was hijacked and effectively sabotaged by Lang, who used it as the platform to launch his own prescription for the nation's economic ills – 'the Lang Plan'.[29] The Lang's programme took shape during the late 1920s,[30] and had three core elements: a significant currency issue, renegotiation of Australia's British war debts from an interest rate of 5% to 3%, and a reduction in interest (to 3%) payable on state and national government loans.[31]

It seems unlikely that Lang matched Theodore's understanding of Keynes's economic theories. And while the two plans had some common ground, the essential difference between them was that Lang's Plan was underscored by a threat that the national and state legislatures should unilaterally 'repudiate' their loan obligations if their respective creditors did not agree more favourable terms. It may be that Lang genuinely thought that the British government and other creditors would be cowed by the prospect of repudiation into accepting reduced or delayed payments, but even if bona fide, the belief was manifestly unrealistic.

While disavowing repudiation in the Lang sense,[32] Theodore's ideas were (for the time) quite radical, and Gibson indicated that Bank Board support – in the form of a reflationary note issue[33] – would be available only if the plan was modified to include yet further reductions in wage levels and welfare expenditure. Even diluted to accommodate Gibson's conservative sentiments, the economic meat of the Theodore Plan was too strong for the Nationalist and Country parties to stomach. Necessary legislative initiatives were blocked in the Senate, and on 6 March 1931 the Nationalists moved a no-confidence motion. The motion – which dragged on through successive adjournments over a week of debate – was eventually defeated, but Lyons, Fenton and four other Labour members voted against the government and effectively left the Labour Party.

Scullin had now lost control of the right of the Labour caucus. Shortly afterwards, consequent on Lang's machinations, he lost control of its left.

[29] Nairn (1995) op cit pp 222–24: Clark (1977) 'Was Lang right?' in Radi and Spearitt op cit.

[30] Pp 25–30 above.

[31] Lang explains his plan and events at the Conference in Lang (1962) op cit chs 57–58; (1970) op cit ch 10.

[32] Lang considered that wage cuts or hours increases imposed by employers or contained in awards made by arbitration courts, or reductions in welfare provision, were themselves a 'repudiation', but were not recognised as such in the Niemayer/Gibson scheme or by Scullin's government. Lang's position also had distinctly Australian nationalist/anti-British dimension, in that he consistently argued that Australia's economic difficulties were largely a consequence of deliberate decisions taken by British financiers: see Lang (1962) op cit chs 57–58; (1970) op cit ch 10.

[33] Vol 1 pp 334–36.

'Lang Labour' in the Commonwealth Parliament

The intra-party turbulence Scullin faced in reappointing Theodore was intensified when a youthful, Lang-supporting trade unionist, Eddie Ward, was selected in early February 1931 by the New South Wales Labour Party to contest a House by-election.[34] Ward subsequently campaigned for election, enthusiastically supporting the Lang Plan.[35] Ward's success at the 7 March by-election was a mixed blessing for Scullin and Theodore, who were not willing to accord any legitimacy to either Lang or his plan. Scullin had majority support in the caucus to deny the whip to Ward if not he did renounce Langism. Ward would not do so, and he and four Lang-supporting New South Wales members resigned the party whip and formed a distinct 'Lang Labour' grouping within the House, 'led' by Jack Beasley.[36] There was no immediate indication that 'Lang Labour' would join the 'United Australia Party' in opposing government policy, but Scullin no longer had a reliable House majority.

Then, on 14 March, the New South Wales party conference, heavily populated per the Red Rules by Lang's supporters in the leagues and smaller unions, expelled Theodore from the New South Wales party.[37] This was ostensibly on the (surreal) ground that Theodore refused to back the Lang Plan, although the underlying rationale seems to have been Lang's increasingly uncontrolled antipathy towards Theodore. In such torrid political times, the High Court's judgment in *Trethowan* might be considered almost anti-climactic.

III. The Judgments

The Court divided three to two in Trethowan's favour; judgment was delivered on 16 March 1931. Rich, Starke and Dixon JJ formed the majority, with Gavan Duffy CJ and McTiernan J dissenting. The five judgments shared two common characteristics. None made any reference at all to any statement made by any politician in the lead up to or during the passage of either the 1929 Act or the attempt to repeal it. All of the judges also accepted that since the New South Wales Legislature was not sovereign in the British sense, the British orthodoxy that any statutory provision could at any time be repealed in the simple majority plus royal assent manner had limited relevance to the issue before them.[38]

[34] Lang disclaimed any role in the selection; Lang (1970) op cit pp 102–03.

[35] Lang (1970) op cit pp 104–05; Nairn (1995) op cit pp 225–27.

[36] Ward (1978) op cit pp 183–85; Robertson (1974) op cit pp 316–18; Lang (1970) op cit pp 104–05. Beasley, an electrician by trade, had been active in trade unionism and leftist politics in New South Wales throughout the 1920s. He became close personally and politically to Lang, who helped him into a winnable New South Wales House seat in 1928. Scullin appointed Beasley to the Cabinet in 1929, and then sacked him in March 1930 when Beasley made clear his preference for Lang's economic policy ideas; http://adb.anu.edu.au/biography/beasley-john-albert-jack-9461.

[37] Robertson (1974) op cit p 325; Fitzgerald op cit pp 293–94.

[38] Curiously, perhaps, no attention was given in the judgments or, it seems, the submissions to the significance of the Parliament Act 1911, a measure which, on its face, created a 'second' British Parliament comprised of the Commons and the King. That may be because that second 'Parliament' – like the Council-less Queensland Legislature – was a reduced (ie bicameral to unicameral) rather than enhanced (ie bicameral to bicameral plus referendum) body.

Gavan Duffy CJ

The Chief Justice delivered a slender judgment, in terms of both length and reasoning. The nub of Gavan Duffy's conclusion was:

> Sec. 7A has no more binding force than any other enactment of the Parliament of New South Wales, and the power to make laws respecting its own "constitution, powers, and procedure" as fully authorized the removal of the referendum machinery as it authorized its introduction. That Legislature can prescribe what "manner and form" shall be necessary, and so cease to require what has theretofore been necessary.[39]

The reasoning is cursory and muddled, Gavan Duffy appears to hold – accepting Loxton's s.9 [BAA] submission – that the Legislature's identity is fixed to embrace only the two houses and the Governor, and that for matters internal to New South Wales *that* Legislature has as much authority as the British Parliament:

> If Parliament had erected a new authority within the meaning of the *Colonial Laws Validity Act* 1865 to take its place either wholly or for the purpose of the repeal of sec. 7 A, it might well be that that authority could alone repeal the section; but it has not done so, and though the Legislature as it existed in 1929 could exercise all the powers conferred on it by the *Colonial Laws Validity Act 1865*, it could not derogate from those powers in the hands of the Legislature as it existed in 1930.[40]

An obvious objection to this analysis – on its own terms – would be that s.7A did indeed create, for just two purposes, a 'new authority' in the CLVA 1865 s.5 sense. Gavan Duffy evidently accepts that such a body might be created. However, he gives no indication of what characteristics such a body would have to have for him to recognise it as such, nor any explanation as to why the Assembly plus Council plus referendum plus Governor should not be so regarded.

The judgment also contains an isolated paragraph which asserts that s.7A had not affected the 'Constitution' of the New South Wales Legislature as that term was used in s.5 of the CLVA 1865, but only related to the Legislature's powers. It may be that Gavan Duffy was nudging towards recognising a normative hierarchy within s.5 of the type outlined in volume one,[41] but he does not develop or clarify the point. More prosaically, he offers no explanation for how one might distinguish between 'constitution' and 'powers'.

The judgment concludes with a tortuous paragraph notionally rooted in the text of the CLVA 1865:

> Again, when the Imperial statute deals with the making of a law as a whole it uses the word "make" or "enact," but when it deals with any integral part of the making it uses an expression appropriate to that integral part, such as "passed," "presented to the Governor," "assented to by the Governor," and the antithesis between the words "make" and "pass" appears to be preserved in the language of sec. 5 itself. It may well be that the words "shall have been passed in such manner and form" in sec. 5 mean nothing more than "passed by the House or Houses of Parliament." But in any case it seems clear to me that the proviso has application only to acts

[39] *Trethowan* (1931) 44 CLR 394, 413.
[40] ibid.
[41] Vol 1 pp 111–12.

> of the Legislature or of some branch of the Legislature. Thus, it might include all that is to be done in the course of legislation by any branch of the legislative body, but it cannot include an act required to be done by some person, or persons outside the legislative body, as a condition precedent to any act of the legislative body.[42]

This seems to reiterate his earlier point: namely, that the Legislature's institutional identity is fixed. One assumes he meant fixed in the sense that its components parts could not be increased but could be reduced; that is – following Queensland's example – the Assembly, Council and Governor could enact a valid statute abolishing the Legislative Council. Whether this would be a 'new authority' or just a new version of the old one is not an issue Gavan Duffy addressed.

Overall, the judgment is feeble stuff, and compares poorly – at least at first sight – in terms of analytical rigour with McTiernan's dissent. On closer reading, however, McTiernan's opinion offers only a more complex version of Gavan Duffy's position.

McTiernan J

The judgment begins by acknowledging the obvious point that one could not answer the question before the court by analogy with the position of the Imperial Parliament:

> The power of the Parliament of New South Wales to put a fetter, which is legally binding, on its power to repeal one of its own Acts cannot be denied on the ground that the Parliament of New South Wales enjoys those attributes of sovereignty which reside in the Imperial Parliament. It is the creature of the Imperial Parliament and subordinate to it.
>
> The powers of the Parliament of New South Wales and the rules governing their exercise must be sought in the statutes by which its creator and sovereign gave it life and vested it with power. The Imperial Parliament as a sovereign is supreme over its own Acts. It does not necessarily follow that the legislature which is created by one of those Acts, can attract to itself a legal supremacy over every law which it enacts, so that every one of those laws may be repealed or set aside by a later enactment.
>
> Nor does it follow that the Parliament of New South Wales has power to enact a law which binds itself because it is not a sovereign legislature. It cannot by taking thought add one cubit to its stature. The determination of the questions argued in this appeal must depend upon the true meaning and effect of the Imperial statutes by which the Imperial Parliament conferred a constitution upon New South Wales …[43]

McTiernan then sets up a *McCawley*-esque dichotomy which pervades his analysis between a 'rigid' and an 'uncontrolled' constitution. The distinction is used not in the sense of 'rigid' being perceived as politically 'bad' and 'uncontrolled' being labelled as politically 'good'. Rather, the assumption is that 'uncontrolled' means 'Assembly plus Council by bare majority plus Governor', while 'rigid' means anything else that renders the making of law (or particular types of law) law more difficult.

McTiernan pursued the historical trail rather more determinedly than Gavan Duffy CJ. He referred to the 1855 Act, but went beyond the Act's text to consider the views

[42] *Trethowan* (1931) 44 CLR 394, 414.
[43] ibid pp 434–35.

expressed by Russell in his despatch explaining the Act's purpose. This made it clear in McTiernan's view that the Imperial Parliament intended New South Wales to have an 'uncontrolled' constitution, any part of which could at any time be amended by simple majority Assembly plus Council plus Governor's legislation.

Perhaps ironically – although the irony apparently escaped McTiernan – he tied the notion of an *uncontrolled* 'constitution' with that of (in institutional terms) a very *rigid* notion of what was meant by a 'Legislature'. Like Gavan Duffy CJ, McTiernan considered this notion could be no more expansive than the two houses and the Governor. This reasoning stemmed in part from matters of imperial tradition, but also from the plain words of CA 1902 s.3, even though McTiernan rather ignored the 'unless …' addendum in s.3.[44]

Set against this constitutional background, Trethowan's case appeared very novel:

> The precise statement of counsel for the respondents was that, after the commencement of sec. 5 of the *Colonial Laws Validity Act*, the *Constitution of New South Wales* became "potentially rigid." In support of this submission, it was contended that sec.5 "extended" the power of the Legislature, so that it became competent to bind itself and its successors by a law requiring that the "manner" therein prescribed for the repeal or amendment of an Act of the Legislature should be observed by itself and its successors.
>
> If that view is correct, the Legislature may, whenever it pleases, become a Constitutional Convention and make a fundamental law, and after it has done so, the powers of the Legislature and its successors to repeal or amend this law suffer a serious contraction, and the Legislature becomes legally subordinate to the law …
>
> If the *Colonial Laws Validity Act* empowers the Legislature of New South Wales to do this, and sub-sec. 6 is a legally binding fetter, from the restraint of which the Legislature cannot escape by the exercise of its power as the Legislature but must rely upon the vote of the majority of the electors to release it, the Colonial Laws Validity Act has authorised a radical disturbance in the constitutional position as established by 18 and 19 Vict. c. 54 [the 1855 Act] and explained by the Despatch of the Secretary of State for the Colonies, with which the *Constitution Statute* and the *Constitution* were transmitted to the Governor of New South Wales.[45]

In essence, McTiernan rooted his analysis of the CLVA 1865, and especially of s.5, in a constitutional setting which would make it very surprising indeed for Trethowan's argument to be correct. McTiernan supported this proposition with reference to several Privy Council authorities (including *McCawley* and *Burah*) dealing with the powers of colonial legislatures, all of which he regarded as confirming that deviations from the principle that colonial 'Legislatures' (in the rigid institutional sense identified above) had plenary powers save to the extent that those powers were *expressly* limited by *Imperial* legislation (such as, for example, the referendum provisions in s.128 of the Australia Act 1901). Far from being a device through which representative 'Legislatures' could restrict their powers:

> Sec. 5 … is an overriding charter which keeps the legislature continuously supplied with plenary power to make laws respecting its own constitution, powers and procedure, and no Act of the legislature can destroy or permanently diminish the authority which it derives from the charter.[46]

[44] Vol 1 p 204.
[45] *Trethowan* (1931) 44 CLR 394, 436–37; original emphases.
[46] ibid 440–41.

Given that *McCawley* clearly accepted the possibility of entrenchment being achieved through s.5,[47] and given that *Burah* made no mention of s.5,[48] neither authority seems particularly supportive of McTiernan's reasoning. Nonetheless, that reasoning led McTiernan to two alternative but – for Lang – equally effective conclusions.

The first was that s.7(A)(6) did not create a 'manner and form' for the passing of law, but instead effected a reduction in the Legislature's powers:

> In my opinion, therefore, sub-sec. 6 of sec. 7A is not in substance a law dictating "manner": it is in substance a law depriving the Legislature of power. The words of the section measure the extent to which the power of the Legislature is cut down. It renders the King, the Legislative Council and the Legislative Assembly assembled in Parliament powerless to repeal the section unless an external body intervenes and approves of the repeal. In my opinion the Legislature, consisting of its three constituent elements in Parliament assembled, may, under sec. 5 of the Colonial Laws Validity Act, resume the power to repeal sec. 7A.[49]

If s.7A(6) did not enact a 'manner and form' constraint, there was no 'manner and form' to be complied with in its repeal, and so repeal by simple bicameral majority and the royal assent would suffice. Alternatively, if s.7A(6) was a 'manner and form' proviso, it would be ultra vires CLVA 1865 s.5 precisely because it purported to restrict the powers of the 'Legislature'.

That second conclusion logically leads to the final element of McTiernan's J's judgment, which dealt with the question of whether or not Bavin's government had persuaded the Legislature to enact a measure which created a new or alternative 'Legislature' for the purpose of entrenching the existence of the Council; (he seemed unwilling or unable to countenance the idea that the Legislature had somehow been divided or fragmented).

McTiernan J was wholly unsympathetic to that suggestion: "In my opinion there can only be one Legislature in New South Wales."[50] He did not explain why this was the case, but moved immediately to consider why the Assembly plus Council plus referendum plus Governor could not be a Legislature in any event. The crux of his reasoning appeared to be that the component parts of a Legislature performed particular functions, functions which could not be performed by a referendum. The argument is not especially well developed. One could certainly accept that the s.7A referendum had no power to initiate a bill and it also had no capacity to modify a bill, both of which were important elements of the functions of the Assembly and the Council. The referendum functioned only to approve or reject a bill. That would, however, seem to be just what the Governor would do in the exercise of his legislative function. In McTiernan's opinion, any attempt to draw an analogy between the referendum and the Governor was flawed because (and here his argument moves without acknowledgement from being one about function to one concerned only with form) because the Governor was the personal representative of the Crown and the referendum was not.

[47] Vol 1 pp 308–13.
[48] Vol 1pp 152–53.
[49] *Trethowan* (1931) 44 CLR 394, 442.
[50] ibid 448.

Rich J

Rich J's brief judgment rejected the main plank of McTiernan's reasoning: namely, that the CLVA 1865 had to be construed in the light of the 1855 legislation. He considered (rather optimistically perhaps) that s.5's meaning was obvious and that any inconsistent Imperial legislation had been overruled:

> I regard it as clear that in so far as sec. 5 enables the Legislature of New South Wales to fetter, restrain, or condition the exercise of its power of constitutional alteration, no prior statute of the Imperial Parliament can operate to enable it to ignore or set at nought any restraint, fetter, or condition it has seen fit to impose in the exercise of that power …
>
> Two methods of controlling the operations of the Legislature appear to be allowed by the express terms of the section. The constitution of the legislative body may be altered; that is to say, the power of legislation may be reposed in an authority differently constituted. Again, laws may be passed imposing legal requirements as to manner and form in which constitutional amendments must be passed.[51]

Rich J also dismissed Gavan Duffy's assumption that significance should be attached to the varied use of 'passed' and 'enacted' in the CLVA 1865. The words were simply different ways of saying the same thing:

> In my opinion the proviso to sec. 5 relates to the entire process of turning a proposed law into a legislative enactment, and was intended to enjoin fulfilment of every condition and compliance with every requirement which existing legislation imposed upon the process of law-making.[52]

Nor did Rich J see any merit in the view propounded by Gavan Duffy and McTiernan that a 'Legislature' had to have a particular institutional identity. It might have two chambers, or one or three. And if it could have a third chamber, it might alternatively or even additionally also incorporate: "a body of persons of another character";[53] and it might acquire those additional parts for some or all purposes:

> If the legislative body consists of different elements for the purpose of legislation upon different subjects, the natural method of applying the definition would be to consider what was the subject upon which the particular exercise of power was proposed, and to treat sec. 5 as conferring upon the body constituted to deal with that subject authority to pass the law although it related to the powers of the legislature. An examination of sec. 7A shows that a legislative body has been created for the purpose of passing or co-operating in passing a particular law. There is no reason why this authority need extend to all laws.[54]

Rich J also indicated that McTiernan's J's focus on the functions of a Legislature's component parts was misconceived. The national Parliament's Senate had no power to initiate or amend money bills; its function was limited to approval or rejection. But it could not credibly be contended that the Senate was in that context not part of a Legislature.

[51] ibid 418.
[52] ibid 419.
[53] ibid.
[54] ibid 419–20.

The judgment concluded with the suggestion that the political purpose underpinning Bavin's initiative was entirely legitimate. It was a measure:

> ... [A]imed at restraining improvident or hasty action. There is no reason why a Parliament representing the people should be powerless to determine whether the constitutional salvation of the state is to be reached by cautious and well considered steps rather than by rash and ill-considered measures.[55]

Starke J

Like Rich J, Starke J (in a brief judgment) found the answer to the litigation in s.5's evidently plain meaning, which:

> ... [P]uts the matter, in my opinion, beyond doubt.
>
> Ordinarily, a law is made when it has been passed in accordance with the regular procedure of the legislative body, and has received the royal assent. But the "manner and form" whose observance is required by the proviso to sec. 5 of the Colonial Laws Validity Act is the method prescribed by the Imperial Act or colonial law for the making of the law respecting the constitution, powers or procedure of the legislature which is in question.
>
> The position is stated clearly and, I think, accurately by Professor Berriedale Keith in his work *Imperial unity and the Dominions* at pp 389–90:
>
> "Any rule whatever," he says, "which has been laid down by any legislative authority with regard to the mode of modifying the constitution is a fetter on the freedom of the Dominion Parliament which it cannot break save in the way appointed by the Act imposing the fetter. If a Dominion Parliament enact to-morrow that any Act which it passes must be passed by a two-thirds majority to take effect as an alteration of the constitution, then this condition becomes one which, so long as the Act in question stands, cannot be undone by the Parliament save in the prescribed manner, that is to say if the Act has been careful to make it clear that this provision itself is to be protected in this way."[56]

Dixon J

Dixon produced a similar opinion. S.5's meaning was again the central issue:

> ... [I]n virtue of its sovereignty it was open to the Imperial Parliament itself to give, or to empower the Legislature of New South Wales to give, to the constitution of that State as much or as little rigidity as might be proper.[57]

The Lang government's reliance on s.4 [BAA] was misplaced in Dixon's view. This was not because s.4 had been 'repealed' by the Constitution Act 1902. Dixon's more subtle conclusion was that s.4 [BAA] could be applied only to the provisions in sch.1 of the 1855 Act. But since s.4 [BAA] had been used to enact the 1902 Act, which repealed

[55] ibid 420.
[56] ibid 424.
[57] ibid 427.

sch.1, there was nothing left for that provision to bite on: it had not been 'repealed', but it had been 'exhausted'. There was thus no need for the Court to concern itself with the normative relationship between s.4 [BAA] and CLVA 1865 s.5, nor to try to reconcile the two provisions. The case's outcome would turn exclusively on the meaning of s.5.[58]

Dixon J clearly rejected any simplistic 'flexible v rigid' binary divide. The 'as much or as little' rigidity was a potentially vast spectrum. Although Dixon J did not elaborate on the notion of 'proper', it seems that he used the term to mean 'by whatever lawmaking process is currently required'. Prior to the enactment of s.7A, the abolition of the Council could 'properly' have been secured by simple majority in the Assembly and the Council plus the royal assent. But that process could also 'properly' create other methods of making law, even if the methods chosen reduced or restrained the powers of a simple majority plus royal assent Legislature. And those new methods would then have become 'proper'.

On Dixon J's reasoning, s.7A was a law within the meaning of CLVA 1865 s.5 'properly' enacted, which reduced the powers of the simple majority bicameral Legislature. The bill intended to repeal s.7A(6) was, in essence, a measure intended to remove that restraint and thus alter again the powers of the Legislature. But it could only 'properly' be enacted through a process in compliance with the prior law found in s.7A.

Dixon saw no force in Gavan Duffy/McTiernan's acceptance of Loxton's submission that a referendum could not participate in the enactment of a law in the CLVA 1865 s.5 sense because it was not a legislative chamber, ie the identity of the Legislature was fixed by s.9 [BAA] of the 1855 Act (or CA 1902 s.3):

> … The more natural, the wider and the more generally accepted meaning includes within the proviso all the conditions which the Imperial Parliament or that of the self-governing State or Colony may see fit to prescribe as essential to the enactment of a valid law. Upon this interpretation a full constituent power is given to the representative legislature, but it may determine what shall be necessary to constitute an exercise of that or any other legislative power.[59]

Dixon did not offer any authority as to why that was: "the more natural, the wider and the more generally accepted meaning". He did suggest that the Crown was not part of the Legislature for s.5 purposes, a conclusion which – though Dixon did not note the point – reduces the scope to argue that a Legislature was not representative in the CLVA 1865 s.1 sense. In common with everyone involved in the case, he did not perceive that adding a referendum to the lawmaking process might be problematic in that regard.

Dixon's reference to 'all the conditions' immediately followed a passage in which he had indicated that such matters as laying before the Commons or Lords and reservation of bills could properly be seen as 'manner and form' provisions within s.5. The obvious inference was that many other departures from the ordinary method might also fall within s.5. His allusion to 'essential' or 'necessary' conditions might imply he envisaged that a legislature might prescribe 'inessential' conditions, but if he had such a distinction in mind, he did not elaborate on it.

[58] Dixon did not notice – or thought the point irrelevant – that the 1902 Act did not in terms repeal 'Schedule 1', but rather repealed the 'Constitution Act 1855', legislators' (mis?)perception then being that there was a New South Wales statute of that name; see vol 1 pp 205–06.

[59] (1931) 44 CLR 394, 432–33.

Reactions to the Judgment

Lang, fortified perhaps by two members of the Court having found in his favour, immediately announced the government's intention to appeal to the Privy Council, and also announced that Sir John Simon, who had successfully led for Theodore in *McCawley*, was briefed to argue the case.[60] Bavin, in contrast, described himself as 'gratified' by the result and predicted any Privy Council appeal would fail.[61]

It appears not to have occurred to Lang – or to any of his Cabinet colleagues[62] – that Bavin's success before the High Court was a potentially very double-edged sword. If the High Court's judgment was indeed 'correct', a government commanding both an Assembly and Council majority now had the capacity to introduce all manner of entrenchment devices (other than those introduced by s.7A) relating to matters within the scope of CLVA 1865 s.5. Indeed, if the meaning of powers in s.5[3] extended beyond questions of the legislature's identity to encompass its general competence, Bavin and Peden had handed Lang – so long as he could control such a majority – a powerful constitutional weapon. The point, it seems, passed (almost)[63] everyone by.

A few days before judgment was issued, Lang had announced that Willis would leave the Cabinet to become the New South Wales Agent-General in London. It may be that Lang was becoming increasingly concerned about Willis's loyalty, and used the appointment to sideline a rival. Lang's own explanation was more straightforward:

> In making this announcement, the Premier (Mr Lang) said that, 'In view of the government's policy, it was essential that the, State should be represented in London by' someone able to explain to the British: nation what the New South Wales government had done in regard to overseas creditors, and why it was done. Mr. Willis, by explaining what Labour's policy of reconstruction means, will be able to break down the propaganda regarding repudiation that has been disseminated among British people …[64]

Lang's concerns about 'propaganda' in Britain might be set in the context of the leader in *The (London) Times* three days later.[65] Titled 'Mr Lang's Rebuff', the leader enthusiastically welcomed the judgment: "Mr Lang, the very "red" Premier of New South Wales, has met a check which may seriously interfere with his plans for establishing a dictatorship of the proletariat with himself as dictator in chief …"

[60] *LD* 17 March 1931 p1, https://trove.nla.gov.au/newspaper/article/236952520. The brief perhaps owed more to cost than concerns about Loxton's competence. Lang's Attorney-General had informed the Assembly on 26 March that the state's costs in the case had been and would continue to be very modest: "So far as the costs in the High Court are concerned, each side pays its own costs. Therefore the costs to the Crown in the High Court do not amount to £500, all told … So far as the costs in the Privy Council are concerned, the only costs that will be incurred there are the fees of Sir John Simon and his junior, and the London agent of our Crown Solicitor, for neither myself nor any other person from the state of New South Wales is going to the Privy Council … l"; *NSWLAD* 26 March 1931 pp 2270–71.

[61] *Barrier Miner* (Broken Hill, NSW) 17 March 1931 p1, https://trove.nla.gov.au/newspaper/article/46601189. Bavin's response was widely reported. I have not found any record of Peden commenting to the press on the judgment.

[62] Or, indeed, to Bavin and Peden.

[63] See the comments in the *Daily Worker* (discussed further below) 18 March 1931 p3, https://trove.nla.gov.au/newspaper/article/145996409.

[64] *Maitland Weekly Mercury* 14 March 1931 p8, https://trove.nla.gov.au/newspaper/article/135249401.

[65] 17 March 1931 p5.

Accusing Lang of lacking the courage to put the abolition question to the electorate, *The Times* urged Game to resist any requests for further Council appointees, and also to refuse assent to any bill of: "a confiscatory or revolutionary character". For good measure, *The Times* denounced Theodore as an 'inflationist' and Scullin and his government as 'impotent'.

In the Australian press, few voices other than the *Labour Daily*, still essentially Lang's in-house journal, criticised the judgment. A wild leader appeared in the *Australian Worker* under the unsubtle heading 'THE LAW DISPLAYS ITS ASININITY':[66]

> The absurdity of such a finding is so apparent that only minds obscured by habits of legalistic casuistry can fail to see it. If one Parliament can bind another, as the Judges say it can, then any Parliament could impose such restraints upon its successors that they could do nothing whatever, and the parliamentary system would perish in a complexity of bandages from which no one was able to release it. A government, going to what it knew to be certain defeat at the polls, could thus make sure that the Labor Movement, however sweeping its electoral triumph, would be reduced to parliamentary impotence?

The article nicely captured – albeit implicitly – Loxton's 'competence' reading of 'powers' in CLVA 1865 s.5. From the other side of the political spectrum, the *Daily Telegraph* – equally nicely and equally implicitly – echoed Maughan's 'identity' reading by raising and dismissing the possibility that the judgment might empower Lang's government to impose similarly impassable barriers:[67]

> If, these people say, Mr. Bavin could pass a law about Council abolition that Mr. Lang cannot alter, what is to prevent Mr. Lang passing a hundred laws that a future Nationalist government will be unable to touch? The argument appears reasonable until one remembers that the Bavin law of 1929 was a special kind of law. It dealt with the instrument of government – the state Parliament – and laid down certain procedure by which a change in its nature could be brought about …

The Telegraph passed by the point that any government would need a majority in both houses to avail itself of s.5 entrenchment. And as events promptly showed, Lang's administration could not muster a Council majority.

Implementing (?) the Lang Plan

The government's pursuit of the Lang Plan was unaffected by the judgment. Just days later, Lang introduced his 'Interest Rate Reduction Bill' to the Assembly.[68] The *Labour Daily* greeted the bill ecstatically:[69]

> **How Lang Proposes to tilt Country's Biggest Burden**
>
> **INTEREST BILL BLAZES NEW POLITICAL TRAIL**

[66] 18 March 1931 p3, https://trove.nla.gov.au/newspaper/article/145996409. The paper was the AWU's journal (and so very pro-Theodore), and it is notable – given the enduring hostility between Lang and the AWU – that the leader castigated the judgment while saying not a single approbatory word about Lang's government.

[67] 21 March 1931 p6, https://trove.nla.gov.au/newspaper/article/246317594.

[68] Lang's second reading speech is at *NSWLAD* 18 March 1931 p1967.

[69] 19 March 1931 p5, https://trove.nla.gov.au/newspaper/article/236943272.

PREMIER GIVES DETAILS IN ASSEMBLY
STEVENS, AS SPOKESMAN FOR MONEY MASTERS, PREDICTS "CHAOS"
COSTLY LITIGATION THREATENED

The bill was, presentationally at least, a key element of the Lang Plan:

> Very little is needed to explain the bill itself. Any interest payable to the bondholders of New South Wales is to be reduced to 3 per cent. Various rates are applied to bank loans, both to and from the bank, and a maximum of 5 per cent. is applied to all forms of loans, such as mortgages, crop liens, and other forms of money-lending – excepting a second mortgage, where the maximum of 6 per cent is allowed.[70]

Lang portrayed the measure as in part designed to equalise the hardship precipitated by the depression, his argument being that if the value of assets (owner-occupied homes being his most frequently cited asset) was declining, then the interest payable on the loans which had financed their purchase should be reduced as well. But since the proposed Act would apply both to government loans and private debts, its immediate benefit from the government's perspective would be to reduce significantly is own interest liabilities.

Lang could not seriously have expected the bill to be enacted; and, it seems, he doubted its constitutionality; the bill was intended perhaps as a symbolic rather than practical measure. It passed Assembly second reading by 50–26, and was scheduled for both committee and report stages and third reading (where it passed without amendment by 52–26) the next day.[71] The bill did not, however, pass through the Council, which at second reading on 25 March 1931 voted 35–22 to adjourn second reading for six months.[72]

One of the more thoughtful (from the right) responses to the judgment was a fear that some previously quiescent Council members would now be emboldened to resist Lang's government economic policy bills, which would, in turn, send Lang back to Game with a request for still more Labour appointees to create a majority for all government measures (other than abolishing the Council).[73] The rejection of the interest reduction bill was an example of such action, as was the Council's effective torpedoing of an industrial conciliation and arbitration bill. Lang did indeed promptly press Game for more appointments, albeit initially with no success.[74]

IV. The Fall of the Scullin Government

The judgment also emerged into a continuingly tumultuous national political context. On 27 March, the national Labour Party conference responded to the provocations of the Ward campaign, the Beasley group's defection, Theodore's expulsion and the

[70] *NSWLAD* 18 March 1931 p1974.
[71] ibid 2006. *NSWLD* 19 March 1931 p2055; third reading is at p2082.
[72] *NSWLCD* 25 March 1931 p2197.
[73] *Sydney Evening News* 16 March 1931 p1, https://trove.nla.gov.au/newspaper/article/115398019.
[74] Nairn (1995) op cit pp 239–41.

New South Wales party's continued embrace of the Lang Plan by purporting to expel the New South Wales branch from the national party and establish a new (and de facto) rival national party version of the New South Wales branch. Evidently uncowed and unabashed in anticipating such action, Lang had told Scullin on 25 March that New South Wales could not (or more likely would not) pay an interest bill of some £800,000 due on 1 April in respect of a London loan. Repudiation was now to be a reality rather than an idle threat within the Lang Plan.[75]

Lang Labour: Repudiation; Consolidation; Isolation

Despite the rift with the national party leadership, Lang enjoyed an extraordinary level of support within the formal structure of the New South Wales (expelled or Lang) party. At the annual conference on 3 April, conference endorsed Theodore's expulsion, expressed fulsome support for the Lang Plan and then approved the loan default by a vote of 122–1.[76]

The United Australia Party

As the Labour Party lurched towards civil war, Lyons had busied himself since the 6 March no-confidence vote in establishing how firmly rooted support for him as the leader of the anti-Labour opposition actually was within the Nationalists. By early May, he was sufficiently reassured to throw in his lot with a notionally new political party. The Nationalists (which Lyons had not formally joined) dissolved themselves, and reappeared as the United Australia Party (UAP), led by Lyons, accompanied by Fenton and the other Labour deserters. The party's name was obviously designed to appeal to disaffected Labour voters, and the rebranding also enabled Lyons to court such voters on the basis that it was Scullin's Labour Party, and not him and Fenton, which had rejected traditional Labour values. Robert Latham, who had succeeded Bruce as the Nationalists' leader, was regarded by Lyon's backers as much less electorally appealing than Lyons himself. Much like Hughes had been ditched to open the door to Bruce in 1922, Latham was shovelled aside into the post of party Deputy Leader.[77] Lyons's first, immediate, parliamentary foray in his new role was to move a censure motion against the government and its increasing flirtation with reflationary, Keynes-inspired economic policy.[78]

[75] Robertson (1974) op cit pp 325–26; Fitzgerald op cit pp 294–95.

[76] Nairn (1995) op cit pp 239–31.

[77] Ward (1978) op cit pp 185–86; Robertson (1974) op cit pp 324–25. Shortly afterwards, Latham was appointed Chief Justice of the High Court on Gavan Duffy's retirement, the obvious inference being that he was promised the role in consideration for stepping quietly aside as leader.

[78] *HRD* 8 May 1931 p1714. Lyons's speech was devoted to arguing that Scullin's government had abandoned principles of sound finance and that he (Lyons) as a loyal Australian was left with no choice but to join the new party; ibid pp 1714–15. He lauded Gibson, condemned Theodore's 'mad schemes' and suggested that Scullin's government was treading, albeit more slowly, along the in his view disastrous path taken by Lang in New South Wales.

The Premiers' Plan

For a brief period in May and June, harmony of sorts between Lang and the national party was seemingly restored when Lang agreed to support a so-called 'Premiers' Plan' on economic policy. In addition to inviting the state Premiers, Scullin and Theodore asked Lyons and Latham to attend to lend the proceedings a 'national', non-partisan character.

The plan – which secured Gibson's approval – was a curious mix of policies. Its headline measure was a 20% reduction in Commonwealth and state employment and welfare spending; it also included a reduction on interest payable on the government's domestic loans to 4%; some increases in personal taxation; and protection against foreclosure for homeowners and small businessmen unable to meet their mortgage payments. What it notably lacked was any reflationary stimulus through an increased note issue.

The Premiers' Plan was thus hardly a reflationary measure, and Lang's initial support for it was perhaps surprising.[79] In part, Lang's support was based on short-term necessity. He also took New South Wales back into the Loan Council and immediately secured a loan which enabled the state to meet its wage obligations to its employees. Lang also attempted to spin the 20% reduction commitment in a more radical direction, by promoting a bill to ensure that the reduction would be achieved largely by capping state employees' salaries at £500 per year. And despite his nominal adherence to the Premiers' Plan, Lang and his supporters did not abate their criticism of the Scullin government in general and of Theodore in particular.

Scullin's political and economic policy difficulties were again compounded by Theodore's absence from the Cabinet in July. The Queensland government's civil action against Theodore over the Mungana affair began on 22 July. The claim was for £30,000 – then a substantial sum. What was really at stake was Theodore's political career. The trial[80] was presided over by William Blair, some 10 years after Theodore had appointed him to the bench[81] (Blair subsequently became Chief Justice of the State Supreme Court in 1925). Proceedings dragged on until 24 August, when the jury found in Theodore's favour.[82]

Despite his 'victory'. Theodore's political standing – and, by extension, the credibility of Scullin's government – was further damaged by the trial, not least because Theodore declined to give evidence in his own defence. More significantly perhaps, the trial, rather than the government's economic policy, had preoccupied Theodore's mind for two months, during which both the economic crisis and the national party's split with Lang grew more intense.

[79] For his account, see Lang (1970) op cit ch 12.

[80] P31 above. The episode is described in detail in Fitzgerald op cit pp 270–78. For a sense of the case's contemporary political importance to national political issues, and of the sensation it generated, see *BC* 23 July 1931 p14, https://trove.nla.gov.au/newspaper/article/21721207; *Queensland Times* 23 July 1931 p7, https://trove.nla.gov.au/newspaper/article/116148256.

[81] Vol 1 p 330.

[82] *BC* 25 August 1931 p11, https://trove.nla.gov.au/newspaper/article/21717825; *Queensland Times* 25 August 1931 p7, https://trove.nla.gov.au/newspaper/article/116152933. The *Labour Daily* gave the verdict little coverage, but reported it – perhaps surprisingly, given Lang's influential editorial voice – in triumphalist terms: *LD* 25 August 1931 p5, https://trove.nla.gov.au/newspaper/article/236595808: "Over five thousand people thronged the old Supreme Court and its precincts, and waited for the decision. And when at last it was given and … Theodore emerged, pandemonium broke loose. The principals in the great Mungana drama, vindicated at last of a charge which had hung over their heads for years, were given a triumph that any victorious general of ancient Rome would have envied."

Theodore and Lang (and Personality and Politics), and the End of Scullin's Government

Game eventually acceded to Lang's repeated requests for a further tranche of Labour appointees to the Council. Twenty-five additional Labour members took office on 19 November – enough, assuming they all acted as government loyalists, to give Lang a small majority. By this point, however, Lang's formal adherence to the Premiers' Plan was devoid of all substance. In early October, he had called for early national elections, and made it clear that 'Lang Labour' would field candidates to oppose both the UAP and the national Labour Party.

Notwithstanding Theodore's acquittal, he and Scullin were now seeing Labour's initially large House majority splintering away both left and right. The threat from the UAP rested essentially on ideology over economic policy. The tentative Keynesianism of the Theodore Plan was far too radical for Lyons and his backers. For the Lang Labour members, Theodore's policies were too timid. But it was seemingly the man himself – seen then by Lang as: "my most bitter enemy"[83] – who they found intolerable. The feeling was apparently mutual. In a speech on 9 October, anticipating opposition from a Lang Labour candidate at the next House election, Theodore castigated both Lang and his supporters:

> Lang typifies a form of reckless, destructive, unintelligent autocracy. The Lang faction is only a crowd of leather lunged lowbrows … The Lang faction has attempted to foist their views on the labour movement. They have travestied the name of Labour …[84]

The *Labour Daily* responded predictably. Theodore was:

> an infliction to be tolerated just so long as the term of the present misfits called a "Federal labour government" lasts … The whole of [Theodore's] vituperative speech reads like the last desperate effort of a thoroughly beaten man …[85]

The article proved prescient. On 25 November 1931, Beasley moved a motion[86] demanding Scullin establish an investigation into allegations that Theodore had improperly influenced the administration of works relief programmes in Sydney to exclude Lang supporters. The allegations had been circulating for weeks, and Theodore equivocated in denying them. Scullin refused to do so, but was provoked during debate to make the matter one of confidence.[87] Any expectation that Scullin had that Lang's supporters would not be so doctrinaire as to trigger an election which would likely return the UAP to power was misplaced. Beasley's motion was carried by 37 votes to 32, with the majority including all of the Lang Labour members.[88] The next day, Scullin advised Isaacs to dissolve Parliament and trigger early elections.

[83] Lang (1970) op cit p94.
[84] *SMH* 10 October 1931 p11, https://trove.nla.gov.au/newspaper/article/16822697.
[85] *LD* 12 October 1931 p4, https://trove.nla.gov.au/newspaper/article/236677794.
[86] *HRD* 25 November 1931 p1888. See Nairn (1995) pp 248–49; Fitzgerald op cit pp 300–02.
[87] ibid 1899: "If honourable members wish to take the business of the House of out the hands of the government, they can have an election."
[88] From the perspectives of the different protagonists, see variously: (Fitzgerald re Theodore) Fitzgerald op cit pp 301–03; (Robertson re Scullin) Robertson (1974) op cit pp 364–71, who suggests Beasley actively conspired with the UAP; (Nairn re Lang) Nairn (1995) op cit pp 247–50. Lang subsequently (and implausibly) claimed not to have played any part in the episode; Lang (1970) op cit ch 13.

The 1931 Commonwealth Election

The 1931 election proved disastrous for the (non-Lang) Labour Party. It retained only 14 seats nationally. The UAP fell just short (34 of 75) of an overall majority, but Lyons formed a minority government with the expected informal support of the Country Party.[89] Lang Labour contested all the New South Wales seats, winning four, and unsuccessfully fought a sprinkling of seats in other states.

The national Labour Party lost 28 of the 42 House seats won in 1929 (although, perversely, it gained three Senate seats). Scullin, retaining his seat, took the result phlegmatically, attributing it largely to having had to govern during the depression.[90] Theodore was the highest profile casualty. In 1929, opposed only by a Nationalist, he had won his Dalley seat with 78% of the vote. In 1931, the Lang Labour candidate, Sol Rosevear, won the seat, taking 48% of the vote to the UAP candidate's 28%, with Theodore languishing in third place on just 19%. For Theodore, the outcome signalled the end of his political career; he did not seek elected office again.[91] With Theodore gone, and the caucus ranks heavily depleted, Scullin had no obvious rival as Labour leader, and was re-elected by the caucus unopposed.

Table 4.1 The 1931 Commonwealth election (19 December 1931)

House of Representatives	**% vote**	**Seats won**	**Change**
United Australia	36.0	34	+17[a]
Labour (National)	27.1	14	–28[a]
Labour (Lang)	10.6	4	
Country	12.2	16	+5[a]
Emergency Committee[b]	6	+6	
Independents	8.2	1	–
Senate[c]			
United Australia/Country	30.2	6	+6
United Australia	25.2	20	–4
Country	–	–	–5
Labour (National)	29.3	10	+3
Labour (Lang)	12.1	0	–

[a] I have equated United Australia with the Nationalists and Independent Nationalists of the 1929 election, aggregated Lang Labour seats with National Labour seats and included the one Country Progressive from 1929 as a Country Party seat.

[b] A party which contested only South Australia seats. It was, in essence, the South Australian Country Party, and fielded candidates with UAP and Country Party backing.

[c] 18 seats contested.

[89] Page linked that support to a government commitment to pursue plans to subdivide New South Wales into several distinct states, hiving off Sydney and its hinterlands from the rural areas; Page op cit ch 23. Of the newly elected House members, Holman, a UAP candidate in a New South Wales seat, was the most notable addition. Hughes, hoping for a Cabinet position, was also returned for the UAP. Hughes was disappointed, and likely infuriated that Bruce was given a Cabinet post, Assistant Treasurer (Lyons appointed himself Treasurer).

[90] Robertson op cit pp 378–82.

[91] He subsequently made several substantial fortunes – in mining in Fiji and, unexpectedly, by establishing a best-selling women's weekly magazine; see Fitzgerald op cit ch 9.

The primary electoral effect of the Lang Labour candidates had been to split the Labour vote in New South Wales. The national Labour Party held only three of the 20 seats gained in 1929; and even if the national and Lang parties could have coalesced around a shared policy agenda – a most unlikely scenario – the four seats won by the Lang-ites added to the three for the national party still represented a catastrophic performance for Labour in the state.

Table 4.2 The 1931 Commonwealth election in New South Wales (19 December 1931)

House of Representatives	% vote	Seats won	Change
United Australia	35.4	13	+11[a]
Labour (National)	16.3	3	−17
Labour (Lang)	24.7	4	+4[b]
Country	17.5	8	+4
Independents	5.6	–	–
Senate[c]			
United Australia/Country	52.7	3	–
Labour (National)	15.1	1	−2
Labour (Lang)	30.7	2	+2

[a] Equated with the Nationalists at the 1929 election.
[b] I have treated Lang Labour as an entirely new party for the purposes of the 'change' column.
[c] 6 seats contested.

Yet for Lang and his supporters, the outcome was regarded almost as a triumph. This was in (very large) part because of Theodore's defeat. The personal antipathy between Lang and Theodore had reached new heights (depths might be a better metaphor) in the election campaign, almost to the point of obscuring policy differences between them. Any 'victory' that Lang had won was essentially pyrrhic. His relative strength in the New South Wales party might have increased, but his electoral prospects in the state were seriously damaged and any hope he harboured of becoming leader of a united national Labour Party was utter fantasy. Similarly fantastic was Lang's supporters' patently absurd presumption that a UAP government's economic policies would be no more hostile to unemployed and impoverished Australians than those adopted by Scullin's government. That presumption was promptly proven ill-founded.

The Lyons Government's Financial Agreements Enforcement Act 1932

There was no prospect that the UAP government would pursue any economic policy other than continued and intensified retrenchment. Nor was there any prospect that Lang's administration would cooperate with that position. Substantial New South Wales loans were soon due for repayment, and Lang had indicated to Lyons that the state could not repay them.[92] The immediate consequence was new national legislation authorising the national government to meet any loan repayments defaulted upon by a state and to recoup the funds from the state's resources.

The Financial Agreements Enforcement Act 1932 was promoted as a matter of urgency after the 1931 Commonwealth election. Its immediate purpose was to provide the Commonwealth with a remedy to retrieve from a state any moneys it paid out to cover that state's default on loans for which the Commonwealth assumed responsibility under the financial agreement underlying s.105A.[93] Since New South Wales was the only state then in that position, the Act was essentially a means to preclude Lang's repudiation policy from having any long-term effect.

The Act's preamble expressly rooted the measure in s.105A. Its key provision was s.5. S.5(1) empowered the Treasurer to identify any unpaid moneys owed by a state to the Commonwealth under a financial agreement. S.5(3) permitted the Treasurer to seek a High Court declaration that such sum was owed. S.5(5) then provided that:

> [S]uch declaration shall be a judgment of the High Court in favour of the Commonwealth against the state, and shall be enforceable as a judgment, and shall, in addition to any other remedies for enforcing such judgment by law provided, operate as a charge upon all the revenues of the state.

S.6 contained a most unusual provision. It provided that, *prior to* any judgment being made under s.5, the House and Senate, by a resolution accepting that the amount identified was owed, could authorise the Commonwealth government to issue a proclamation to that effect. Among the various consequences of the proclamation were that: per s.10, no person owing any liability to the state should pay that sum to the state; per s.12, any state official accepting any such payment would commit an offence; and per s.15, the Treasurer could order any bank holding any state deposits to transfer such deposits to the Commonwealth.

The speed with which the measure was enacted was matched by the alacrity with which the Lyons government identified unpaid New South Wales debts and successfully promoted s.6 resolutions in the House and Senate, and by Lang's prompt challenge to the Act's constitutionality.

[92] Lang (1970) op cit ch 16.
[93] Pp 334–36 above.

5

Trethowan before the Privy Council

> I never had any doubt about the result. The measure was carefully thought out before introduction …
>
> Francis Boyce, Attorney-General in the 1927–30 Bavin administration, commenting in the *Sydney Morning Herald* of 1 June 1932 on the Privy Council's judgment in *Trethowan.*

Trethowan was argued for eight days before the Privy Council in April 1932.[1] But, important though the case was in Lang's estimation, it was unlikely his top priority. The continuing schism between Lang Labour and the national Labour Party, both nationally and in New South Wales, was a more pressing concern. Relatedly, Lang's personal and political relationships with Game were becoming increasingly difficult. Additionally, although an election was not due for a year, Bavin's prospects of leading a Nationalist/Country Party coalition to victory were growing amid indications that Lang Labour's electoral approval was diminishing. And pervading those three questions was the state's increasingly fragile economic viability.

Game faced repeated calls from conservative political circles – often prominently voiced by the *Sydney Morning Herald* – to dismiss Lang from office. As a matter of law, Game could do so. The Statute of Westminster 1931 had not yet been adopted in Australia, but even if it had been so adopted and thereby freed Australia as a Dominion (and more precisely the Commonwealth Parliament and the s.128 constitutional amendment mechanism) from the restrictions of CLVA 1865 s.2, it would not have had that effect on the states. Nor had the 1931 Act instituted any legal change in the powers of the Governor-General or State Governors. As George V's resistance to Isaacs's appointment as Governor-General had indicated, British governments were then reluctant to cede control of that aspect of the governmental process to Australian sources. More pertinently, the 1931 Act had not altered the content of the *Instructions* issued to State Governors concerning the circumstances in which they might exercise the dismissal power.

The relevant instructions from the British government on the dismissal issue to New South Wales's Governor dated from letters patent issued in 1900, which reproduced in part those sent in 1879:

> 10. The governor may, so far as We Ourselves lawfully may, upon sufficient cause to him appearing, remove from his office, or suspend from the exercise of same, any person exercising

[1] [1932] AC 526.

> any office, or place, in the state under or by virtue of any commission or warrant granted, or which may be granted by Us, under Our name, or Under Our authority.[2]

The purpose underlying cl.10 was restated in the state's *Official Yearbook* in 1926 during Lang's first administration:

> The general nature of his position is such that he is guardian of the Constitution and bound to see that the great powers with which he is entrusted are not used otherwise than in the public interest. In extreme cases his discretion constitutes a safeguard against malpractice.[3]

The 1902 New South Wales Constitution Act[4] – like its predecessors – did not constrain the dismissal power. By late 1931, Game was wondering if such 'sufficient cause' might soon arise, but was not satisfied it had already done so.[5] Indeed, on 19 November 1931, Game eventually accepted – albeit only partially – Lang's request for more nominees to the Council; 25 were appointed.[6] And, given the result of the 1930 election, Lang's government commanded a clear Assembly majority.

Lang was unsuccessful during his first administration in lobbying the British government to instruct de Chair to swamp the Council after the first abolition initiative failed; the British government considered that this was a domestic matter for de Chair to resolve.[7] Lang certainly harboured suspicions – perhaps well founded – that the non-intervention was rooted in hostility towards his government. He was similarly suspicious in late 1931 that the MacDonald National administration[8] was sotto voce indicating to Game that dismissal would not meet any disapproval from London.

Trethowan may therefore have been little more than a minor distraction from the maelstrom of Lang's domestic political situation. It was probably not even the litigation most on Lang's mind. Shortly before argument in *Trethowan* concluded on 25 April, the High Court delivered judgment in response to Lang's challenge to the constitutionality of the Financial Agreements Enforcement Act 1932.

I. The Validity of the Financial Agreements Enforcement Act 1932

The High Court heard argument in *New South Wales v Commonwealth (No 1)*[9] for five days between 17 and 29 March. The result was revealed on 6 April, with reasoned

[2] Nairn (1995) op cit p 237.

[3] *Official Yearbook of New South Wales 1925–1926* p 35. My thanks to Anne Twomey, at Twomey (2004) op cit p625, for alerting me to this.

[4] Vol 1 pp 202–05.

[5] Game's thinking is charted in despatches to the Dominions Office, excerpted and analysed in Morrison (1976) 'Dominions Office correspondence on the New South Wales constitutional crisis 1930–1932' *JRAHS* 2; Morrison (1982) 'Further documents and comments on the New South Wales constitutional crisis 1930–1932' *JRAHS* 2.

[6] The appointees – including (for the first time) several women – are profiled at Nairn (1995) op cit pp 249–50.

[7] P 18 above.

[8] By this point, Ramsay Macdonald, Britain's first Labour Prime Minister, had – like Lyons – abandoned the Labour Party to head a Conservative/Liberal/'National Labour coalition', which – again like Lyons's government – saw financial retrenchment as the appropriate way to deal with the depression.

[9] (1932) 46 CLR 155.

judgments delivered on 21 April. Rich, Starke, Dixon and McTiernan were all persuaded that the 1932 Act fell within the Commonwealth Parliament's powers. Gavan Duffy and Evatt dissented. Lang's government was the lead claimant. But the issue was not simply about Lang's economic policy agenda. Both Victoria and Tasmania intervened in support of the New South Wales's position. Neither state was then governed by an administration sympathetic to Lang's political ideas. A larger question relating to the states' economic – and thence political –autonomy was in issue. The majority, however, did not consider the question difficult to decide.

The Majority Opinions

Dixon and Rich's joint opinion approached the issue as essentially just one of textual interpretation, a methodology wholly consistent with *Engineers* and the 1923 'state sovereignty' decision.[10] In their view, s.105A(3)'s power to make laws for the 'carrying out by the parties' of an agreement:

> [A]uthorises the enactment of laws calculated to bring about the performance of their obligations by the parties … [and] … A law which … compels involuntary satisfaction appears to us to be properly described as a law for the carrying out by the parties thereto of the agreement.[11]

Dixon and Rich dwelt only briefly on the case's broader political context: namely, its impact on state fiscal autonomy: "Strong as the measure is, it may fairly be regarded in the conditions which at present prevail, and which we are entitled judicially to take notice, as reasonably necessary to ensure payment of a liability …"[12]

The judges did not identify the 'conditions' to which they referred; Lang's loan defaults and threat of repudiation were likely prominent in their minds. Starke produced a similarly reasoned opinion.

Unlike his majority colleagues, McTiernan began by identifying the 1932 Act's political effects, which he characterised as containing: "drastic provisions, novel in the law of the Commonwealth" because of their impact on states' fiscal autonomy.[13] McTiernan also intimated that he concurred with the Lang government's suggestion that the 1932 Act was not 'fair', as it did not provide any enforcement mechanism to the states. Nonetheless, the: "imperious character of the language"[14] of s.105A was sufficiently expansive to encompass the remedies provided in the Act.

In Dissent

Gavan Duffy delivered a brief opinion. He considered that the 1932 Act was intended to give the Commonwealth coercive powers over the states. But s.105A(3) did not sustain such legislation:

[10] Vol pp 330–32 and pp 8–9 above.
[11] *NSW (No 1)* (1932) 46 CLR 155, 178.
[12] ibid 181–82.
[13] ibid 227.
[14] ibid 228.

> The subsection does not authorise any coercion of the parties to the agreement ... The truth is that the language of the sub-section is not apt to include a statute enforcing obligations against any of the parties to an agreement.[15]

Nor did s.105A(5) provide a source for an enforcement statute. The effect of that provision was simply to validate any agreement that might have been made by a state which contravened its own constitution.

Evatt's dissent set the scene more sweepingly: "Now, the application of such remedies to States possessing the powers of responsible self-government is entirely without precedent in the constitutional history of Britain and the British Dominions."[16]

Evatt invoked a substantial body of Privy Council and High Court authority to suggest that such remedies were not just without, but against such precedent.[17] In his view, s.105A had to be read consistently with that broader – essentially theoretical – constitutional context. In the most forceful part of his judgment, Evatt J echoed Gavan Duffy CJ in finding no merit in the assertion that 'carrying out' in s.105A(3) could encompass enforcement action:

> If the enforcement as against the states of their contractual obligations is the idea behind sec. 105A (3) the language is singularly ill-adapted to hint at, much less express, such a thought. The word "enforcement" would have been the obvious word to use.[18]

Consequences

The judgment's immediate consequence was that state debt 'repudiation' was no longer a policy that could be pursued unilaterally. It would require at least the acquiescence of the national government. And there was no prospect of that indulgence being extended by Lyons's administration to Lang's ministry.

Lang's memoirs record that he hoped Gavan Duffy and Evatt would find for the state, and that McTiernan would join them. Lang was disappointed, if not greatly surprised, by McTiernan's decision. He was certainly indignant about the judgment, and in terms that echoed – in substance if not style –Evatt J's dissent: "So the High Court became the final instrument for the destruction of state rights as originally maintained and asserted by the architects of the Federal Constitution."[19]

Lang's analysis is perhaps critical less of the Court than of s.105A itself. He also suggested that s.105A(3): "had been sneaked through without anyone realising its significance".[20] Lang's comment implies an element of political duplicity rather than lack of legal foresight in Bruce and Page's advocacy of the reform.[21] Nonetheless, after a brief

[15] *NSW (No 1)* (1932) 46 CLR 155, 172–73.

[16] ibid 196.

[17] ibid 196–202.

[18] ibid 204.

[19] The quotation is at Lang (1970) op cit p188. For Lang's overview of the case, see ibid pp 183–91. Lang did not recognise (or accept) that the 'architects' in issue were not those of the original 1901 constitution but of the 1927 amendment.

[20] Lang (1970) op cit p105.

[21] ibid pp 195–97. The charge is perhaps ill-founded. Page – the primary architect of the Agreement and s.105A – recalls that the reform was aimed at the '*co-ordination* of federal and state finance' (that being the

hesitation, Lang's government sought permission to appeal to the Privy Council, but this was refused – only Evatt supported the application.[22]

But while Lang's ministry could not enhance its financial viability by cutting its expenditure on debt repayment, it did formulate both an extraordinary legislative proposal to extend its tax base and various administrative policies to protect the funds it still had. As Lang put it: "We licked our wounds and decided that our only hope was to fight the Commonwealth for survival."[23]

II. The *Trethowan* Hearing

As Lang planned that fight, Bavin 'resigned' as leader of the New South Wales UAP. He was replaced by Bertram Stevens – the civil servant Lang dismissed during his first administration[24] – on 5 April. Bavin bowed out gracefully on the ostensible grounds of ill health, although Stevens had been manoeuvring zealously to replace him for some time.[25] And while these events unfolded in New South Wales, *Trethowan* was progressing towards judgment in the Privy Council.

The Judges

The bench was notably strong, comprising Viscount Sankey (the Lord Chancellor), Lord Hanworth (the Master of the Rolls), Lord Russell of Killowen, Lord Atkin and Lord Blanesburgh. The eminence of the judges indicates that – as in *McCawley* some 10 years earlier – the British government regarded the issue as of major significance.

Sankey was appointed as Lord Chancellor by Ramsay MacDonald in MacDonald's 1929 Labour administration.[26] An Oxford-educated barrister from humble origins, Sankey was appointed to the High Court in 1914 and to the Court of Appeal in 1928. In the context of his domestic judgments, he is perhaps best known for the so-called 'Golden Thread' speech in *Woolmington v DPP*,[27] which reiterated in stirring language the common law presumption in English criminal law that the onus to prove guilt rests

title of ch 14 of Page (1963) *Truant surgeon*), not at the *subordination* of the states to the Commonwealth. Page does not suggest that he had in mind (prior to 1927) that s.105A could sustain such intrusive Commonwealth legislation, although he does claim for himself a major role in subsequently securing the passage of the 1932 Act; ibid pp 208–09.

[22] *SMH* 8 April 1932 p 9, http://nla.gov.au/nla.news-article16854132; 23 April 1932 p14, http://nla.gov.au/nla.news-article16858165. The appeal application (*New South Wales v Commonwealth (No 2)* [1932] HCA 8 (1932) 46 CLR 235) was heard with a second case (*New South Wales v Commonwealth (No 3)* [1932] HCA 12 (1932) 46 CLR 246) brought by New South Wales seeking an injunction to prevent various New South Wales banks from paying any moneys to the Commonwealth per s.15 of the 1932 Act. On that issue, the Court divided on the same basis.

[23] Lang (1970) op cit p188.

[24] P 15 above.

[25] See Nairn (1995) op cit pp 254–55.

[26] Heuston (1963) *The lives of the Lord Chancellors* ch x: Stevens (2004) 'Sankey, John, Viscount Sankey' *ODNB*.

[27] [1935] AC 462.

squarely on the prosecution. On the Privy Council, Sankey's most celebrated opinion was in *Edwards v Attorney-General of Canada*,[28] in which – reversing the judgment of Canada's Supreme Court – the Privy Council adopted a very expansive approach to the interpretation of the British North America Act 1867 to conclude that women could be appointed to the Canadian Senate. Sankey was politically a moderate social democrat. He had also played a prominent role in the 1930 Imperial Conference, and in drafting the Statute of Westminster 1931. Sankey suffered little anxiety about following MacDonald into the latter's national government in 1931, and served as Lord Chancellor until 1935. Although that would indicate he would have little sympathy with Lang's government in party political terms, there was no reason to assume that it would affect his approach to the question raised in *Trethowan*.

Lord Hanworth, the Master of the Rolls, was born Ernest Pollock in 1861,[29] the grandson of the renowned jurist Sir Frederick Pollock. After attending Charterhouse and Cambridge, Pollock was called to the Bar in 1885. He coupled practice with a political career, and was elected as a Conservative MP in 1910. Pollock was appointed as Solicitor-General in 1919[30] and then Attorney-General in 1922 in Lloyd-George's post-war coalition government. Pollock did not contest the 1923 election, and was then appointed Master of the Rolls later that year during Stanley Baldwin's Conservative administration. He was not an especially eminent practitioner (although he was briefed by Ryan to argue *Taylor* in the Privy Council),[31] and the appointment attracted some substantial controversy on the basis of his qualifications (or lack thereof) for the post. He proved an able administrator, but produced no judgments of lasting significance.

Lord Russell was one of a grandfather, father and son triumvirate who all served as Law Lords. The Russell who sat in *Trethowan* was the second of the three, Frank Russell, who was born in 1867 and was called to the Bar, where he practised primarily in chancery matters, in 1893. Russell was appointed to the High Court in 1919 and, after just one year on the Court of Appeal, to the Lords in 1929.[32] Russell was conservatively inclined on political and social issues, but had never sought political office.

Lord Atkin was to become something of an icon in British constitutional law theory for his dissenting judgment in the notorious 1942 House of Lords decision *Liversidge v Anderson*.[33] That dissent was premised on an orthodox – indeed, very conservative – approach to the task of statutory interpretation, but had been couched in language which had made Atkin distinctly unpopular with his fellow judges. Atkin had been born in Brisbane in 1867; his parents had emigrated to Australia from Kent in 1864. Atkin's father, of Irish descent, earned some distinction in Brisbane, editing a newspaper and being elected to the State Assembly.[34] Atkin's mother returned with her children to England in 1871, shortly before the father's death. The family was neither particularly

[28] [1928] SCR 276, [1930] AC 124. See the brief discussion at p 14 n 60 above.

[29] Wrottesley (2008) 'Pollock, Ernest Murray, First Viscount Hanworth' *ODNB*.

[30] In which capacity he had appeared for the British government qua intervener in *McCawley*, supporting Theodore's position.

[31] Vol 1 p 278.

[32] Gibson P (2004) 'Russell, Francis Xavier Joseph [Frank] Baron Russel of Killowen' *ODNB*.

[33] [1942] AC 206. The best guide to *Liversidge*, and to Atkin's role in I, remains Heuston (1970) 'Liversidge v Anderson in retrospect' *LQR* 33. For a condensed account, see Loveland (2015) op cit pp 69–72.

[34] http://adb.anu.edu.au/biography/atkin-robert-travers-2908.

wealthy nor well connected, and Atkin won scholarships for public school and to Oxford. He was called to the Bar in 1891, and pursued a career primarily in commercial law, taking silk in 1909, and being appointed to the High Court in 1913 and the Court of Appeal in 1919. Atkin was widely regarded as an outstandingly able appellate judge, and was promoted to the House of Lords in 1928.[35]

Lord Blanesburgh, perhaps the panel's least intellectually distinguished member,[36] was born Robert Younger, a Scot of wealthy parentage, who was called to the Bar after attending Oxford. He was appointed to the High Court in 1915, and served on the Court of Appeal between 1919 and 1923 before being appointed as a Law Lord. He had not pursued a political career.

Counsel

Both parties – presumably in part as a nod to colonial deference[37] – had briefed eminent members of the English Bar. Although Lang had initially instructed Sir John Simon, Sir Stafford Cripps[38] eventually led for New South Wales. Cripps was born into a well-connected political family. His father, Charles Cripps, had been a successful barrister, a Conservative MP and – after a change of political heart – a Labour cabinet minister in MacDonald's first and second Labour administrations. Stafford Cripps was educated at Winchester and UCL, where he took a science degree. He was called to the Bar in 1913, and spent the war years variously as an ambulance driver in France and managing a munitions factory. After the war, his practice was sufficiently successful that he took silk in 1927, and on the recommendation of Herbert Morrison, the then Labour leader of the London County Council (for which Cripps had often acted as counsel), Cripps was appointed by MacDonald as Solicitor-General in 1930 and found a safe Labour seat. Unlike Sankey – but like his father Charles – Cripps had refused to follow MacDonald into the National Labour/Conservative coalition government in 1931, and from that point onwards his political views veered sharply leftwards. After some years of increasingly quixotic political activity, Cripps was appointed as Ambassador to Moscow in 1940, and subsequently served in Churchill's wartime Cabinet and as Chancellor of the Exchequer in Atlee's post-war Labour government.

Cripps's 'junior' was Dennis Pritt, by then both a silk (since 1927), having built a practice largely in commercial law, and the defeated (in the previous year's general election) Labour Party candidate for Sunderland. Pritt's embrace of leftist politics came late in life. He won a seat for Labour in 1935, and enjoyed the dubious distinction of being expelled from the party in 1940 because of his overt communist sympathies.[39] Like

[35] Lewis (2004) 'Atkin, James Richard, Baron Atkin' *ODNB*.

[36] Robert Stevens has described him thus: "It has been said that his career was largely a tribute to his personality and the charm it radiated. [A]s a judge Younger was competent rather than distinguished. As a lord of appeal he sat from 1923 to 1937 … Blanesburgh was overshadowed by his peers. His vision of the role of an appeal judge was to look for the current law. He saw little role for any creative function in the final Court of Appeal" (2004) 'Younger, Robert, Baron Blanesburgh' *ODNB*.

[37] Although Lang's motivation was partly financial; see p 87 n 60 above.

[38] Clark and Toye (2004) 'Cripps, Stafford' *ODNB*.

[39] Morgan (2004) 'Pritt, Dennis Nowell' *ODNB*.

Cripps, Pritt had no particular reputation as a constitutional lawyer in 1932, and there is an obvious suspicion that Lang's brief to them may have owed more to their presumably sympathetic politics than to their specific expertise.

Trethowan's case was led by Wilfrid Greene, assisted by Maughan.[40] Born in 1883, Greene had excelled academically at Oxford, being elected a Fellow of All Souls. His early career at the Bar was interrupted by the war, in which he served with conspicuous distinction, rising to the rank of major. He subsequently developed an extensive practice in equity and commercial law. He took silk in 1922 and was appointed directly to the Court of Appeal in 1935, subsequently serving as Master of the Rolls from 1937 to 1949 before being appointed to the Lords. In 1932, Greene had no particular reputation as a constitutional lawyer, although as Master of the Rolls he subsequently authored a seminal judgment in the field of administrative law.[41]

The seriousness with which the case was regarded in Britain was underlined by an invitation from the Privy Council to the Commonwealth government to intervene in the proceedings. Their case was argued by Robert Latham, then Attorney General in the Lyons government. The British government also intervened in the case, represented by Sir Thomas Inskip, the Attorney-General.

Submissions

That submissions[42] consumed so many days of the court's time was attributable to a style of presentation that would nowadays be regarded as quite absurd. As the *Herald* reported in its coverage of proceedings on 14 April:

> As an instance of the detail with which their Lordships are studying the case, there was no demur when Sir Stafford Cripps proceeded to read ten *complete* judgments [from the courts below], five each from the Supreme Court, and the High Court.[43]

Despite the change of counsel, neither party markedly departed from or added to the positions pressed before the High Court. Cripps and Pritt offered several distinctly unpersuasive propositions.[44] The first was that the CLVA 1865 did not override or amend s.4 [BAA], but had to be construed in a manner that left the s.4 [BAA] method of lawmaking (in the ordinary way) continuously intact. The second, seriously misreading or misrepresenting both Isaacs's judgment in *McCawley* and the subsequent Privy Council decision, was that *McCawley* supported the proposition that a colonial legislature could not 'abdicate' its capacity to make any law in the ordinary way. Cripps also invoked *Taylor* to support this argument, which seems quite bizarre, given that *Taylor* expressly approved such an 'abdication'. As in the High Court, Lang's strongest point

[40] Lever (2004) 'Green, Wilfrid Arthur, Baron Greene' *ODNB*.

[41] *Associated Provincial Picture Houses v Wednesbury Corporation* [1948] I KB 223.

[42] The account of submissions in the official report *Trethowan* [1932] AC 526 is brief – some six pages – and does not record any questions from the bench. There are daily accounts of the submissions in the *SMH*, which is the primary source I use here. There are no records at all of submissions in the official Commonwealth Law Reports report of the case (1932) 47 CLR 97.

[43] *SMH* 16 April 1932 p13 (emphasis added), https://trove.nla.gov.au/newspaper/article/16856538.

[44] *Trethowan* [1932] AC 526, 529–30.

appeared to be the submission with which Pritt ended the hearing: namely, that the notion of 'manner and form' in s.5[45] encompassed only alterations to the originally constituted legislature's proceedings and did not – as was the effect of s.7A – subject the legislature's lawmaking capacity to the approval of an external body: a 'referendum' could not be part of the legislature (that conclusion would obviously mean that *Taylor* was wrongly decided in the High Court). Pritt optimistically (or just wrongly) contended that *In re Initiative and Referendum Act*[46] supported that assertion.

Greene's rebuttal emphasised that the referendum was a well-known lawmaking device in Australia by this point. Quite correctly, he cited *Taylor* as an obvious authority for the legality of such a mechanism. More broadly, he contended that s.5's 'manner and form' proviso embraced all sorts of departures from the ordinary method of legislating, although Greene chose to present such departures as placing a 'fetter' on the legislature rather than redefining it for particular purposes. Greene also – entirely understandably – invoked *McCawley*, borrowing Birkenhead's terminology, as an authority supporting the validity and effectiveness of s.7A:

> The judgment of the Board in McCawley ... recognised that under s.5 of the Act of 1865 a flexible constitution could by appropriate legislation be made rigid pro tanto. The constitutional principle that parliament cannot bind its successor has never been applied to a legislature which has not sovereign but derived powers. Where a legislature of that kind purports to pass an Act having that effect, the validity of the Act depends upon the statutory powers under which it operates, not upon general principle.[47]

Latham and Inskip did little more than endorse Greene's submissions.

The hearing attracted little attention in the British press, but the submissions were carefully and approvingly reported in the *Herald*.[48] There was, however, little time for politicians, lawyers, the press and the public to speculate about the constitutional and political implications of the forthcoming decision. The case was almost immediately eclipsed by other events. On 13 May 1932, Lang was dismissed as Premier by Governor Game.

III. The End of the Second Lang Government

The first months of 1932 had been marked by increasingly frantic manoeuvrings by Lang's government to shore up its financial position, and by Game's growing concern that the 'sufficient reason' to exercise the dismissal power referred to in his *Instructions* was ever more likely to arise as Lang's control over the practicalities of governing the state became increasingly compromised. The details of those government activities and of Game's ruminations are too complex to explore fully here,[49] but two matters merit discussion.

[45] ibid 532.
[46] [1919] AC 935; pp 66–67 above.
[47] *Trethowan* [1932] AC 526, 531–32.
[48] 'PRIVY COUNCIL. UPPER HOUSE CASE. A Day at the Hearing. GREAT JUDGES; BRILLIANT PLEADERS': *SMH* 22 April 1932 p9, http://nla.gov.au/nla.news-article16857693.
[49] For a full account see Nairn (1995) op cit ch 11.

The Mortgages Taxation Bill

The 'extraordinary legislative initiative' alluded to above was entitled the Mortgages Taxation Bill.[50] The measure would require all mortgage lenders to pay – within 14 days – a one-off tax equivalent to 10% of the sum loaned. If the tax was not paid, the mortgage would be forfeited to the State Treasury. The apparent target of the proposed legislation was the banks, by far the most substantial mortgage lenders.

Lang introduced the bill on 11 May 1932. Hansard records[51] that it was presented as a matter of considerable urgency:

> **EXTENSION OF SITTING HOURS.**
>
> Motion (by Mr. Lang) agreed to:
>
> That so much of the sessional orders be suspended as would preclude the continuation of the present sitting after 6 o'clock, p.m.
>
> **MORTGAGES TAXATION BILL.**
>
> Standing orders suspended to permit of the bill being passed through all its stages in one sitting.

Lang informed the Assembly that the proposed Act was designed to raise funds – £7,000,000 – to enable the government to do what the opposition parties had been urging: namely, to end repudiation and meet the state's overseas debts. Furthermore, there would be sufficient funds left over to assist destitute widows and children, and to provide work for the unemployed: "If there is anyone who stands for the poor, he must stand by this measure."[52]

Lang's speech was coupled with a splenetic attack on the integrity of the High Court majority in the enforcement litigation.[53] Lang bluntly accused Dixon of political bias, suggesting that he had been deeply and mendaciously involved in drafting the original legislation[54] and alleged that another judge, who Lang declined to name,[55] had been wined and dined by Bruce to secure his support.

The bill completed its Assembly passage at around 2 am on 12 May.[56] It passed through the Council with similar dispatch later that day.[57] It seems doubtful that Lang seriously thought that the banks could find such sums so quickly: the bill was likely an exercise in gesture rather than practical politics. It nonetheless provoked widespread and near-hysterical press opposition. The opposition spilled beyond state boundaries. Lang's bill was met by a measure promoted by the Lyons government, enacted as the Financial Emergency (State Legislation) Act 1932. S.3 provided that: "Notwithstanding anything in any law of a state or anything done under any such law", a mortgage could

[50] For Lang's account, see Lang (1970) op cit ch 20. I have drawn here on Nairn (1995) op cit pp 259–64.
[51] *NSWLAD* 11 May 1932 p9264.
[52] ibid p9265.
[53] ibid pp 9267 et seq.
[54] Page's autobiography does not mention Dixon playing any role. The alleged mendacity was that Dixon drafted s.105A in terms which hid its potential centralising effect.
[55] Rich is the most likely candidate.
[56] *NSWLAD* 11 May 1932 p9311.
[57] *NSWLAD* 12 May 1932 p9402 (second reading vote); p9415 (third reading).

not be subject to any tax in excess of that applicable under state law on or prior to 30 April 1932. The validity per se of the Commonwealth Act and its effectiveness in countering Lang's proposed law were never tested;[58] it received the royal assent on the day that Lang was dismissed.

Game was clearly perturbed by the substance of Lang's bill, and very concerned that he could not properly refuse assent to it or reserve it. The *Labour Daily*'s front page on 14 May 1932[59] certainly suggested that Game dismissed Lang in order to prevent the bill becoming law:

> **LANG SACKED AT MOMENT OF VICTORY**
>
> *Governor Allies Himself With Enemies To Save Banks From Mortgage Tax*

That the dismissal occurred the day after the bill passed in the Council lends obvious, if circumstantial, force to that analysis; as does Game having met – without Lang's permission – with British companies holding many New South Wales mortgages on 13 May itself.[60] The bill in effect fell with the government that promoted it. However, on Game's account, the reason for the dismissal was Lang's knowing decision to breach Commonwealth law in trying to sidestep the provisions of the Financial Agreements Enforcement Act 1932.[61]

Lang's April Circular and Lyons's May Proclamations

On 12 April 1932, Lang's government issued a Circular to all its department heads with some unusual instructions:[62]

> Will you please instruct your departmental officers and officers of your sub-departments, and other collecting officers, including industrial undertakings, to
>
> (1) Refrain from meeting any governmental expenditure by the drawing of cheques …
> (3) Under no circumstances to pay receipts into any bank.
> (4) All collections to be made in cash or, if in any case it is necessary to take a cheque, such cheque must be cashed, if practicable …
> (5) All cash and cheques collected to be delivered to the Treasury, either direct or to the departmental head office. Banks must not be used for this purpose, but safe and suitable arrangements should be made for forwarding cash and cheques to the Treasury.

[58] Evatt, writing extrajudicially, doubted its validity (1936) *The King and his Dominion Governors* pp 161–64.
[59] https://trove.nla.gov.au/newspaper/article/236985153.
[60] Evatt (1936) op cit p161, citing a report in the *SMH* 14 May 1932.
[61] One commentator has suggested that Game was motivated primarily by an officially unacknowledged concern: namely, that if Lang remained in office, a quasi-fascist and distinctly militaristic organisation styling itself the New Guard would provoke violent public disorder which would threaten the integrity of the entire governmental system; McCarthy (1974) 'A "law and order election": New South Wales June 1932' *JRAHS* 105. At an 80-year distance, it is difficult to reach any authoritative conclusion as to how credible a threat the New Guard posed. One might, however, note that immediately prior to the Mortgages Taxation Bill being debated in the Assembly, the Assembly had discussed the threat that the New Guard posed to the social order and democratic politics; *NSWLAD* 11 May 1932 p9246 et seq. See further Nairn (1995) op cit pp 253–66; Lang (1970) op cit ch 15.
[62] *SMH* 14 May 1932 p13, https://trove.nla.gov.au/newspaper/article/16863357.

Lang's intention was avowedly to prevent state revenues from being attached by the Commonwealth government, his (surely well-founded) presumption being that any bank receiving such revenues would remit them immediately to the Commonwealth Treasury. Game had sought advice from Street on whether such practices would breach the state's Audit Act 1902.[63] No legal proceedings on that point ensued, but in Lang's view the mere fact that Game asked for Street's advice was constitutionally problematic, since Lang considered that the Governor's duty was to act on the advice of his ministers, such minister on legal issues being the state's Attorney-General.[64]

The manoeuvre led – for a short period – to the remarkable spectacle of large amounts of cash being delivered to and stored in the State Treasury offices, and of the government paying its bills (and its employees' – and ministers' – salaries) by doling out notes and coins.[65] For Game, the issue of the Circular's conformity with state law was rapidly eclipsed by another, graver, potential problem.

Lang's initiative prompted Lyons (qua Commonwealth Treasurer) on 5 May 1932 to issue a Proclamation purportedly rooted in powers granted by the Financial Agreements Enforcement Act 1932.[66] The Proclamation identified a long list of revenues payable to New South Wales which would in future: "become payable to the [Commonwealth] Treasurer, or, if the Treasurer, by notice in the *Gazette*, so directs, to authorized persons, and in accordance with such directions as are contained in the notice". The 5 May *Gazette* also contained a 'Notice',[67] purportedly rooted in the Proclamation, which required all such moneys to be paid into the Commonwealth Bank. A Notice on 6 May ordered all officers and employees of the New South Wales government to comply with the 5 May Notice,[68] and a further Notice on 12 May applied that order to "the Public".[69] The Notices made the issue one of criminal law, not simply of inter-governmental relations, since, per s.10 of the Financial Agreements Enforcement Act 1932, "any person" who failed to comply with such directions committed a criminal offence.

Lang's government responded defiantly to the Proclamation and the May 5 and 6 Notices. In a melodramatically phrased statement issued on 10 May,[70] the Cabinet equated the Lyons government's actions with imposing slavery on the state and instructed all state employees to comply with the April Circular. The statement did not offer any legal basis for the instruction, either in terms of justifying the instruction's validity or questioning the validity of the Proclamation and Notices.

A flurry of correspondence between Lang and Game followed on 12 and 13 May.[71] Its gist was that Game asked Lang either to provide a legal opinion that the instructions in

[63] Ss.17 and 20 required the (State) Treasurer to arrange for any such moneys to be paid into a bank, and s.30 required public employees who received such funds to pay them into a Treasury-approved bank account.

[64] Then Joseph Lamaro. Lamaro, born in 1895 of working-class Sicilian immigrant parents, worked as a civil servant and took his LLB at Sydney, before qualifying as a solicitor and then barrister. He was first elected to the Assembly in 1927. That he was a Lang loyalist rather than an accomplished lawyer seems (for Lang) to have been Lamaro's primary qualification to be Attorney-General; http://adb.anu.edu.au/biography/lamaro-joseph-7013.

[65] Lang (1970) op cit pp 189–90.

[66] *CAG* 5 May 1932 (No 41) p633.

[67] ibid p636.

[68] *CAG* 6 May 1932 (No 43) p 637.

[69] *CAG* 12 May 1932 (No 45) p 677.

[70] Reproduced in Lang (1970) op cit p190.

[71] The letters are reproduced at Lang (1970) op cit ch.21. They are also at *SMH* 14 May 1932, p13https://trove.nla.gov.au/newspaper/article/16863357; *LD* 14 May 1932 p6, https://trove.nla.gov.au/newspaper/article/236985255.

the April 12 Circular did not breach the Commonwealth government Proclamations of May 5 or to withdraw the Circular. Lang declined to do either. Game thereupon asked Lang to offer his government's resignation. Lang refused. Game then promptly dismissed him and invited Stevens to form a caretaker administration pending a prompt Assembly election. The *Government Gazette* of 13 May 1932 announced simply:[72]

> HIS Excellency the Governor directs it to be notified that he has this day withdrawn the Commission of the Honorable John Thomas Lang, M.L.A., Premier and Colonial Treasurer, and has commissioned the Honorable Bertram Sydney Barnsdale Stevens, to form a ministry.

Lang's final action in the Premier's 'office' – in the geographical rather than occupational sense – was to provide a hovering *Herald* reporter with a parting comment: "Well, I must be going. I am no longer Premier, but a free man. I have attempted to do my duty."[73]

Stevens's first action as Premier was to announce that the April Circular was withdrawn; this announcement was immediately followed by confirmation from Lyons that the Proclamations issued under the 1932 Act would also be revoked.

Lyons refrained from triumphalist comments. Latham, then in London, was less restrained.[74] For Scullin and the national Labour Party, the dismissal's implications were complicated. Scullin had denounced Lyons's emergency measure countering Lang's Mortgage Taxation Bill as 'panicky' and unnecessarily far-reaching, and, while happy to see Lang out of office, felt there was little prospect of national Labour scoring any electoral success in New South Wales. The principle that a Governor might dismiss an elected Premier was also hard to reconcile with traditional Labour Party policy. Scullin eventually sheltered behind the assertion that this was a matter best resolved by state electors.[75]

With the predictable exception of the *Labour Daily*,[76] there was little press support or sympathy for Lang. Holding fast to its Theodore loyalties, the *Australian Worker* denounced Lang rather than Game,[77] accusing Lang of deliberately flouting the law, adopting: "all manner of extraordinary expedients" to frustrate Commonwealth attachment of state funds and ultimately creating: "chaos".

Unsurprisingly, the *Sydney Morning Herald* greeted the dismissal ecstatically:[78]

> **DISMISSAL OF MR. LANG.**
>
> **Wave of Relief Sweeps Australia**
>
> **GOVERNOR'S ACTION PRAISED.**
>
> **New Cabinet to be Announced To-day.**
>
> **ENFORCEMENT ACT TO BE SUSPENDED**

[72] https://trove.nla.gov.au/newspaper/article/220367424.

[73] *SMH* 13May 1932 p13, https://trove.nla.gov.au/newspaper/article/16863359.

[74] *The Age (Melbourne)* 14 May 1932 p13, https://trove.nla.gov.au/newspaper/article/203750156.

[75] Robertson op cit pp 407–08. Theodore did not offer any public comment; Fitzgerald op cit pp 332–33.

[76] A wonderfully hysterical rant in the *Labour Daily* harangued Game for the dismissal, but reserved most opprobrium for McTiernan and his judgment in the Financial Agreements Enforcement case, describing him – echoing the criticism the right-wing press made of McTiernan's Court appointment (pp 68–69 above) – as: "probably the poorest lawyer on all the Australian Benches"; *LD* 14 May 1932 p4, https://trove.nla.gov.au/newspaper/article/236985218.

[77] 18 May 1932 p17, https://trove.nla.gov.au/newspaper/article/146154866.

[78] 13 May 1932 p9, https://trove.nla.gov.au/newspaper/article/16863431.

Election Date Probably June 11.

> A great wave of renewed confidence swept over the financial world on Saturday, the Stock Exchanges throughout Australia and in London showing marked activity, and shares appreciating greatly. The constitutionality of the Governor's action is widely acclaimed in the British Press, and in Great Britain Mr. Lang's dismissal has already enhanced Australian credit.

The *Herald's* sentiments were shared by many newspapers. The *(Sydney) Daily Telegraph* trumpeted loudly (but misinformedly) the headline: "GOVERNMENT PROVED GUILTY OF BREAKING THE LAW",[79] and informed its readers that the dismissal had prompted crowds to dance joyously in the streets not only in Sydney, but also in Melbourne.[80] *The (Sydney) Sun* found such delight further afield, reporting that: "The New Zealand business community heaved a sigh of relief" at Game's action.[81]

The dismissal was also welcomed in the British press, which praised Game and castigated Lang in equal measure. A *Times* leader asserted:[82]

> The Governor took the view that there was no ground for him to interfere while the Ministers kept within the bounds of law. He has now interfered because Mr Lang exceeded those bounds. It is difficult to see what other course Sir Philip Game could have taken. There could be no security for the rights and liberties of the people if Ministers were entitled to remain in office while defying and violating the law.

For the *Daily Telegraph*, the political and constitutional arguments were equally clear:[83]

> Only a sense of the gravest necessity could have induced Sir Philip Game to take so extreme a measure. The Lang government made itself an outlaw. It firstly defied the superior authority of the Commonwealth government, and repudiated the Premiers' Financial Agreement. But it was the spectacle of the wreckage Langism was making of New South Wales's finances and the ruinous handicap it imposed on the whole effort to re-establish Australian credit that compelled this remarkable exercise of the prerogative of the Crown.

The 'Constitutionality' of the Dismissal

That Game's action was indeed 'remarkable' is uncontentious. Whether it was constitutionally defensible is a much more problematic question. Had Lang's actions ever been put to a legal test, it is quite plausible that his government would have been found in breach of national law.[84] They were never so tested, however, either before or after the dismissal. Game had in effect taken it upon himself to undertake a court's role and conclude that Lang's administration was designedly breaching the Financial Agreements Enforcement Act 1932.

[79] 14 May p1, https://trove.nla.gov.au/newspaper/article/246335947.
[80] ibid p6, https://trove.nla.gov.au/newspaper/article/246336056.
[81] 14 May 1932 p7, https://trove.nla.gov.au/newspaper/article/230113404.
[82] 14 May 1932 p3.
[83] 14 May 1932 p5.
[84] Whether s.105A of the Constitution could have sustained the proviso in s.10 of the 1932 Act, which purportedly empowered the Treasurer to criminalise the actions of *individuals* (other than state officers and employees), as was done in the Notice of 12 May 1932, would likely have been a much more contentious issue.

Lang was convinced that Game had been – if not pushed – then guided to that conclusion by Street, and suspected that Isaacs (qua Governor-General) had played a similar role.[85] There is no obvious documentary evidence to support Isaacs's involvement, but it is clear that Game was in regular contact both with Street[86] and with the Dominions Office in London about the scope of his power and the propriety of its use.[87]

The 'advice' offered to Game from London was drafted in opaque terms, culminating in a draft letter[88] overtaken by the dismissal itself. That letter at first glance might suggest that Game's action would not be approved by the British government:[89]

> The courts of law are the proper tribunal to settle whether any particular action of Ministers is or is not a breach of the law. So long as the courts have not settled this issue … it could not, I think, be said to be unconstitutional if a Governor refrained from taking the initiative in restraining his Ministers from any action alleged to be illegal. If the courts had pronounced against the legality of any particular action and Ministers still persisted in continuing to perform such action the position would, of course, require further consideration.

More careful reading might suggest that Game was also being told that exercising the dismissal power prior to the courts settling the issue would not be unconstitutional either.

Game's decision was also approved by various constitutional 'experts'. Earlier in 1932, Berriedale Keith[90] had argued that Game had no proper basis on which to succumb to media pressure to dismiss Lang because of the repudiation policy. In an article printed in the *Melbourne Argus* on 9 February 1932,[91] Keith suggested that while the Governor had the legal power to dismiss the government, the constitutionally appropriate remedies for what he described as Lang's 'unprecedented' policies were judicial proceedings and the electorate's votes at the next election. By 14 May, the dismissal having occurred, Berriedale Keith changed his mind.[92] Citing – as Game had not – the potential effects of the Mortgage Taxation Bill, and ignoring the point that the lawfulness of the April Circular instruction had not been resolved, Keith argued that:

> The Premier doubtless was entitled to contest the validity of the Commonwealth legislation to enforce the Financial Agreement before the Courts, but once a decision adverse to his contentions had been delivered he was under an absolute obligation to obey the law of the Commonwealth. But instead of accepting the law of the land he attacked the impartiality of the High Court and made successive attempts to defeat the steps adopted by the Commonwealth to enforce the performance of his duties of State. His proposed taxation on mortgages was clearly due to a desire to inflict a maximum of loss on his political opponents in the state. In these circumstances it would have been impossible for the Governor to justify acquiescence. In the Premier's continued tenure of office the Governor was under a clear obligation to secure observance of the law of the Commonwealth …

[85] Lang (1970) op cit p205. Lyons bluntly denied that Isaacs was involved; *SMH* 16 May 1932 p10, https://trove.nla.gov.au/newspaper/article/16863612. He also forcefully denied that there had been any national government intervention in the episode; *Newcastle Morning Herald* 16 May 1932 p8, https://trove.nla.gov.au/newspaper/article/136578069.

[86] A letter of 15 May 1932 from Game's wife to her mother records that Game was up all night discussing the matter with Street; cited in Morrison (1982) op cit p129.

[87] Morrison (1976) op cit; (1982) op cit.

[88] Reproduced in Morrison (1982) op cit pp126–27.

[89] See eg the analysis in Ward (1977) 'The dismissal' in Radi and Spearritt op cit.

[90] Vol 1 p227 n 95.

[91] P7, https://trove.nla.gov.au/newspaper/article/4429323.

[92] *SMH* 16 May p10, https://trove.nla.gov.au/newspaper/article/16863608.

Evatt stood squarely in the opposing camp. In 1936, he published the first edition of what became widely regarded as an authoritative treatise – *The King and his Dominion Governors*. The book ranged widely in both a chronological and geographical sense. The chapter dealing with Lang's dismissal took Game's explanation for his action at face value and found it constitutionally wanting:

> … [T]he power of dismissal can hardly be regarded as properly exercised if a Governor justifies it merely by reliance upon the Ministers having broken the law, and it appears that there is available a competent legal tribunal which can determine the issue of legality … and issue appropriate orders and injunctions.[93]

Less temperate criticism of Game's actions came from Albert Piddington. Since withdrawing from his nomination to the High Court in 1912,[94] Piddington had taken silk in 1913, been active both at the Bar and in Labour political circles nationally and in New South Wales, and had run (unsuccessfully) against Hughes in the 1922 election. Piddington had been an early and fervent advocate of child endowment policies,[95] and Lang appointed him as the state's sole Industrial Commissioner in 1925, giving him in effect complete control over many industrial arbitration awards. (Bavin's government had subsequently reduced that influence by promoting an Act[96] enlarging the Commission to three members, albeit with Piddington as the presiding judge.) In a rather quixotic gesture, Piddington resigned his post,[97] on the not obviously relevant basis that Game's dismissal of Lang was unconstitutional, as what was in issue was a legal question to be resolved by the courts. Lang drew obvious comfort and justification from Piddington's resignation;[98] although its primary practical consequence was enabling Stevens to appoint a new presiding judge on the Industrial Commission.[99]

With Lang out of office, a caretaker Stevens-led coalition in temporary power and an election imminent, the long-awaited Privy Council judgment in *Trethowan* rather lacked the significance it might have enjoyed in more stable political times. But whatever the court's decision might be, there was now no immediate prospect of the Council being abolished.

IV. The *Trethowan* Judgment

Notwithstanding Cripps and Pritt's best endeavours, the court decided the matter in short order for Trethowan, issuing its decision on 31 May 1932.[100] Following Privy

[93] Evatt (1936) op cit p174.

[94] Vol 1 pp 256–57.

[95] See Jelley (1977) 'Child endowment' in Radi and Spearritt op cit.

[96] Industrial Arbitration (Amendment) Act 1927 s.2.

[97] Piddington's resignation letter is summarised in the *SMH* 21 May 1932 p13, https://trove.nla.gov.au/newspaper/article/16865254.

[98] He devotes a chapter of his memoirs (Lang (1970) op cit ch 23) to Piddington ("Of the many men with whom I had come into contact during my political career none impressed me more than Albert Bathurst Piddington KC"; ibid p223) and his resignation, reproducing the resignation letter in full.

[99] Piddington was then a few months away from the statutory retirement age (70).

[100] The date given in the AC report is 21 May 1932, but this does not seem to be when the judgment was released.

Council tradition, a single opinion, authored by Lord Sankey, was handed down. The judgment is – in several senses – very brief.

Sankey began by identifying the question before the court, namely:

> [W]hether the legislature of the state of New South Wales has power to abolish the Legislative Council of the state or to alter its constitution or powers without first taking a referendum of the electors upon the matter. This question depends upon the true construction and effect of certain statutes, both Imperial and local, and, before dealing with it, it is necessary for the sake of clearness to set out such portions of the said statutes as are material to the present matter.[101]

Adopting Dixon's account in the High Court judgment,[102] Sankey then quoted what he regarded as the key legislative provisions, these being respectively s.4 [BAA] and s.9 [BAA] of the 1855 Act, s.5 and s.6 of the CLVA 1865, and s.7A itself. He referred also to the 1857 repeal of s.36 and to the enactment of the Constitution Act 1902, which he initially characterised as having repealed such parts of the 1855 Act as were then still in force.[103]

Lord Sankey's account of the political background to the litigation was extremely terse: "Towards the end of 1930 the government then in power were anxious to get rid of this legislation, and they promoted two Bills for this object, both of which passed both houses of the legislature."[104] The opinion then summarised the parties' submissions.

The reasoning in the judgment begins at p539 of the report, and ends some three pages later. Other than a short quotation from Rich's *Trethowan* opinion and his adoption of Dixon J's history, Sankey does not cite a single case in his judgment, be it Australian, British, Canadian or from any other jurisdiction. Nor did Sankey refer to any of the academic commentaries cited by counsel in their submissions. This seems to be because, in Sankey's opinion:

> [T]he point involved in the case is … really a short one namely, whether the legislature of the state of New South Wales has power to abolish the Legislative Council of the said State, or to repeal s. 7A of the Constitution Act, 1902, except in the manner provided by the said s. 7A.[105]

In the court's view, the answer to the question before it depended "entirely" on the meaning of s.5 of the CLVA 1865 and s.4 [BAA] of the New South Wales Act 1855 if – as Sankey implied, somewhat inconsistently with his earlier observation – that provision had not been repealed in 1902. S.5 was: "the master section to consider for the purpose here in hand".[106] Sankey nonetheless saw no need to give any consideration to the historical origins of s.5, nor to the Act itself.

The economy of 'authority' which the Privy Council felt was required to resolve the case might be taken either as an indication of that court's acuity in identifying the matters in issue – an acuity clearly not shared by the High Court – or as betokening

[101] *Trethowan* [1932] AC 526, 533. No one had suggested that the legislature might not be representative per s.1 when the number of Councillors exceeded the number of Assembly members; ibid 535.

[102] ibid 534.

[103] ibid 536.

[104] ibid 537. The 'then in power' phrase reflecting, one assumes, the fact that in between the conclusion of argument and the handing down of judgment that government had been removed from power.

[105] ibid 539.

[106] ibid.

a rather lackadaisical approach to their Lordships' treatment of the controversy. The methodology obviously echoes that deployed in *McCawley*, in which the Privy Council had not even seen the need to engage with *Cooper* or *Taylor*. There is some symmetry in this. *McCawley's* analysis of CLVA 1865 s.5 and its endorsement of s.5 as a source for 'meticulously precise' 'shackles' being imposed by colonial legislation on the ordinary way of lawmaking were obviously very relevant to the effect of s.7A; yet the *Trethowan* judgment ignored *McCawley* just as the *McCawley* judgment ignored *Cooper* and *Taylor*. In contrast, however, to Birkenhead's characterisation of the losing party's argument in *McCawley* as essentially imbecilic,[107] Sankey refrained from denigrating any of the parties' submissions.

Within 'the master section', Sankey was particularly concerned to determine the meaning of the "second sentence" in s.5.[108] This may have been merely a slip of the pen which escaped all their Lordships' attention, but there is no 'second sentence' in s.5. The section is a single – but very long – sentence.[109] Sankey was presumably referring to the (third) clause (identified in this book as s.5[3]).

The Privy Council spared itself the rigorous task of trying to make sense of s.5's many individual elements. As suggested in chapter four of volume one,[110] that task would have been an unrewarding one because of the sloppy way that s.5 – indeed, the entire Act – had been drafted. Sankey avoided that difficulty by concluding that:

> [I]n their Lordships' opinion it is impossible to read the section as if it were contained in watertight compartments. It must be read as a whole … [I]t gives to the legislature of New South Wales certain powers, subject to this, that in respect of certain laws they can only become effectual provided they have been passed in such manner and form as may from time to time be required by any Act still on the statute book.[111]

The 'certain laws' comment may be read as intimating that s.5[2] was limited to 'identity' issues in relation to legislatures, but Sankey does not expand on this. Nor did he offer any view as to which departures from the 'ordinary way' of legislating could be encompassed by the notion of 'manner and form'. He concluded simply that:

> Beyond that, the words "manner and form" are amply wide enough [to] cover an enactment providing that a Bill is to be submitted to the electors and that unless and until a majority of the electors voting approve the Bill it shall not be presented to the Governor for His Majesty's assent.[112]

Nor did Sankey address questions relating to the legitimacy of any such departures from the 'ordinary way'. Rich's allusion below to the propriety of preventing the enactment of 'rash' laws did not detain Sankey's attention.[113]

[107] Vol 1 pp 308–12.
[108] *Trethowan* [1932] AC 526, 539.
[109] Vol 1 p 108.
[110] Vol 1 pp 108–112.
[111] *Trethowan* [1932] AC 526, 539.
[112] ibid 540.
[113] In contrast, Sankey did invoke Rich to dismiss (Gavan Duffy's) rather tortuous notion that a meaningful distinction could be drawn between the use of 'passed' and 'enacted' in s.5. Rich's conclusion that the two terms meant the same thing was preferred; ibid 542.

The legal consequence which flowed from this curt – or perhaps insightful – analysis of s.5 and s.7A was presented in a rather topsy-turvy way. Had the Governor assented to the first of Lang's bills, the document he signed: "would not be a valid Act of the legislature". But that result flowed from the anterior fact (albeit it is presented subsequently in the judgment) that: "the presentation of the Bill to the Governor without such approval [in a referendum] would be the commission of an unlawful act".[114]

Those two circumstances are quite distinct. Trethowan, all the way back in his initial application for an injunction, was asserting simply that Professor Peden qua President of the Council would be acting unlawfully – as would anyone else – in putting either bill before the Governor. He was not *sensu stricto* challenging the validity of an 'Act'. Sankey did not explicitly consider whether the Governor would, in turn, be acting unlawfully if he assented to such an unlawfully presented bill, but presumably if the resultant 'Act' was not valid then the prior assent to the bill would not have been valid either.[115]

The issue which had been so hard and bitterly fought in New South Wales political circles, and which had so exercised the minds of counsel and judges in the Australian courts, was dispatched by Sankey and his colleagues in just three pages of authority-free legal reasoning. This might be regarded as yet another example – perhaps the best of the bunch – of the Privy Council being a court of statesmen rather than jurists.[116] But for audiences in New South Wales, it was the result rather than the reasoning that was important.

Reactions in New South Wales

Despite Lang's dismissal, the judgment generated feverish speculation in New South Wales. Rumours circulated that the judgment had been finalised, but for unexplained reasons withheld from publication, and media organisations made special plans for prompt reporting which pushed at the limits of contemporary communications technology:[117]

> **PRIVY COUNCIL DECISION OVER AIR**
>
> Arrangements are announced by station 2CH for broadcasting this evening the Privy Council's decision … The special cable news which 2CH has arranged may reach Sydney about 9 o'clock. If received earlier it will be at once broadcast and will be repeated at 10 and 10.30 p.m.

According to the *Herald*, Lord Sankey read out his judgment on 31 May at: "a tremendous rate" to an almost empty room, his face hidden behind a sheet of paper: five

[114] Both ibid 541.

[115] The Privy Council perhaps considered that its own analysis should be bound by the limited nature of the permission to appeal granted by the High Court; p 72 above.

[116] Sankey's most well-known judgment on the Privy Council, the aforementioned *Edwards v Attorney-General* [1930] AC 124, was reasoned on a similarly non-legal basis, with Sankey invoking the metaphor of the British North America Act 1867 being a 'living tree' for interpretive purposes, which metaphor essentially equipped a court to dispense with concerns of narrow textualism or contradictory prior judicial authority, adopting, one assumes – to use Haldane's terminology – the methodology of the 'statesman' rather than the 'jurist'; vol 1 pp 177–79.

[117] *The (Sydney) Sun* 31 May 1932 p7, https://trove.nla.gov.au/newspaper/article/230121016.

minutes had sufficed.[118] Latham, one of the few attendees, greeted the decision in apocalyptically political terms, praising the Privy Council for saving New South Wales from (Lang's): "personal dictatorship".[119] Back in Sydney, Boyce had seemingly forgotten his embarrassing uncertainty about s.7A's legal effects during s.7A's Council passage. He told the *Herald* that: "I never had any doubt about the result. The measure was carefully thought out before introduction ..."[120] Sir John Peden, although the subject of a brief biography in *The Sun* days after the judgment had been issued, does not seem to have offered any public comment.[121] Bavin, evidently restored to health, welcomed the judgment as a vindication of his policy and promised Stevens his wholehearted support in the election.[122]

Lang's immediate response was terse: "I am not surprised. I expected it."[123] The *Labour Daily*, whether out of ignorance or mendacity is not clear, fiercely criticised the Privy Council on the basis that the court had both ignored and overridden its own judgment in *McCawley*. *Trethowan* was, of course, entirely consistent with *McCawley* in purely legal terms. The *Labour Daily* was on firmer ground in teasing out the implications of the judgment: "This possibility opens up unlimited resources for displays of fine work by the legal lights who also dabble in politics. Any law no matter how brutal or how intensely subversive, may be entrenched till the crack of doom."[124]

This was very much the minority view in the state's press. The *Herald*, having reported crowds dancing in the streets at Lang's dismissal, recorded the reaction of a presumably more rarified audience to the judgment:[125]

> **APPLAUSE AT HER MAJESTY'S.**
>
> The announcement of the decision of the Privy Council was thrown on to the screen at Her Majesty's Theatre last night, in the words "Lang's appeal dismissed," during one of the Intervals in the performance of "Don Pasquale". The news was received with sustained applause from all parts of the house, and from the members of the orchestra.

The fate of the Legislative Council, and more broadly of Lang's political career, now lay in the short term in the political arena.

[118] *SMH* 1 June 1932 p11, http://nla.gov.au/nla.news-article16920123.
[119] ibid.
[120] ibid.
[121] 5 June p12, https://trove.nla.gov.au/newspaper/article/230113298.
[122] *SMH* 7 June 1932 p9, https://trove.nla.gov.au/newspaper/article/16901564.
[123] *SMH* 2 June 1932 p10, https://trove.nla.gov.au/newspaper/article/16895946. Willis, then still the New South Wales government's Agent-General in London and also in attendance when the judgment was delivered, did not accept the *Herald*'s invitation to comment.
[124] 1 June 1932 p 4, https://trove.nla.gov.au/newspaper/article/236975838. The derogatory reference to lawyers makes one wonder if Lang authored the piece; p 56 n 38 above.
[125] 1 June 1932 p11, https://trove.nla.gov.au/newspaper/article/16920088.

6

Aftermaths

> [T]here is no difference between what this government is trying to do with this measure and what the Mussolinis and Hitlers and others have done and are trying to do in European countries. Such attempts to stifle the voice of the people, whether by constitutional or extra-constitutional means, can have only one outcome. If this measure becomes law, no matter what the people may say, it will result in the Labour Party always being in a minority in the Legislative Council.
>
> Jack Lang in the second reading debate on the Constitution Amendment (Legislative Council) Bill; *NSWLAD* 15 December 1932 p2970.

Although no longer Premier, Lang did not face any immediate challenge to his leadership of (his faction of) the state Labour Party. Lang was dismissed on 13 May 1932. Game appointed Stevens as Premier on the understanding that there would be an immediate dissolution and election. The election was held on 11 June.

I. The 1932 New South Wales Election

In a limited – and, in practical terms, useless – sense, the election was a triumph for Lang's Labour Party, which comfortably won the largest share of the vote. In another, more narrow sense, namely the relative popularity in New South Wales of the Lang and national factions of the state 'party', the election was again a success for Lang: the national faction won a derisory share of votes and no seats.

Table 6.1 The 1932 New South Wales Legislative Assembly election (11 June 1932)

Party	% vote	Seats won	Change
State (Lang) Labour	40.2	24	–31
United Australia (Nationalist)	36.2	41	+18
Country Party	13.1	23	+11
(Federal) Labour	4.2	0	[–55][a]
Independents	2.7	0	
United Australia/Country Party[b]	1.7	2	+2

[a] On the assumption that the 55 seats won in 1930 could be classified as (national) Labour.

[b] I have treated these two members as United Australia members for the purposes of the change column.

Such victories were scant consolation to Lang and his supporters. The election's primary consequence was that a United Australia Party (UAP) and Country Party coalition – the parties having agreed not to oppose each other in many constituencies and to field a joint candidate in others – formed a new ministry, headed by Stevens, controlling 66 of the Assembly's 90 seats. Labour's tally fell from 55 to only 24. Some seats were lost because the national Labour Party gained more votes than the gap between the second-placed Lang candidate and the victorious UAP/Country Party candidate;[1] but many long-standing members in what were prior to the election regarded as safe Labour seats were defeated by more votes than were gained by the national Labour Party, and indeed for a while during the count it seemed that Lang's own seat might fall.[2]

The campaign was fought on a starkly polarised basis.[3] Lang was hysterically portrayed by the UAP and the Country Party as the harbinger of a communist dictatorship. He, in turn, presented Stevens as favouring economic policies designed to subordinate New South Wales to the dictates of London financiers and to force working-class people into penury. Suggestions have been made that significant numbers of members of the New Guard would have engaged in violent insurrection if Lang Labour had won the election.[4] This likely exaggerates both the scale of public support for the New Guard and the determination of its core members[5] (although Lang records in evident seriousness that he had been advised by the state police service to take precautions against a planned New Guard kidnapping).[6]

The election defeat further undermined Lang's standing even among his former loyalists, whose numbers had already fallen. His ardour for abolishing the Council and for the Lang Plan remained undiminished, however. In a rabble-rousing speech to his local constituency party on 1 August, Lang had reportedly said, inter alia:

> If I could have got rid of those old birds upstairs, I would have shown you what could be done, and what I would have done … They think that because we are defeated, that they have got away with it all … Labor must go the whole hog. If you play you are going to fall. It is a fight, a bitter fight, and next time you must use all your weapons.[7]

Not all of Lang's former allies joined him in the fight. A personal rift[8] with Willis culminated in an extraordinary slander action – *Willis v Lang*[9] – argued before the High Court on appeal from the State Supreme Court.[10] The suit arose when Willis, having resigned his Council seat,[11] secured the national Labour Party nomination to fight an Assembly by-election, while the Lang-dominated state Executive put forward its

[1] McCarthy (1974) op cit pp 110–11, 114.
[2] Nairn (1995) op cit pp 265–66.
[3] See generally the account in McCarthy (1974) op cit.
[4] McCarthy (1974) op cit.
[5] See inter alia McCarthy (1971) '"All for Australia"; some right-wing responses to the depression in New South Wales, 1929–1932' *JRAHS* 160: McCarthy (1974) op cit.
[6] Lang (1970) op cit ch 18.
[7] *The Sun* 2 August 1932 p7, https://trove.nla.gov.au/newspaper/article/228875322.
[8] Charted in Nairn (1995) op cit pp 268–70.
[9] (1934) 52 CLR 637.
[10] The case does not feature in the state reports. For contemporaneous newspaper coverage of the initial trial, see *SMH* 26 September 1933 p15, https://trove.nla.gov.au/newspaper/article/17009888; *LD* 27 September 1933 p1, https://trove.nla.gov.au/newspaper/article/237906646.
[11] *NSWLCD* 22 June 1933 p7.

own candidate. In the ensuing squabble, Lang levied myriad 'defamatory' allegations against Willis.[12] Lang's candidate took the seat, and in apparent pique Willis sued Lang for libel. Lang successfully defended the claim by relying on an unusual provision in s.5 of the Defamation Act 1912. Originally enacted by the Legislative Council in 1847, s.5 provided that defamatory accusations would not found any liability if they were made in circumstances where they would not (in the jury's view) damage the claimant's reputation. S.5 in effect enabled a court to conclude that the rough and tumble of political argument in the state was habitually so fierce and so rooted in personal abuse, and so many politicians were presumptively seen by the wider public as scoundrels, that having one's honour, honesty or competence traduced by one's political opponents in an election campaign would not inflict any meaningful damages on a politician's reputation. Both Willis and Lang were such scarred political figures in 1934 that likely anything defamatory either said about the other's political beliefs and activities would fall within s.5. The litigation's almost surreal quality was heightened by Willis's choice of leading counsel – one Thomas Bavin KC.[13]

After the Election – Reforming the Legislative Council

Stevens had been making a pre-election speech at a Sydney theatre when the Privy Council's *Trethowan* judgment was revealed. While welcoming the decision, he offered a clear pledge that if a UAP government was elected it would introduce meaningful reform to the Council's composition and powers:

> We will make the Legislative Council a deliberative house of review … not merely a place for the registration of the decision of the trades hall coterie and or political partisanship. I do not doubt that when our proposals are put to a referendum of the people they will be carried by an overwhelming majority.[14]

Stevens' government moved promptly ahead – in evident accord with s.7A – with its proposals to reform the Council. Somewhat ironically, one of Stevens' first acts as Premier was to request Game to appoint sufficient new UAP/Country Party members to the Council to create a notional government majority there. A total of 20 appointments were made, increasing the Council's size to 125 members.[15] Stevens justified the appointments on the basis of a need to secure a government majority against anticipated Labour obstruction to the reform plans.[16] He did not acknowledge that he was

[12] For a flavour of the campaign, see *Daily Telegraph* 25 May 1933 p9, https://trove.nla.gov.au/newspaper/article/246241509; *(Grafton) Daily Examiner* 27 May 1933 p5, https://trove.nla.gov.au/newspaper/article/195023376; *Northern Star* 30 May 1933 p5, https://trove.nla.gov.au/newspaper/article/94217748.

[13] Bavin was subsequently appointed to the Supreme Court by the Stevens government in October 1935, where he sat for some years prior to his death in 1941.

[14] *(Sydney) Daily Telegraph* 1 June 1932 p1, https://trove.nla.gov.au/newspaper/article/246329425.

[15] *SMH* 7 September 1932 p13, https://trove.nla.gov.au/newspaper/article/16917795. Ten were Country Party members, increasing the party's Council strength from just 4 to14; on the appointees, see Davy (2006) *The Nationals: the Progressive, Country and National parties in New South Wales 1919–2006* pp 78–79: *SMH* 7 September 1932 p13, https://trove.nla.gov.au/newspaper/article/16917790. It had apparently still not occurred to anyone in New South Wales political or legal circles that the Legislature might no longer be representative per CLVA 1865 s.1.

[16] *SMH* 7 September 1932 p13, https://trove.nla.gov.au/newspaper/article/16917794.

'swamping' the Council. And Governor Game apparently felt no difficulty in granting the request.

The reform proposals on which the Stevens government eventually settled were broadly those proposed by Bavin's administration in 1929: namely, to alter the Council's composition to a 60-member body 'elected' by the existing Council and Assembly members; and to make provisions to overcome any legislative deadlock between the two houses. The bill completed its passage through the Assembly and Council on 16 December 1932. The government thereafter promoted several machinery bills to make arrangements for a referendum so that any Council reforms would comply with the manner and form mandated by s.7A. The requisite s.7A referendum was held on 13 May 1933. The vote produced a small majority – 717,000 to 676,000 – in favour of the bill, which was subsequently enacted as the Constitutional Amendment (Legislative Council) Act 1933 (hereafter CALCA 1933).[17]

The Deadlock Provisions in (the Amended) s.5 of the Constitution Act 1902

The reforms subsequently enacted to deal with the problem of impasse between the two houses on the passage of bills were contained in an amendment to CA 1902 s.5[18] introduced by CALCA 1933. S.5A was a straightforward measure. It related solely to appropriation bills, and provided that if the Council rejected, failed to pass[19] or voted to amend an appropriations bill in a manner with which the Assembly disagreed, that bill could be presented (unamended) to the Governor for assent and would on assent become an Act.

S.5B was a distinctly more complicated provision, which applied to all other types of bill (including those falling within s.7A).[20] Read in the light of *Trethowan*, s.5B might – insofar as it applied to s.7A issues – be thought to have been intended by legislators to introduce into New South Wales law a new 'manner and form' provision rooted in CLVA 1865 s.5, even though CALCA 1933 does not at any point describe its provisions as being 'manner and form' matters. However, since s.5B applied to *all* bills (other than appropriation bills per s.5A), it is not immediately obvious that CLVA 1865 s.5 provided

[17] Royal Assent (the bill having to be reserved per the Australian States Constitutions Act 1907 s.1) was reported to the Assembly on 22 June 1933; *NSWLAD* 22 June 1933 p12.

[18] CA 1902 s.5 (vol 1 p 204) reproduced the text (italicised below) of s.4 [BAA] of the 1855 Act: "*The Legislature shall*, subject to the provisions of the Commonwealth of Australia Constitution Act, *have power to make laws for the peace, welfare, and good government of New South Wales in all cases whatsoever* …"Whether the 1902 Act had repealed the still extant [BAA] sections of the 1855 Act was still (then) an unresolved question.

[19] Per s.5B(4), a bill 'failed to pass' if more than two months within the current parliamentary session had elapsed since it was sent to the Council. The consequence of this was that the Assembly could not invoke s.5A (or s.5B) for last-minute measures.

[20] That point was expressly made in s.5B(5). Since s.5B was enacted through the s.7A procedure, it obviously introduced – through the old manner and form (ie Assembly bare majority plus Council bare majority plus referendum bare majority plus royal assent) – a new (and additional) manner and form (ie Assembly bare majority twice plus Council failure to pass twice plus referendum bare majority plus royal assent). The new Act therefore – bizarrely perhaps – seemingly made future abolition of the Council *easier* to achieve than in the past.

a legal root for it in that general sense. The High Court's judgment in *Taylor* seemed to source Queensland's Parliamentary Bills Referendum Act 1908 (hereafter PBRA 1908) in the CLVA 1865 s.5,[21] and the PBRA 1908 was also of general scope rather than being limited to CLVA 1865 s.5[1] and [2] issues. The correctness of that conclusion would depend on adopting a broad reading of the 'powers' element of CLVA 1865 s.5[2], ie as pertaining to the issue of a representative legislature's competence rather than just its identity. That seemed to have been assumed rather than argued and decided in *Taylor*.[22]

Whatever s.5B's legal source actually was, its deadlock procedures had several distinct elements, each of which ostensibly might be considered to meet Birkenhead's 'meticulous precision' test in *McCawley*:[23]

> S.5B (1) If [1] the Legislative Assembly passes any Bill other than a Bill to which section 5A of this Act applies, and [2] the Legislative Council rejects or fails to pass it or passes it with any amendment to which the Legislative Assembly does not agree, and if [3] after an interval of three months the Legislative Assembly in the same Session or in the next Session again passes the Bill with or without any amendment which has been made or agreed to by the Legislative Council, and [4] the Legislative Council rejects or fails to pass it or passes it with any amendment to which the Legislative Assembly does not agree, and if after [5] a free conference between managers there is not agreement between the Legislative Council and the Legislative Assembly, [6] the Governor may convene a joint sitting of the Members of the Legislative Council and the Members of the Legislative Assembly. The Members present at the joint sitting may deliberate upon the Bill as last proposed by the Legislative Assembly and upon any amendments made by the Legislative Council with which the Legislative Assembly does not agree. No vote shall be taken at the joint sitting.
>
> (2) [7] After the joint sitting and either after any further communication with the Legislative Council in order to bring about agreement, if possible, between the Legislative Council and the Legislative Assembly, or without any such communication the Legislative Assembly may by resolution direct that the Bill as last proposed by the Legislative Assembly and either with or without any amendment subsequently agreed to by the Legislative Council and the Legislative Assembly, shall, at any time during the life of the Parliament or at the next general election of Members of the Legislative Assembly, be submitted by way of referendum to the electors qualified to vote for the election of Members of the Legislative Assembly …
>
> (3) [8] If at the referendum a majority of the electors voting approve the Bill it shall be presented to the Governor for the signification of His Majesty's pleasure thereon and become an Act of the Legislature upon the Royal Assent being signified thereto, notwithstanding that the Legislative Council has not consented to the Bill.

The 'ostensibly' caveat is used above because on anything more than a cursory reading the drafting of CA 1902 s.5B(1)[24] is conceptually very sloppy in several specific instances once one reaches [5].[25] The word 'shall' in the sense of imposing what one might take to be an essential or mandatory procedural step appears only twice in s.5B.

[21] Although Ryan had submitted and Isaacs had apparently accepted that the power to enact the PBRA 1908 could also be found in cl.22 of the 1859 Order/s.2 of the Constitution Act 1867; vol 1 pp 259–60.

[22] Vol 1 pp 260 and 263.

[23] Vol 1 p 310. The [1], [2] etc inserted into the text are my addenda.

[24] Which does at least manage to divide its 201 words into two sentences, rather than just the one which contains all 128 words of CLVA 1865 s.5 (vol 1 pp 108–09).

[25] It is linguistically sloppy throughout.

The first is in [7], which provides that a referendum '*shall*' be held if the Assembly passes a resolution to that effect (although that '*shall*' is prefigured by the '*may*' relating to the making of the resolution, which presumably is used to denote that the Assembly could decide to discontinue the bill at this point).[26] The second is at [8], when we are told an unspecified person or persons '*shall*' present the bill to the Governor for assent if a referendum majority approved it. [1]–[4] seemingly allude simply to ordinary aspects of the legislative process and envisage that the Assembly might decide not to press on with the bill after [2] or [4], so there would be no need for s.5[B] to lend a mandatory character to such steps. S.5B is silent as to whether [5] (the free conference) is a mandatory or optional step, as it refers neither to '*shall*' nor to '*may*'; nor does it specify by whom any such conference *shall* (or *may*?) be called. [6] (the Governor calling a joint sitting), in contrast, expressly uses '*may*' rather than '*shall*', which might readily be taken to mean that such a sitting was not an essential precursor to the bill being put to a referendum.[27]

The sloppiness also has a more general element. No explicit provision was made anywhere in the amendments to the 1902 Act to clarify what role should be played by the state's courts if a challenge was brought to the 'lawfulness' of a s.5B measure, either as a bill was undergoing its passage or after it had emerged as an 'Act'. This omission was, of course, consistent with the entire drafting history of 'manner and form' provisions in Australian colonial law (as were the aforementioned individuated instances of linguistic sloppiness), but, given that *Trethowan* in the High Court and Privy Council had not clearly decided if pre-enactment injunctive relief should be available for such challenges, the Legislature's failure to resolve the point in clear terms was unfortunate. The speeches made during the measure's enactment cast little light on the Stevens government's intentions as to s.5B's enforceability and are similarly uninformative about what legislators regarded as the source of the legislature's power to enact the s.5A and s.5B provisions.

In the Legislative Council

The bill began its passage in the Council. The government's case at second reading was led by the then Attorney-General, Henry Manning.[28] Beyond noting on several occasions that the referendum was the 'ultimate' element of s.5B – a term which might simply denote a question of timing rather than importance – Manning said nothing about enforcement of the deadlock provisions beyond noting their details might be considered further in committee. Concannon,[29] replying for Labour, dwelt on the likely

[26] S.5B says nothing about whether a resolution could be rescinded prior to the referendum being held.

[27] The text of s.5B has obvious similarities to Kidston's 1908 amendments to Queensland's Constitution in the PBRA 1908 (vol 1 pp 233–36) (amendments which were upheld as valid by the High Court in *Taylor*; vol 1 pp 262–64), although that legislation did not have the additional requirements of the free conference and joint sitting prior to the referendum.

[28] *NSWLCD* 13 September 1932 p157 et seq. Manning was the son of a prominent financier who had also sat in the Assembly. Manning was a family friend and protégé of Barton. After reading law at Sydney University, Manning was called to the Bar and worked briefly as O'Connor's assistant on the High Court. He combined his successful legal career with several failed attempts to win election to the Assembly as a Liberal before the war. Having taken silk in 1929, Manning was eventually elected as a UAP candidate in 1932 and was called straight into Stevens's Cabinet as Attorney-General; http://adb.anu.edu.au/biography/manning-sir-henry-edward-7776; Clune and Griffith op cit p323.

[29] See n 85 at p 42 above. [ch.12]

unrepresentative character of the reformed chamber and its size, which he suggested was far too big. Second reading, which took up lengthy periods over several days, concluded on 21 September with a 53–28 vote for the bill to proceed.[30]

The committee stage began on 27 September and concluded the next day.[31] Little attention was given to the enforceability issue. Manning alluded to the point when addressing the question of what would happen if the two houses disagreed as to whether a bill fell within s.5A or s.5B. Informing members that this issue: "has received consideration from those responsible for drafting the bill", Manning's evident hope was that any such disagreement would be amicably resolved within the Legislature:

> But ultimately, when Parliament has expressed its will in an Act of Parliament, the only means by which persons or bodies seeking to transgress the limits can be restrained is by resorting to the courts of the land. There comes a time when the functions of Parliament shall have been exerted to the full. Every care has been exercised, and the results of the deliberations have been embodied in an Act of Parliament that sets out in express language, without ambiguity, the rights conferred on the respective Chambers. When that has been done, if by any breach of constitutional propriety or any disregard of the functions of the Chamber concerned, there should be an attempt to usurp functions that are not by legislative enactment conferred upon that particular body, the only resort is to the supremacy of the rule of law. If resort is made to the supremacy of the law courts, the courts have power to interfere to the proper extent.

"Those responsible …" – Manning did not identify who they were[32] – apparently saw no need to propose enactment of specific remedies to deal with alleged breaches of either s.5A or s.5B.

In committee, Concannon put a specific question concerning how s.5B would impact on the conventional presumption that bills affecting the composition or powers of the Council should begin their passage in that house, given the implication in s.5B's text that they would pass the Assembly *before* going to the Council. His evident concern was that the President of the Council might rule that any bill affecting the constitution of the Council should begin its passage in that house, and that the Council's refusal to consider a bill for that reason would not amount to a 'failure to pass it', which would, in turn, render the deadlock provisions inapplicable:

> The Hon. J. M. CONCANNON: The Vice-President of the Executive Council has not yet answered my question as to whether it would be possible for the Legislative Assembly to introduce a bill to abolish the Legislative Council.
>
> The Hon. H. E. MANNING: I will deal with that![33]

Manning was unable to deal with the question immediately as the day's proceedings adjourned at that point. Replying the next day, and noting that the issue had not occurred to the government before Concannon raised it, Manning suggested that if the Council invoked that point as a justification to refuse to consider a bill, that would amount to

[30] *NSWLCD* 21 September 1932 p407.

[31] *NSWLCD* 27 September 1932 p511 et seq.

[32] Peden presided as President of the Council over the second reading debate. It seems likely that he was involved in the drafting, especially as much of the bill replicated Bavin's discarded 1929 measure. But he gave no indication of that involvement during the bill's passage, and there is nothing in his personal papers to confirm the presumption.

[33] *NSWLCD* 27 September 1932 p537.

a failure to pass the bill for the purposes of s.5B. Noting that the proposed s.5B made 'express' and 'exact' provision for bills to begin in the Assembly, Manning asserted that its effect would be to override any question of privilege.[34] The reply was overstated, since s.5B is neither 'express' nor 'exact' as to where bills should begin; although it does raise an obvious and strong presumption that bills would be introduced in the Assembly.[35] No amendment was suggested to confirm the point. The bill subsequently passed third reading without division the next day.[36]

In the Legislative Assembly

Second reading in the Assembly began on 14 December. Displaying a selective political memory, Stevens opened the debate just after 7.30 pm, asserting that the need for reform was caused by Labour's swamping (or 'flooding', as he sometimes styled it) of the Council, which had both undermined the Council's utility and legitimacy,[37] and – evidently equally importantly for Stevens – had placed successive Governors in an invidious political position. His professed objective was to create a Legislative Council free from the more venal aspects of electoral politics:

> The development of the partisan spirit in the Upper House has been one of the most disturbing and disappointing characteristics of recent politics, and the growth of this element in the House has been accompanied by a loss of the prestige of the deliberative body as a whole. The Upper House, while as much an instrument of the will of the people as the Lower House, should not be affected by the transient political alliances and animosities of the Assembly.[38]

Stevens devoted only one paragraph of his speech to the deadlock provisions. He offered no view at all as to their legal enforceability, presenting them simply as a political device which ensured that the Council could not frustrate the political wishes of the 'people': "These provisions will vest complete control in the people, and it will not be possible for the Legislative Council to oppose the popular sentiments of the electorates if the electors so determine."[39]

[34] *NSWLCD* 28 September 1932 pp 590–91.

[35] That is put most strongly in what became s.5B(4): "… the Legislative Council shall be taken to have failed to pass a Bill if the Bill is not *returned to the Legislative Assembly* within two months *after its transmission to the Legislative Council* …" (emphasis added). cf the comment of James Ashton (ibid p592): "as a matter of courtesy each House has allowed the other to introduce measures dealing with its constitution, but that on several occasions the right of one House to interfere with the powers of the other has been admitted. That shows it is not as matter of law but simply of courtesy between the two houses. When the law is changed, as it will be when these deadlock provisions come into operation, it is inconceivable to me that any President would rule a bill out of order. If he did, the deadlock provisions would come into operation immediately, and the law could be passed without reference to the Legislative Council at all." Ashton was a newspaper owner, pastoralist and banker elected to the Assembly as a free trader in 1894. He remained in the Assembly until 1907, having also served as a minister, and was appointed to the Legislative Council in 1907, from where he fiercely opposed Lang's abolition plans; http://adb.anu.edu.au/biography/ashton-james-5069.

[36] *NSWLCD* 28 September 1932 p647.

[37] *NSWLAD* 14 December 1932 p2958 et seq. Stevens overlooked Holman's appointments in 1917 (p 5 above) and his own 20 nominations granted in September.

[38] *NSWLAD* 14 December 1932 p2961.

[39] ibid pp 2965–66.

Stevens yielded the floor to Lang after an hour.[40] Lang's hour-long speech was also devoted to issues of high politics rather than legal efficacy. His focus was entirely on the composition of the reformed Council, which he characterised as designed to ensure that the UAP and Country Party would have a permanent majority that would prevent any future Labour ministry implementing a radical legislative programme. His language was avowedly unrestrained:

> In objective there is no difference between what this government is trying to do with this measure and what the Mussolinis and Hitlers and others have done and are trying to do in European countries. Such attempts to stifle the voice of the people, whether by constitutional or extra-constitutional means, can have only one outcome. If this measure becomes law, no matter what the people may say, it will result in the Labour Party always being in a minority in the Legislative Council.[41]

Lang also denounced the deadlock proviso as – in practical terms – a sham, on the basis that the cost of conducting a referendum would be so great that the mechanism could hardly ever be used.[42]

Bavin then held the floor for the rest of the evening's proceedings.[43] His contribution, like those of Lang and Stevens, was concerned primarily with the composition of the reformed Council. Debate resumed on 15 December.[44] The contributions echoed those made the day before, and the bill (evidently) passed second reading by 34 votes to 20,[45] without any discussion of the means of enforcing the deadlock provisions.

The bill went immediately into committee.[46] The discussion, in fractious terms, centred primarily on Lang's rejected proposal that the size of the reformed Council be set at two-thirds of the numbers of Assembly members. Lang also echoed Concannon's concern that the deadlock provisions might be frustrated by the Council insisting that any bill affecting its own composition should begin its parliamentary passed in that chamber. That intervention was firmly rebutted by Lewis Martin,[47] Stevens's Minister of Justice:

> That … is a misapprehension. It is true that that has been the customary practice. It was radically and emphatically departed from in the case of the Parliament Bill, in the British House of Commons, and there is no necessity under our constitutional law to follow it here. This House is competent to introduce and pass through, and when this bill is passed will be competent to introduce and pass through, any proposed law whatever.[48]

[40] ibid p2969 et seq.

[41] ibid p2970. The suggestion that Labour could *never* gain a Council majority in the reformed chamber was an exaggeration. But since the original reformed Council would be chosen by an 'electorate' in which Labour was a minority in both chambers and so would surely contain a clear anti-Labour majority, and as only a quarter of the 60 founding members would be replaced every three years, Labour would have to win several successive Assembly elections before it had any realistic prospect of acquiring a Council majority.

[42] *NSWLAD* 14 December 1932 pp 2971–72.

[43] ibid p2973 et seq.

[44] *NSWLAD* 15 December 1932 p3045.

[45] ibid p3085. The 'evidently' is because Hansard records: "Ayes 34. Noes 20. Majority 10." The entry is a nice illustration of the evidential difficulties that might arise in legal proceedings in which the validity of a measure was dependent on the level of support it had received in a legislature.

[46] ibid p3085.

[47] http://adb.anu.edu.au/biography/martin-lewis-ormsby-7505.

[48] *NSWLAD* 15 December 1932 p3090.

Some Labour members, including Lang,[49] were unpersuaded by this assertion. However, it did not occur to any member of the Assembly to propose an amendment to what became s.5 to put the matter beyond doubt. The committee stage concluded the next day, the debate being primarily ill-tempered bickering between Lang and Bavin as to their respective political records. Third reading followed straight away without debate, the bill passing by 33 to 19.[50]

The Referendum

The referendum vote was subsequently held on 13 May 1933. The campaign rehearsed the arguments aired during the bill's parliamentary passage. Lang additionally attached some weight to a matter that had not been considered in either house, his concern being that a UAP/Country Party majority in the reformed Council could frustrate the deadlock process by failing to participate in the free conference stage of the s.5B process.[51] Lang was likely drawing on Piddington's advice on this matter.[52] The claim was fiercely rebutted by Mitchell in a *Herald* article on the eve of the poll.[53] Dismissing Lang's arguments as having: "no merits and no substance. They are mere bogeys and red herrings", Mitchell continued:

> The supposition that any Upper House at any time would ever be so insane as to refuse to enter into conference with the other House is so fanciful and so nonsensical that no rational person could imagine that such a situation could ever materialise into fact.

This legalistic dispute seems unlikely to have swayed many voters. When the referendum vote was finally counted, the bill was approved by a narrow majority,[54] albeit amid allegations in the *Labour Daily* of improper administration of the voting process.[55]

'Lang's' Legal Challenges to the Reform

The *Labour Daily*'s claims seemed to have little weight behind them, and with the political battle lost in both houses and in the referendum, Lang's Labour Party had – despite Lang's personal distaste for lawyers – no reluctance about taking the dispute into the courts.

Piddington v Attorney-General

Having denounced Game's dismissal of Lang as constitutionally improper,[56] Piddington qua claimant (joined by four Lang Labour Council members) immediately launched a legal challenge to Stevens's reform plans after the referendum result approving the 1932

[49] ibid p3092.
[50] *NSWLAD* 16 December 1932 p3166.
[51] *SMH* 10 May 1933 p12, https://trove.nla.gov.au/newspaper/article/16984400.
[52] *SMH* 2 May 1933 p10, https://trove.nla.gov.au/newspaper/article/16979346.
[53] 12 May 1933 p11, https://trove.nla.gov.au/newspaper/article/16962208.
[54] 716,938 to 676,034; Clune and Griffith op cit p330.
[55] *LD* 24 May 1933 p6, https://trove.nla.gov.au/newspaper/article/236559760.
[56] P 111 above.

bill was announced. The composition of the State Supreme Court that heard *Piddington v Attorney-General*[57] on 25 and 26 May 1933 was changed from the one that had argued *Trethowan*. Street had announced that he would retire as Chief Justice in July 1933, and did not sit in *Piddington*. His expected successor, John Harvey, English-born and Oxford-educated, who was appointed to the Supreme Court bench by McGowen's Labour government in 1913,[58] presided. Harvey had never actively engaged in party politics.[59] He was joined on the bench in *Piddington* by Long Innes and Sir Colin Davidson. Davidson, born in Sydney and a graduate of Sydney University, had run a combined career at the Bar and in academia, taking silk in 1926 and being appointed immediately thereafter to the Supreme Court during Lang's first administration.[60] Like Harvey, he had no obvious party political affiliations. Neither Harvey nor Davidson had been involved in *Trethowan*.[61]

Piddington engaged Loxton to argue his cause, which was to have the Court injunct presentation of the bill (post-referendum) to the Governor for assent. The primary contention was that the referendum element of the lawmaking process was invalid because the bill had not been 'submitted' to the electorate as required by s.7A(3) and (4).[62] Piddington's assertion was that 'submitted' required a copy of the bill to be provided to electors in some formal and explicit fashion prior to any vote being taken. The ingenious basis for that argument was that if the referendum was to be regarded (as *Trethowan* suggested) as a third legislative chamber, then voters could not perform their (impliedly) designated legislative function if they had not considered the bill's contents (as would the Assembly and Council) prior to voting on it.

Loxton's argument met obvious scepticism from the bench.[63] David Maughan who led for the government, was not much pressed in reply. The Court announced it would not grant the injunction when argument concluded. Its reasons, issued on 30 May, were brief:

> In our opinion, the words of the section requiring submission of the Bill to the electors on the day of the voting mean nothing more than this, that the authority in charge of the voting should submit the Bill to the vote of the electors; in other words, should take a vote of the electors whether they assented to or disapproved of the Bill.[64]

The Court was also unpersuaded that s.7A contained any implied term that explicit provision had to be made to enable voters to deliberate on the bill's merits. The two-month delay provided for in s.7A(3) between the bill completing its Assembly and Council

[57] (1933) 33 SR NSW 317.

[58] *The Sun* 9 April 1913 p1, https://trove.nla.gov.au/newspaper/article/229835715.

[59] http://adb.anu.edu.au/biography/harvey-sir-john-musgrave-6594.

[60] http://adb.anu.edu.au/biography/davidson-sir-colin-george-watt-5896. It is perhaps symptomatic of the low regard in which Lang held lawyers as a class (see p 56 n 38 above) that he devotes barely any space in his memoirs to the judicial appointments made during his administration. An exception is his explanation of the appointment of Street's son, Kenneth, to the Supreme Court in 1931, which Lang says was done to remove Kenneth Street from his position on the State Industrial Commission, where it was feared he would make unwanted arbitration awards; Lang (1970) op cit p 224. There was no suggestion in the New South Wales press that Davidson's appointment had any partisan dimensions.

[61] I have not been able to discover why. There is an obvious inference to be drawn that Street kept them off the bench on the basis that they might have been inclined to resolve that matter in Lang's favour.

[62] P 34 above.

[63] *Piddington* (1933) 33 SR NSW 317, 319. There is an extensive account of the submissions and questions in *LD* 26 May 1932 p10, https://trove.nla.gov.au/newspaper/article/236568705.

[64] *Piddington* (1933) 33 SR NSW 317, 324 (Harvey ACJ).

passage and being put to a referendum vote indicated that it was quite proper for the Legislature to assume in any machinery legislation that voters would use that time period to familiarise themselves with the bill's contents.

The government had not taken any steps to have the bill passed to Game for his assent while the litigation was ongoing. Formally that responsibility lay again with Peden, once more President of the Council.[65] Peden subsequently passed the bill to Game, who sent it to London for the King's assent.[66]

Doyle v Attorney-General

Piddington did not seem unduly disheartened by his defeat and the bill's enactment. Rather than press the matter to the High Court, Piddington took a brief from one of Lang's 1926 Council appointees, Thomas Doyle,[67] to argue a slightly different case before the State Supreme Court. *Doyle v Attorney-General*[68] was heard on 30–31 August and 4–5 September. Doyle's challenge was targeted at the machinery legislation which made arrangements for the referendum to be conducted.

Piddington's argument repeated – to no obviously useful purpose – the 'submitted' point made in his own case.[69] However, on Mr Doyle's behalf, he also argued the peculiar notion that the relevant Act's[70] creation of an electoral college of the two houses voting secretly was ultra vires because of its inconsistency with – in essence – the common law and 'British constitutional tradition'. The argument might have appealed to Boothby's constitutional predilections,[71] but, given CLVA 1865 s.2 limited 'repugnancy' to inconsistency with Imperial statutory provisions in force in New South Wales,[72] the submission was a hopeless one. Doyle also appeared to submit that the reform bill had been invalidly passed because – and here it seemed irony was being pressed beyond the most extreme limits – the majority supporting it in the Council had been artificially created by the 20 swamping appointments made immediately after the 1932 election. Maughan, again leading for the Stevens government, used his submissions to denounce the suit as a 'scandalous' abuse of the judicial process.[73]

The Court was apparently with Maughan in substance, if not in tone. The judgment, which spans barely three pages of the law reports, was issued on 5 September.

[65] There is a letter to Peden from Piddington in Peden's papers, dated 27 May 1933, in which Piddington requested Peden not to present the bill to the Governor prior to any appeal being finalised; Peden Family Collection (Legal Papers; Legislative Council Bill) ML Mss 1663 1.

[66] Per s.1 of the Australian States Constitution Act 1907 (vol 1 pp 208). Game left office in 1935, and returned to London to become Commissioner of the Metropolitan Police.

[67] Doyle, a member of the state party Executive when appointed, was a Lang loyalist in the 1926 abolition vote; Radi op cit pp 105–09.

[68] *Piddington* (1933) 33 SR NSW 484.

[69] The bill having received the assent, the claim was seeking to have the ensuing 'Act' invalidated rather than to injunct giving of the royal assent.

[70] This being s.3 of CALCA 1933, which inserted the secret ballot provision as an amended s.17A(4) into the Constitution Act 1902.

[71] Vol 1 pp 80–85.

[72] Vol 1 pp 107–08.

[73] The account of Maugham's submissions in the *SMH* is rather more forceful than the one offered in the law reports: see *SMH* 1 September 1933 p12, https://trove.nla.gov.au/newspaper/article/17003221; *SMH* 5 September 1933 p12, https://trove.nla.gov.au/newspaper/article/17004356.

Harvey's sole opinion curtly rejected all of Doyle's submissions. Even if the electoral process chosen to create the new Council was an unusual one, the objections that Doyle was raising were political questions for the electorate and not legal questions for a court. It was clear from *Trethowan* that s.4 [BAA] and CLVA 1865 s.5 had given the Legislature: "the most complete power … of altering its own constitution subject only to the limitations contained in those statutes".[74] With admirable tenacity, Doyle took his case to the Privy Council,[75] where it was (albeit politely) dismissed as without merit on all grounds.

The First 'Elected' Legislative Council

The 'elections' for the reformed Council, scheduled to meet for the first time in April 1934, were held in November and December 1933. The 'electorate' comprised 208 voters: 90 from the Assembly and 118 from the Council. For the UAP and the Country Party, the results unsurprisingly closely reflected the electorate's party composition. Of the 60 elected Legislative Councillors, 25 were UAP members; 11 Country; 17 (Lang) Labour; five (national) Labour; and two Independent.[76] Lang Labour's return was lower than its formal share of the electorate, and national Labour's higher – an outcome result which suggests that some (formally) Lang Labour Councillors hid behind the secret ballot to support national Labour candidates. Peden, Playfair and the barrister EM Mitchell took seats for the UAP; Trethowan was elected for the Country Party.

In effect, Lang's plans to abolish the Council had proven hugely counterproductive. In 1934, New South Wales was left with a Council which offered no short- or medium-term prospect of a working Labour majority and which, because of the Lang government's defeat in *Trethowan*, enjoyed a firmly entrenched legal status. More galling perhaps for Lang in a personal sense was the impetus *Trethowan* then provided to the Queensland Labour Party to safeguard the abolition initiative which Theodore had successfully introduced a decade earlier.

Table 6.2 'Electors' and elected: the 1933 New South Wales Legislative Council election[a]

Party	Assembly voters	Council voters	Total voters	[–%]	Seats won	[–%]
UAP	41	46	87	[42]	25	[43]
Country	25	12	37	[18]	11	[18]
Labour (Lang)	24	48	72	[35]	17	[28]
Labour (national)	–	8	8	[3.5]	5	[8]
Independent	–	4	4	[1.5]	2	[3]

[a] The table is sourced from the *SMH* 18 December 1933 p9, https://trove.nla.gov.au/newspaper/article/17033424.

[74] ibid 499–500.

[75] *Doyle v Attorney-General (NSW)* [1934] AC 511. Piddington led for Doyle. Greene led for the Stevens government, but was not called upon to reply to most of Piddington's submissions. Of the *Trethowan* bench, only Russell sat in *Doyle*; he was joined by Lords Tomlin (who authored the judgment), Macmillan and Alness, and Sir Lancelot Sanderson.

[76] *SMH* 18 December 1933 p9, https://trove.nla.gov.au/newspaper/article/17033424.

Entrenching Abolition in Queensland

Labour's defeat at the 1929 Queensland Assembly election which had led to such difficulties for Theodore[77] was reversed in 1932, when Labour won a slender majority. The new Premier, William Forgan Smith,[78] moved promptly (in response to the Privy Council's *Trethowan* judgment) in a fashion which had not occurred to Theodore and his Cabinet 10 years earlier after *McCawley*. The disagreement between the Nationalists (now UAP) and Country Party when faced with Theodore's abolition initiative in 1921[79] had continued with sufficient force to prevent any measure reinstating the Council during the 1929–32 coalition administration.

Forgan Smith's government made any such future reinstatement more difficult by using its single chamber majority to have the Constitution Act Amendment Act 1934 passed. The Act expressly stated in s.1 that it was amending the state's Constitution. S.3 was introduced as a 'manner' (if not – linguistically – a 'manner and form') proviso:

> 3(1) The Parliament of Queensland … constituted by His Majesty the King and the Legislative Assembly of Queensland in Parliament assembled shall not be altered in the direction of providing for the restoration and/or constitution and/or establishment of another legislative body (whether called the " Legislative Council," or by any other name or designation, in addition to the Legislative Assembly) except in the manner provided in this section.

The specified manner was a simple provision precluding presentation of any such bill to the Governor unless it had first been approved by a majority of voters at a referendum. And in presumably coincidental numerical symmetry, s.3(6) – like s.7A(6) of Bavin's 1929 legislation – provided that the section itself could only be repealed in the manner specified by the section.[80]

Opening the second reading debate, Forgan Smith rooted the political case for the bill in a celebration of direct democracy:

> The basic principle that power rests with the people is one that should not be violated, although it is being questioned in certain quarters to-day, where we find a form of mental snobbery which frequently adopts the method of impugning the sense or intelligence of democracy generally.[81]

He then quoted extensively from the Privy Council's judgment in *Trethowan* – and briefly from Birkenhead's opinion in *McCawley* – to root the legal basis of the bill in CLVA 1865.[82]

[77] P 31 above.

[78] Whose entry in the *Australian Dictionary of Biography* engagingly begins: "… painter and decorator and Premier …"; http://adb.anu.edu.au/biography/smith-william-forgan-bill-8489. Smith was a Scots émigré, first elected to the Assembly in 1915, who had served as a minister from 1922 to 1929. He became party leader in 1930.

[79] Vol 1 pp 325–27.

[80] Also like Bavin's 1929 Act and CALCA 1933, the Queensland legislation did not create any specific remedy for enforcing the 'manner' proviso.

[81] *QLAD* 20 September 1933 p 479.

[82] He did not seem alert to the possibility that the power might also derive from cl.22 of the 1859 Order.

The bill also proposed that the maximum period of years between elections should be set at three years, and that the three-year period be entrenched in the same manner. Much of Forgan Smith's speech and the ensuing second reading debate focused on the latter issue.

The notion of 'debate' is used guardedly here. Second reading was passed without division or dissent,[83] as the opposition parties had decided to boycott the proceedings. The then leader of the opposition and former Premier AE Moore reserved his views for a comment in the *Courier-Mail*:

> If one government can tie the hands of a future government the effective governing of a country will be made impossible … If we should decide to make the restoration of the Upper House the main issue of an election, we would not be entitled on our return to power to repeal the referendum clauses of the Bill now before Parliament and constitute a Legislative Council in the same manner as a Labour government abolished the Upper House in 1922. The Bill now before the House is as puerile as it is stupid. We do not wish to waste the time of the House on an absolutely worthless measure when such urgent problems as unemployment are awaiting the attention of Parliament.[84]

That he was making much the same case as Lang had made in opposing the 1929 amendments in New South Wales seemed to pass Mr Moore by. He did not take his party back into the debate. The committee stage, passing without discussion or division, occupied barely 10 lines of Hansard when the measure came back to the Assembly on 27 October.[85] Third reading passed in the same way four days later.[86]

II. The End of Lang's Political Careers?

The schism between Lang and national Labour in New South Wales showed no immediate signs of healing after the 1932 election, and the party remained divided in the 1934 national election. That election provided a vindication of sorts for Lang, whose candidates took two House seats from national Labour (leaving Scullin with just one New South Wales member in the House) and one each from the UAP and the Country Party. The modest overall gains that the national Labour Party recorded in 1934 pushed Lyons and the UAP back into a formal coalition government with the Country Party. Scullin, beset by worsening ill health, stepped down from the national leadership in September 1935. A few months earlier, Stevens had led the UAP to another victory in the 1935 New South Wales Assembly elections. Lang Labour had gained five more seats than in 1932, but with only 29 it remained far from any realistic prospect of being re-elected to government.

[83] ibid 490.

[84] *Courier-Mail* 21 September 1933 p19, https://trove.nla.gov.au/newspaper/article/1121593. The *Courier* and the *Mail* had merged in August 1934.

[85] *QLAD* 27 October 1933 p1082.

[86] *QLAD* 31 October 1933 p1083.

Table 6.3 1935 New South Wales Legislative Assembly election (11 May 1935)[a]

Party	% vote	Seats won	Change
State (Lang) Labour	42.4	29	+5
United Australia (Nationalist)	33.1	38	–3
Country Party	12.9	23	–
(Federal) Labour	5.0	0	–
Independents	4.4	0	–

[a] The ostensibly remarkable discrepancies between votes and seats won by Lang Labour and the UAP/Country Party arose because: the UAP/Country Party did not contest many safe Lang Labour seats; in contested seats first-preference UAP/Country Party voters were most unlikely ever to nominate Lang Labour as second choice; and Lang Labour candidates winning a plurality but not majority of first preference votes were overtaken by the sole UAP/Country Party candidate when second preference votes were taken into account.

Early in 1936, the national Labour Party formally disbanded its New South Wales branch, thereby in effect restoring Lang Labour as the official branch of the party. The rapprochement was at best precarious. Within the state party, opposition to Lang's leadership coalesced around Robert Heffron. Born in New Zealand, where he had been active in trade union circles, Heffron had continued that activism after emigrating to New South Wales in 1917. He was initially elected to the Assembly as a Lang loyalist in the 1930 election, but by 1936 had become sufficiently vocal in expressing his disenchantment with Lang that he was expelled from the party. With several like-minded colleagues, Heffron formed the Industrial Labour Party to contest seats at the 1938 Assembly election.[87]

In the interim, Lyons had again led the UAP/Country Party coalition to victory in the 1937 House election, taking 44 of the 75 seats. That outcome was reflected in the 1938 New South Wales Assembly election. The Stevens coalition government won a comfortable majority: United Australia taking 37 seats, the Country Party 22 and Labour 28. Lang's star was increasingly waning by this point, in part because he had lost his effective control of the *Labour Daily* newspaper earlier that year. Heffron's Industrial Labour Party won two Assembly seats at the election, defeating Lang's candidate as well as the UAP in doing so. When Heffron's party won two further seats in by-elections in 1939, the national party was moved to try to effect a reconciliation to bring the two factions back under a single organisational roof.

The so-called unity conference in August 1939 drew the Lang and Heffron parties back together, and – crucially – approved a change to party rules which once again placed the election of the leader solely in the hands of the Assembly caucus. The rule change had obvious adverse implications for Lang's position as leader, as his support was much stronger among the now disenfranchised local memberships than among his parliamentary colleagues. At the subsequent leadership election in September 1939, Lang lost the ballot by 20–12 to William McKell.[88]

[87] http://adb.anu.edu.au/biography/heffron-robert-james-10476.

[88] McKell was born in New South Wales and grew up in desperately straitened financial and family circumstances. Initially apprenticed as a boilermaker, his involvement in union activities and his anti-conscriptionist position led to his election to the Assembly in 1917. He served as a minister in both Storey

Despite losing the leadership, Lang did not retire from active parliamentary politics. Instead, having retained his Assembly seat in 1941, he quit the national party once more to found yet another Labour Party in 1944, styling it the 'Australian Labour Party'. Lang's new party ran a slate of candidates and took over 9% of the vote at the 1944 Assembly elections, but won only two seats; Lang was returned again as the member for his Auburn constituency.

On the national stage, the Labour Party had won an overwhelming victory in the 1943 House election, taking 49 of the 75 seats.[89] The national party was then led by John Curtin, a Western Australian first elected to the House in 1928. Curtin, one of the few politicians then well versed in Keynesian economic theory, was closely aligned with Theodore, and had been prominent in efforts to have Lang expelled from the national party in 1931 and 1932. To the surprise of many observers both in the party and in the national press, Curtin was chosen as Scullin's successor in October 1935, when Scullin's ill health forced his resignation.[90]

Unsurprisingly, Lang's political and personal relations with Curtin were no more positive than they had been with Scullin, and they remained equally hostile with Ben Chifley, who succeeded Curtin as Labour leader and Prime Minister on Curtin's death in 1945. Despite his alienation from the leadership of both the state and national parties, Lang retained a considerable personal following in New South Wales. He successfully contested a New South Wales House seat in the 1946 national elections (in which Labour had retained 43 of the 49 seats won in 1943). Lang served only a single term, notable primarily for his evidently hostile relationship with many of his former party colleagues and his constant, almost hysterical obsession with communist infiltration of the Labour Party and government institutions. He lost his seat at the 1949 election by a substantial margin to the official Labour Party candidate.[91]

Although no longer holding elected office, Lang maintained a loud – if, during the 1950s, not much listened-to – voice on the fringes of Labour politics, primarily through his ownership and editorship of a new newspaper, *Century*, to compensate for his loss of influence over the *Labour Daily*. By 1960, Lang had long outlived Theodore, Scullin, Lyons and Bavin.[92] He was a no doubt interested bystander when, in 1960, Robert Heffron, the man who had done much in the mid- to late 1930s to bring Lang's dominance of the New South Wales Labour Party to an end, initiated another attempt to abolish the Legislative Council, which once again brought the notion of 'manner and form' to the forefront of constitutional debate.

and Dooley's governments. McKell took advantage of Labour's subsequent period in opposition to read for the Bar and emerged in 1925 as a Lang loyalist and Minister of Justice. After some very visible wavering, McKell stood with Lang during the 1927 resignation imbroglio (Lang (1956) op cit ch 61), and was again a minister in the 1930–32 administration; http://adb.anu.edu.au/biography/mckell-sir-william-john-15293.

[89] Lyons had died in office in April 1939. He was succeeded as leader of the UAP by Robert Menzies, who had initially come to prominence as leading counsel (aged only 26) in *Engineers* (vol 1 pp 330–33) and who in political terms stood very much to Lyons's right.

[90] http://adb.anu.edu.au/biography/curtin-john-9885.

[91] Nairn (1995) op cit pp 302–14.

[92] Who had died respectively in 1950, 1953, 1939 and 1941. Stevens was still alive at that point, although his political career had effectively ended in 1939, when he lost a UAP leadership election and resigned as Premier. Lang might have derived a certain pleasure that Stevens had lost support within his party because of a perception that he was drifting dangerously towards a Keynesian centre ground on economic policy issues. Stevens resigned his seat in the Assembly shortly afterwards and, on failing to win a House seat in 1940, he withdrew entirely from electoral politics. He died in 1973 after some years of very poor health.

7

Still not Abolishing the New South Wales Legislative Council

> … [I]t is plain from the character and terms of the section, the circumstances in which it was enacted, and the purpose which it was designed to achieve, that it was not intended that the Legislative Council should be at liberty to interpose at any stage a Bar to the achievement of that purpose by a mere refusal to concur in one of the preliminary steps prescribed …
>
> Herbert Evatt, qua Chief Justice of New South Wales, in *Clayton v Heffron* [1961] SR (NSW) 768, 814.

The Labour Party remained in opposition in New South Wales until 1944, when it won a comfortable 54–36 Assembly majority.[1] It also won the ensuing five Assembly elections, albeit that its majority after the 1959 election was only four seats.[2] Defying Lang's 1932 predictions,[3] the Labour Party had also, since 1952, maintained a Council majority.[4] This led to the ostensibly unlikely position that in 1952 the state party's annual conference had overwhelmingly passed a motion *not* to abolish the Council because of its potential value as a Labour-controlled obstacle to bills promoted by a non-Labour government if Labour lost control of the Assembly. That position was maintained for only six years. The party restored its abolition position at the 1958 conference, and made the issue a prominent part of its March 1959 Assembly election campaign.[5]

I. Heffron's Abolition Initiative

An abolition bill was introduced by the then Premier Robert Heffron in November 1959. After his successful manoeuvrings to remove Lang from the state party in the

[1] Two of the 38 were Lang Labour.

[2] The balance was: Labour 49; Liberal (UAP) 28; Country 16; Independent 1. The government's effective majority was often more than four, as the Liberal and Country parties did not always function as a bloc.

[3] P 124 above.

[4] The Council's bizarre 'electoral system' meant that if a party could maintain a majority in the Assembly over several elections it would gradually increase its representation in the Council as well and could eventually secure a Council majority that would survive even swingeing defeat in the next Assembly election.

[5] See generally the discussion in Twomey (2006a) 'Clayton v Heffron' in Winterton (ed) *State constitutional landmarks*; Currey (1960) 'The most recent attempt to abolish the Legislative Council of New South Wales' *The Australian Quarterly* 21; Evans and Lovelock (2008) *Legislative Council practice* pp 35–37.

mid-1930s, Heffron had served continuously in the New South Wales Cabinet since 1944, becoming deputy leader in 1952 and party leader and Premier in October 1959.[6] The abolition bill was his first major initiative as Premier.[7] The bill had two main provisos. The first, repeating Lang's failed measures, was simply to abolish the Council and the office of Legislative Councillor. The second, following Queensland's 1933 legislation, provided that a future Act recreating the Council would have to be approved by a referendum as well as by the Assembly.

Heffron led for the government at first reading. He immediately met an objection from Charles Cutler, then leader of the Country Party, that the bill should as a matter of parliamentary privilege begin its passage in the Council.[8] Some bickering across the floor then followed in relation to Erskine May and matters of inter-house courtesy. No member who spoke referred either to the text of s.5B or the Stevens government's explanation during the passage of the 1932 bill as to how the Act would override any such objections.[9] First reading lasted for several hours; much of it involved histrionic denunciation of the bill from the Country Party as a communist plot to establish a dictatorship in the state.[10] The Liberal party (as the UAP renamed itself in 1945) was content for the bill to proceed, given that, irregardless of whether it was passed by the Council or not, it would have to be subjected to a referendum before being enacted. The eventual vote in favour of first reading was 55–15.[11] Second reading occurred on 1 and 2 December, which it passed by 71–15. There was no committee stage, and the bill immediately passed third reading without division.[12] That same evening, the Council returned the bill to the Assembly without giving it any consideration. The Council's stated reason for doing so was that:

> [I]in accordance with long established precedent, practice and procedure, and for that reason, declines to take into consideration a Bill which affects those sections of the Constitution Act providing for the constitution of the Legislative Council unless such bill shall have originated in that House ...[13]

Echoing the fate that befell Lang's abolition attempt in 1926, seven Labour members of the Council supported the Council's resolution, and were promptly expelled from the party for their pains.[14] Since the resolution was carried by 33–25,[15] the seven Labour members' decisions to support the opposition altered the outcome of the vote.

The government then proceeded on the basis that the Council's stance amounted to a rejection or failure to pass the bill within s.5B.[16] The bill was reintroduced in the

[6] http://adb.anu.edu.au/biography/heffron-robert-james-10476.

[7] Heffron was among the most vocal Labour Assembly members in critiquing the terms of CALCA 1932 during the Act's parliamentary passage; see inter alia *NSWLAD* 14 December 1932 pp 2974–75, 2978, 2980.

[8] *NSWLAD* 12 November 1959 p1982.

[9] Pp 122–23 and 124–25 above.

[10] See especially Cutler at *NSWLAD* 12 November 1959 pp 1987–89.

[11] *NSWLAD* 12 November 1959 p126.

[12] *NSWLAD* 2 December 1959 p2611.

[13] *NSWLCD* 2 December p2549 et seq.

[14] *Tribune* 16 December 1959 p11, https://trove.nla.gov.au/newspaper/article/236734046; *The Biz* 16 December 1959 p22, https://trove.nla.gov.au/newspaper/article/189925689. Twomey (2006) op cit p 173, citing an *SMH* article (12 December 1959), records that the expulsion process was begun and concluded in ten minutes.

[15] *NSWLCD* 2 December 1959 p2561.

[16] Pp 122–23 above.

Assembly on 31 March 1960, and once again passed through the house (on 6 April 1960). It immediately received the same response as before from the Council. Following the scheme of s.5B, the Assembly requested that the Council participate in a free conference. That request was rejected. Shortly afterwards, Heffron advised the then Governor to call a joint sitting per s.5B. The Council responded by resolution that the Governor had no power to do so, although 23 (Labour) members of the Council subsequently joined 85 members of the Assembly in what the participants (and Hansard)[17] described as a 'joint sitting' on 20 April.[18] The joint sitting approved the bill in its original form, and on 12 May the Assembly made what it presented as a s.5B request to the Governor that a referendum be held.[19]

And then, just as had occurred when Lang's government had sought to abolish the Council without holding a referendum in 1930, Heffron's administration found itself facing a legal challenge led by a member of the Council.

II. *Clayton v Heffron* in the State Courts

Hector Clayton, born in Sydney in 1885, qualified and practised as a solicitor. After serving with distinction in World War I, Clayton returned to legal practice and was 'elected' to the Council in 1936 as a UAP member. He subsequently (formally) resigned the party whip on the basis that Council members should be politically non-partisan. Clayton never held government office, although his 're-election' in 1948 and 1960 and subsequent self-identification as leader of the non-Labour members indicate that he remained in substance very much a Liberal. Clayton was personally and politically close to Playfair, and as a lead plaintiff in *Clayton v Heffron* was picking up Playfair's shared *Trethowan* mantle.[20] Clayton had also moved and been the primary speaker in support of the resolutions in the Council refusing to consider the bill.[21]

Clayton and his co-plaintiffs offered the New South Wales courts a lengthy list of arguments supporting an application for an injunction to prevent the government proceeding with its referendum plan. The most striking was that s.5B was per se invalid, both as a matter of general constitutional principle and because of its incompatibility

[17] *NSWLAD* 20 April 1960 p ii et seq.

[18] The siting was brief and ill-tempered. Hansard does not record the start time, but does record a pre-lunch end time of 12.50 pm. Proceedings began with an opposition challenge from Cutler to their legality; ibid pp ii–iii: "Mr. C.B. CUTLER: I have taken the point of order that, not only have standing orders been infringed, but also that the meeting as at present constituted is illegal under the Constitution. The CHAIRMAN: It is not for this joint sitting to determine whether or not it is illegal. That is a matter for the judges, applying their forensic skill. My task this morning is to determine whether the standing rules and orders of the Legislative Council are being complied with. If the hon. gentleman will intimate to me a particular standing order that he claims has been infringed, I can judge the point; so far he has not done so. Mr. C.B. CUTLER: Mr. Chairman, I take the point again that the whole meeting this morning, which has been convened by His Excellency the Governor under section 5B, is illegal. (Interruption.) The CHAIRMAN: Order! Let me make the position quite clear. I am not a jurist. I do not know whether today's meeting is legal or illegal; neither does the hon. gentleman. That is a matter for vital consideration by the courts to which the point might be taken …"

[19] Since s.7A was still in force, a referendum would have had to have been held even if the Council had passed the bill.

[20] http://adb.anu.edu.au/biography/clayton-sir-hector-joseph-9759.

[21] *NSWLCD* 2 December 1959 p2549 et seq; ibid 6 April 1960 p3631 et seq.

with the CLVA 1865. The plaintiffs also contended that neither the free conference nor the joint sitting provisos of s.5B had been complied with and that those provisions were (in respect of Heffron's bill)[22] 'manner and form' requirements per CLVA 1865 s.5[3] enforceable by the court. Clayton also contended that the bill was unlawful because (the point Concannon and Lang had raised in 1932) any bill abolishing the Council should begin its parliamentary passage in that house.[23]

The 1932 Act neither specified the legal consequences of non-compliance with any s.5B procedure nor created a precise judicial mechanism to assess those consequences. Clayton's claim pursued alternative remedies: it sought firstly to persuade the Court that it could injunct any continuation of the legislative process if s.5B was per se invalid or if a s.5B step had not been complied with; and secondly – alternatively – to have any 'Act' that might eventually be produced declared invalid on either of those bases. *Trethowan* had not settled the question of whether any remedy could be provided prior to enactment, and *Clayton* proceeded on the basis of a government concession that such a remedy was in principle available. *Clayton* followed the procedural path taken in *Trethowan*. An application was made (presumably per s.16 of the Equity Act 1901)[24] for an injunction before a single judge, and was immediately set down (per s.6 of the Equity Act 1901) for argument before a five-judge Supreme Court panel. The case was argued for eight days in May and June. Judgment was handed down on 29 September.[25]

The Judges

Evatt's career following his appointment to the High Court[26] took him back into the party political arena. He left the Court in 1940 to take a seat in the House, serving successively as Federal Attorney-General and Foreign Secretary in the wartime Labour government. Evatt subsequently played a leading part in establishing the United Nations, and became the national Labour Party leader in 1950. However, he proved unsuccessful in that role, leading the party to three consecutive election defeats.[27] Having decided finally to retire from the national political stage, Evatt accepted the appointment as Chief Justice of the New South Wales Supreme Court at Heffron's invitation in January 1960.[28]

By 1960, the number of senior judges in New South Wales who had previously held political office was notably smaller than in the *Trethowan* and earlier eras. Of the four other judges who sat in *Clayton*, only one had a party political identity, and that of a rather lukewarm kind. The one was William Owen, appointed to the Court in 1937. A Stevens appointee, Owen had unsuccessfully sought selection as a UAP candidate for the

[22] Which was a CLVA 1865 s.5[2] matter.
[23] Pp 122–23 and 124–25 above.
[24] P 54 above.
[25] *Clayton* [1961] SR (NSW) 768.
[26] Pp 53–54 above.
[27] Evatt also produced several notable academic works while on the court and in government, especially (1934) *The King and his Dominion Governors* and (1947) *Rum rebellion*; he also published a major biography of Holman: (1940) *Australian Labour leader*.
[28] Tennant op cit pp 348–55. Evatt's tenure was short-lived. In fragile health when appointed, Evatt became increasingly unwell and retired in March 1962. He subsequently died in 1965.

1932 Assembly election.[29] Leslie Herron was appointed in 1941 by a UAP government. Born and educated in Sydney, Herron established a successful practice at the common law Bar and served briefly as a lower court judge. He had never sought political office and had no obvious political affiliations.[30] Bernard Sugerman also made his way to the Court without dabbling in party politics, having built a career as both a practitioner and an academic lawyer. He became King's Counsel in 1943, and sat on the Commonwealth Court of Arbitration and Conciliation before being appointed to the Supreme Court in 1947 by a Labour administration.[31] Charles McLelland had a similarly non-party political identity. He had emigrated to Queensland from Scotland as a child in 1912. After attending Sydney University, McLelland qualified as a solicitor and was called to the Bar in 1932. He took silk in 1950 and was appointed to the Supreme Court (also by a Labour government) in 1952. He was the first instance judge in *Clayton*.

The Majority Judgments

Four of the judges dismissed Clayton's claim on all counts. Evatt and Sugerman gave the first (joint) opinion, in terms suggesting they saw little merit in the plaintiff's contentions. This spared Evatt and Sugerman from having to resolve a question they raised at the outset: namely, whether, if any of the plaintiff's grounds were well founded, the Court could properly intervene prior to the 'Act' coming into force.

Evatt and Sugerman

Evatt and Sugerman's analysis began[32] with the proposition that s.5B's "ultimate source" lay in CLVA 1865 s.5, "read in conjunction with" s.4 [BAA] of the 1855 Act. Quoting Sankey's judgment in *Trethowan*, they described CLVA 1965 s.5 as: "the master section to consider for the purpose here in hand".[33]

Clayton's first contention as to s.5B's invalidity built on Haldane's observation in *Re the Initiative and Referendum Act*.[34] The argument was essentially that the Legislature could not – while maintaining its own existence – create an additional legislature (which was how Clayton portrayed the Assembly plus referendum plus assent process). Evatt doubted that this characterisation of s.5B's effect was accurate. S.5B did not create an alternative legislature – nor, indeed, was the referendum an additional element of the ordinary legislature. Following Isaacs's judgment in *Taylor*, Evatt viewed the referendum simply as a means to break the deadlock between the two houses.[35] As such, it fell squarely within the *Burah* notion of a colonial legislature's competence.[36] That is a curious conclusion. The (Indian) legislature in issue in *Burah* was 'colonial' per CLVA

[29] http://adb.anu.edu.au/biography/owen-sir-william-francis-11324.
[30] http://adb.anu.edu.au/biography/herron-sir-leslie-james-10492.
[31] http://adb.anu.edu.au/biography/sugerman-sir-bernard-11799.
[32] [1961] SR NSW 768, 799.
[33] [1932] AC 526, 539; p 112 above.
[34] [1919] AC 935; pp 66–67 above.
[35] *Clayton* [1961] SR (NSW) 768, 800–02.
[36] (1878) 3 App Cas 889, 905; on *Burah*, see vol 1 pp 152–53.

1865 s.1; but it was not 'representative' per CLVA 1865 s.5 and so could not root any of its legislation in CLVA 1865 s.5. Evatt and Sugerman may have been implying in citing *Burah* that the New South Wales legislature could have sourced s.5B in its s.4 [BAA] power – assuming that power still to exist[37] – without any resort to CLVA 1865 s.5; but the point is certainly not made clear.

Taylor also provided Sugerman and Evatt with the basis to reject Clayton's claim that s.5B was inconsistent with CLVA 1865 s.5. *Taylor* raised a question that was 'indistinguishable' from that arising here.[38]

Nor were Evatt and Sugerman impressed by the assertion that the bill had to have begun its passage in the Council, given that it would, if enacted, affect that house's powers. That there might be such a privilege – based on courtesy and past practice – was a perfectly credible proposition. However, s.5B could only operate as a device to break legislative deadlocks if the bill in issue originated in the Assembly:

> The existence of a privilege such as is claimed, or of a similar rule of law would deprive s.5b(5) of all effect. Assuming here in favour of the plaintiffs, but without deciding the question, that the privilege relied upon was an existing privilege of the Legislative Council in 1932, it is plain that, by its concurrence in the enactment of s.5b, that House must fairly be taken as having waived or abandoned its privilege for the future to the extent necessary to give that section efficacy.

Clayton also made various submissions which assumed that s.5B was valid, but that the way the bill's passage had been conducted did not conform to s.5B's requirements.

The first was that the Council's refusal to consider the bill at all was not 'rejection' or 'failure to pass' in the s.5B sense. The assertion was that these terms bore a special 'parliamentary' meaning, applicable only when the Council had evaluated a bill's merits and decided not to pass it. If there was – as here – no such evaluation, neither rejection nor failure to pass could occur. Evatt saw no basis to construe s.5B's words in anything other than their ordinary sense:

> It may be suggested that a Bill is rejected if, by whatever mode and for whatever reason, positive action is taken by way of demonstrating and giving effect to non-concurrence with it, with the result that the Bill can proceed no further and is prevented from passing into law.[39]

Clayton also argued that the various procedural steps outlined after 'rejection' had occurred had a mandatory character; that they were in the context of a CLVA 1865 s.5[2] issue 'manner and form' requirements per CLVA 1865 s.5[3] and so their breach invalidated any subsequent legislative steps. The consequence of this – in remedial terms – would be both that any resultant 'Act' would be invalid and that pre-enactment relief could be granted to terminate the s.5B process. The particular foci of Clayton's submission were that no free conference had taken place and therefore the Governor had no power to call a joint sitting as a free conference having been held was a precondition to that power arising.[40] Clayton also argued that since the Council had passed a resolution

[37] The Privy Council had expressed doubts on that point in *Trethowan*; p 112 above.
[38] *Clayton* [1961] SR (NSW) 768, 804–05.
[39] ibid 811.
[40] These being the points raised by Lang just prior to the referendum, which Mitchell had dismissed at the time as: "insane … fanciful and … nonsensical"; p 125 above. Mitchell had died in 1943.

refusing to participate in a joint sitting, no such sitting had occurred, which, in turn, meant that the Assembly had no power to ask the Governor to initiate the referendum process.

Evatt and Sugerman sidestepped the potentially difficult question of deciding whether the free conference and joint sitting provisos of s.5B were mandatory 'manner and form' requirements. On the latter point, Evatt observed simply that there had been: "in fact a 'joint sitting' …"[41] On the former, the judges resolved the issue by interpreting the free conference proviso in accordance with what they regarded as the: "purpose and object of s.5B":

> … [I]t is plain from the character and terms of the section, the circumstances in which it was enacted, and the purpose which it was designed to achieve, that it was not intended that the Legislative Council should be at liberty to interpose at any stage a bar to the achievement of that purpose by a mere refusal to concur in one of the preliminary steps prescribed …[42]

Insofar as s.5B's free conference requirement had a mandatory character, its 'true construction' was satisfied *so long as the Assembly had requested such a free conference*, which request the Council had rejected: "without cause or for a cause which is not sufficient".[43] Since the requirement had been met, there was no need to decide if it had a mandatory character.

Herron and McLelland

Herron's judgment recited the facts at length and concurred broadly with the outcome and reasoning offered by Evatt and Sugerman, although his own analysis on whether the free conference and joint sitting elements of s.5B had a mandatory character was rather muddled. Herron spent some time trying to identify whether the provisos had a mandatory character – and concluded that they did not – but then rendered the question redundant by adopting an interpretive technique which read additional words into s.5B's text:

> … [T]o give effect to the intention of s. 5b, sub-s. (1) should be read as if after the words "if after a free conference between managers there is not agreement between the Legislative Council and the Legislative Assembly", there appeared the words "or if a free conference having been requested by the Legislative Assembly the Legislative Council refuses or fails to agree to a conference being held …". Similarly, sub-s. (2) should be read as if after the word "sitting", there appeared the words "or after a joint sitting has been duly convened and the members of the Legislative Council refuse or fail to attend such a joint sitting". This method of approach is not to re-draw the section; it is simply a means of expressing the construction which the Court places upon the section having regard to the true meaning which is to be found upon an examination of the section as a whole in the context in which it appears.[44]

[41] *Clayton* [1961] SR (NSW) 768, 811.
[42] ibid 814.
[43] ibid 813. Mitchell's 1933 opinion (p 125 above) had indeed argued that s.5B only required that the Council be offered an *opportunity* to participate in a free conference; *SMH* 12 May 1933 p11, http://nla.gov.au/nla.news-article16962208.
[44] ibid 842–43. Herron also concluded that there had actually been a joint sitting.

McLelland spent much of his long judgment rehearsing and copying out verbatim elements of New South Wales's legislative history. His judgment's analytical parts were in contrast succinct. He agreed with Evatt and Sugerman's conclusion on all points, and for the most part with their reasoning. His approach to the question of whether the free conference proviso had a mandatory character was also rather muddled, albeit differently from Herron's. McLelland considered the proviso mandatory. He then negated that conclusion by assuming that s.5B's overall object was to preclude the Council from preventing a bill's passage, and so he should read into s.5B additional words to the effect that the free conference was not mandatory if the Council did not do: "all things necessary to be done on its part for the holding of such a conference".[45]

In Dissent

Owens agreed with his colleagues both that s.5B was not invalid per se and that there was no legally enforceable basis to hold that a s.5B measure affecting the Council's powers should originate in that house.[46] However, he dissented on the 'rejects or fails to pass' issue. In a notably incoherent passage,[47] Owen accepted Clayton's assertion that those words presumed that the Council would have to undertake a merits-based evaluation of a bill before that bill could be rejected or fail to pass. On this reasoning, the bill's continued passage became unlawful at that point, and so Owen saw no need to consider the "difficult questions"[48] of whether the free conference and joint sitting proviso had been complied with.

Conclusion

All the judgments devoted substantial space to offering a long-term legislative history of the New South Wales Constitution. None referred to the 1932 parliamentary debates as an aid to determining the meaning of s.5B in relation to the question of whether its terms were supposed to be legally enforceable and, if so, how and to what extent. As had been the case in the 1930s, that would not have been regarded as permissible (either in Britain or in Australia) in 1960.[49] But, as suggested above, little assistance would have been gleaned from the debates as to legislators' intention concerning s.5B's enforceability. It seems unlikely that the imprecision of s.5B's drafting and the limited analytical rigour which attended its passage through the Council and Assembly were aspects of a deliberate strategy by Stevens's government to create an unenforceable deadlock proviso.[50] Incompetence rather than mendacity would seem the more probable explanation.

[45] ibid 861.
[46] ibid 815–26.
[47] ibid 824–25.
[48] ibid 826.
[49] On the more recent position in UK law see Loveland (2018) op cit pp 210–215.
[50] Although Heffron seemingly held this view; see Twomey (2006) op cit p166; citing Heffron's speech at *NSWLAD* 18 November 1959 pp2089–90.

III. *Clayton v Heffron* in the High Court

Clayton promptly received the High Court's permission to appeal. *Clayton* was argued episodically in Melbourne and Sydney in October and November 1960; judgment was given on 15 December.[51] Three *Trethowan* protagonists sat on the High Court in 1960. McTiernan, 30 years into his tenure, remained on the bench, as did Dixon, Chief Justice since 1952.[52] The third was Frank Kitto, Evatt's junior before the state courts, who was appointed to the Court in 1950.[53] Their four fellow judges[54] had not been involved in any fashion in *Trethowan*.

The Majority Opinion

Dixon and McTiernan were joined by two colleagues, Taylor and Windeyer, in a majority opinion which rejected all of the plaintiffs' contentions.[55] The majority was concerned with both substantive and remedial issues; if an unlawful action had occurred at some point in the lawmaking process, was the proper course for the court to follow to await 'enactment' of the 'law' and then assess its validity or to grant injunctive relief prior to completion of the measure's passage? Indeed, the opinion can credibly be read as being concerned more with the remedial issue than the substantive one; although in some parts the opinion seemed to merge the two matters together.

Dixon stressed at the outset that *Trethowan* was not a binding precedent for this case on the remedial issue:

> It is evident enough that such a case has no analogy to Attorney-General (N.S.W.) v. Trethowan (1932) AC 526 (1932) 47 CLR 97 (1931) 44 CLR 394 (1930) 31 SR (NSW) 183. The injunction was there granted by the majority of the Supreme Court because a definite statutory prohibition made, so it was held, the step of presenting that Bill to the Governor for his assent unlawful: in the opinion of the Supreme Court, to enforce this *distinct and imperative negative duty* the remedy of injunction was available.[56]

[51] *Clayton* (1960) 105 CLR 214.

[52] McTiernan eventually retired in 1976, after 46 years in office. Dixon retired because of ill health in 1964.

[53] Kitto was appointed straight from practice by the (Liberal) Menzies government. Kitto's practice had been largely in equity and tax matters, and he had not held or sought political office.

[54] William Windeyer (appointed 1958); Alan Taylor (appointed 1952); Douglas Menzies (appointed 1958); Wilfred Fullagar (appointed 1950). Fullagar was a Labour government appointee; the three others were Liberal (formerly UAP) government appointees. Windeyer had been active in Liberal party politics (seeking selection to stand for the Senate in 1949). Fullagar, in his early years at the Bar a protégé of Dixon, had – like Taylor – no overtly partisan political affiliations. Menzies was a cousin of the (Liberal) Prime Minister who appointed him, but was not a partisan figure and had never held political office.

[55] Dixon was likely the prime mover in and author of the majority opinion, and I use the attributions 'Dixon' and 'the majority' interchangeably hereafter. In the period between *Trethowan* and *Clayton*, Dixon had authored several academic papers exploring and explaining the basis of judicial review of legislation and legislative action in the Australian colonies. None of them had cast any doubt on the correctness of the High Court and Privy Council's judgments in *Trethowan*: (first published 1935) 'The law and the constitution' in Dixon (1965) *Jesting Pilate*; (first published 1955) 'Concerning judicial method' in Dixon (1965) op cit; (1957) 'The common law as an ultimate constitutional foundation' *Australian Law Journal* 240.

[56] *Clayton* (1960) 105 CLR 214, 233; emphasis added.

What Dixon termed this 'distinct and imperative negative duty' was an exception to the relevant general principle that a colonial court should not:

> … enter upon an inquiry into the lawfulness and regularity of the course pursued within the Parliament itself in the process of legislation and before its completion. It is an inquiry which according to the traditional view courts do not undertake. The process of law-making is one thing: the power to make the law as it has emerged from the process is another. It is the latter which the court must always have jurisdiction to examine and pronounce upon. Of course the framers of a constitution may make the validity of a law depend upon any fact, event or consideration they may choose, and if one is chosen which consists in a proceeding within Parliament the courts must take it under their cognizance in order to determine whether the supposed law is a valid law; but even then one might suppose only after the law in question has been enacted and when its validity as law is impugned by someone affected by its operation.[57]

The principle was perhaps derived from *Wauchope*,[58] although Dixon did not cite that case – or any other authority – to sustain his proposition. Dixon was clearly correct in identifying the State Supreme Court judgment in *Trethowan* as unusual in providing pre-enactment injunctive relief to uphold a 'manner and form' departure from the ordinary lawmaking process. The overwhelming trend in Australian colonial judicial review of 'legislation' was that courts granted post- rather than pre-enactment remedies.[59]

The remainder of the judgment collapsed the remedial and invalidity issues into several composite questions arising from Clayton's various assertions, which questions were resolved with varying degrees of clarity.

The majority was certain that there was no traction in the suggestion that any remedy – whether pre-enactment injunction or post-enactment invalidation – could arise simply because the bill began its passage in the Assembly rather than the Council. Clayton's submission on this point was construed as asserting that commencement in the Council was a 'manner and form' requirement per CLVA 1865 s.5. Dixon concluded with obvious justification that Council commencement had no legal basis of any sort and so did not fall within s.5. He also accepted that s.5B's scheme implicitly provided that any bill would begin in the Assembly.[60]

Dixon took this point further, however, by suggesting that Clayton was also submitting that insofar as Council commencement was an aspect of parliamentary privilege, it might support a conclusion that such an invocation of privilege in the shape of refusing to consider a bill at all might mean that the bill had not been 'rejected' or had not 'failed to pass' in the s.5B senses. While Dixon began by saying: "the argument has an importance which is considerable",[61] he and his colleagues had little difficulty dismissing it. To accept the contention would entail lending 'rejected' or 'failed to pass' meanings conditioned by parliamentary practice. Like the Supreme Court judges, the majority considered that these terms should bear their ordinary meaning, although Dixon's reasoning was rooted more in s.5B's text than – as in the Supreme Court – in a more

[57] ibid 234.

[58] (1842) 8 ER 279; vol 1 p 52 above.

[59] The point is true starting with Pedder and the Dog Act, through to Lutwyche's judgments in early 1860s Queensland, Boothby and Gwynne's contemporaneous opinions in South Australia, and then on to *Cooper, Taylor* and *McCawley* in early 20th-century Queensland; vol 1 pp 24–27, 76–80, 80–85, 214–227, ch 8 and ch 9.

[60] *Clayton* (1960) 105 CLR 214, 233–34.

[61] ibid 241.

amorphous notion of the Act's purpose.[62] On that basis, a refusal to consider a bill at all could be equated with rejection.

The analysis of Clayton's submissions that s.5B was per se invalid was more elaborate, and tied closely to the reasoning in other parts of the judgment which dealt with the legal consequences arising if any of s.5B's procedural mechanisms were not complied with during a bill's passage.

Dixon was much concerned to identify *precisely* the legal source for enactment of s.5B. S.7A was rooted in CLVA 1865 s.5. As such – reiterating the point and extending the point made earlier in the judgment – respect for s.7A's referendum requirement was "essential" for any resultant statute to be valid; ie that requirement was, as Dixon put it earlier, a "distinct and imperative negative duty". Moreover, breach of such a duty would also found pre-enactment injunctive relief. But Dixon also appeared to be suggesting that non-compliance with *any* procedural requirement that was a 'manner and form' proviso per CLVA 1865 s.5[3] would have the same effect.[63]

He then reasoned that it did not necessarily follow that all procedural devices departing from the 'ordinary way' of legislating were rooted in CLVA 1865 s.5[3]. S.5[3] could apply only to matters substantively within s.5[1] and [2]. In Dixon's view, CLVA 1865 s.5[2] dealt with 'identity' rather than 'competence' issues.[64] However, s.5B applied to legislation on any topic. Therefore, if it was valid for those purposes, it would have to be sourced elsewhere than in CLVA 1865 s.5.[65] That source, in Dixon's view, was s.5 of the CA 1902.

Dixon construed CA 1902 s.5 as conflating s.4 [BAA] and s.1 of sch.1 of the 1855 Act:[66]

> [CA 1902] s.5 confers a complete and unrestricted power to make laws with reference to New South Wales. There is doubtless a territorial limitation implied in the reference to New South

[62] "The question is what does s.5B mean to cover by its use. The provision is concerned with a refusal or neglect of the Council to give effect to the Assembly's will in lawmaking. It is because the assent of the Council to a bill may be withheld otherwise than by rejection that the alternative "fails to pass" is added and that the provision deals specially with amendment. Pursuing the same purpose, sub-s.(4) provides a period of inaction as conclusive of failure to pass a bill. These are considerations which point to an intention to cover entirely the withholding by the Legislative Council of its consent to a measure sent up to it by the Legislative Assembly"; ibid 243.

[63] He made this assertion in the 1935 paper, 'The law and the constitution' op cit p50: "If a requirement of the existing law is one that goes to manner and form of legislation, then that requirement cannot be disregarded and any attempt to legislate which does not comply with it, is void."

[64] Dixon seemed to take a different view in *Trethowan*, where he had construed the 'powers' element of CLVA 1865 s.5[3] as a general competence provision: "The power to make laws respecting its own *powers* would naturally be understood to mean that it might deal with its own legislative authority. Under such a power a legislature, whose authority was limited in respect of subject matter or restrained by constitutional checks or safeguards, might enlarge the limits or diminish or remove the restraints. Conversely, the power might be expected to enable a legislature to impose constitutional restraints upon its own authority *or to limit its power in respect of subject matter*" (1931) 44 CLR 394, 430 (emphasis added).

[65] Dixon doubted that the effect of Heffron's bill – which left the original legislature intact while establishing an alternative means of legislating – fell within CLVA 1865 s.5[2] in any event, and intimated that he thought the decision in *Taylor* was incorrect on that point (1960) 105 CLR 14, 249–50. Ryan's submission in *Taylor*, it may be recalled, had rooted the PBRA 1908 either in CLVA 1865 s.5 or in cl.22 of the Order/s.2 of the Constitution Act 1867 (Queensland's equivalent of New South Wales's CA 1902 s.5), and Isaacs had expressly approved that submission; vol 1 pp 260 and 263. Dixon did not acknowledge either source.

[66] Dixon referred to ss.1–9 of the 1855 Act (which I have called the [BAA] elements in vol 1 p 45 n 46) as the *Constitution* Statute *1855* and to sch.1 of the Act (the New South Wales bill as amended) as the *Constitution* Act *1855*. I adopt that labelling here. In *Trethowan*, Dixon had referred to s.4[BAA] as being 'exhausted' or 'spent' and subsumed within CA 1902 s.5; (1931) 44 CLR 394, 427.

> Wales but there is no limitation of subject matter. The laws may be constitutional or at the other extreme they may deal with subjects of little significance. Clearly the power extends to laws altering the Constitution Act itself: cf. McCawley v. The King ...[67]

The term 'complete and unrestricted' does not appear in CA 1902 s.5's text, and is obviously an incorrect characterisation in that the state legislature's power was (in 1902, in 1932 and in 1960) constrained by the terms of the national constitution and CLVA 1865 s.2. The imprecision in Dixon's terminology is perhaps surprising, given his eminence as a jurist and judge, and is presumably a stylistic not substantive error. But Dixon saw no reason to assume that the CA 1902 s.5 general power did not extend to altering the Legislature's composition, even though that issue was dealt with in a particularistic way by CLVA 1865 s.5. The definition of the legislature in CA 1902 s.3[68] was evidently as amenable to alteration by legislation rooted in CA 1902 s.5 as any other provision of New South Wales law:

> What ground is there for supposing that the Legislature must always be defined in terms of two Houses? ... [O]nce it is seen that s.5 gives the Legislature a full constituent power the question why should the power of the Legislature not extend to the enactment of s.5B almost answers itself. What it means is that the power to legislate, including the power to legislate for the abolition of the Council, may be exercised by the Crown with the consent of the Assembly provided the proposed law is approved by the majority of the electors voting at a referendum.[69]

Given that CA 1902 s.5 did not – and could not – amend or repeal CLVA 1865 s.5 (and so the two measures coexisted), Dixon's conclusion that CA 1902 s.5 (a general power) displaced CLVA 1865 s.5 (a much more specific power) is a departure from orthodox constitutional principles.

The significance of Dixon's reasoning was not simply that Clayton's arguments concerning s.5B's validity would fail. It also had profound implications for the normative status of the s.5B procedures, which, in turn, conditioned the principles which the Court should invoke to ascertain both (firstly) the meaning of s.5B's provisos and (secondly) the legal consequences flowing from their breach. In essence, Dixon held that because s.5B was rooted in CA 1902 s.5 and not in CLVA 1865 s.5[3], the s.5B procedures were not s.5[3] 'manner and form' constraints and thus were not automatically to be considered as rendering invalid any statute passed in breach of the designated procedures.[70]

CALCA 1933 had not specified what the legal consequences of such a breach would be. As noted above,[71] legislators had not addressed that question during s.5B's passage. S.5B was yet another particularistic example of what Dixon (quite accurately) identified

[67] (1960) 105 CLR 214, 250.

[68] Which provided: "3. In this Act, unless the context or subject-matter otherwise indicates or requires, – 'The Legislature' means His Majesty the King, with the advice and consent of the Legislative Council and Legislative Assembly." Dixon might perhaps have concluded just as readily that s.5B created a 'context' per CA 1902 s.3 that altered the presumptive definition of the 'Legislature's' composition. No significance was attached to the change of wording from the definition of the Legislature in s.9 [BAA] of the 1855 Act, which included the phrase: "... any future Legislature which may be established". If CA 1902 s.5 did grant a 'complete and unrestricted power', it presumably had in some fashion absorbed the capacity to 'establish' a 'future Legislature'.

[69] (1960) 105 CLR 214, 251.

[70] Nor a fortiori as grounds for a remedy for breach through pre-enactment injunctive relief.

[71] Pp 120–121 above.

as a general trend: "commonly no express declaration is to be found in a statutory power as to the effect on validity of departures from the procedure laid down".[72] That effect therefore had to be found in common law principles. Those principles:

> distinguished sharply between invalid attempts to exercise a legislative power and departures from the prescribed course for its exercise which may not or do not bring invalidity as a necessary consequence … The question is then determined by reference to the nature of the power conferred, the consequences which flow from its exercise, the character and purpose of the procedure prescribed.[73]

That list of ingredients in Dixon's interpretive recipe conspicuously does not include the literal wording of the contested provision. Dixon's subsequent analysis seemed less concerned with textual than with contextual considerations; all of which considerations seemed to him to point to the free conference being merely a directory rather than an imperative procedural requirement.[74]

Dixon's first concern was a floodgates argument of sorts:

> The power here is to enact a public general statute and the power to do this extends to a statute altering the constitution of the Legislature so that if the statute is to be void every future piece of legislation passed by the Legislature of the state so constituted will have no force or effect.[75]

This would presumably be – Dixon did not immediately spell out the conclusion – a most undesirable consequence and thus a reason for not regarding the proviso as imperative.[76] A second matter pointing in the same direction was that if the free conference were an imperative requirement, the Court would have no choice but to involve itself in evaluating the Legislature's internal proceedings, which would require it to accept a very unusual jurisdiction. This, too, apparently – Dixon again does not make the point explicitly – would also be undesirable. A third concern – which in substance echoes Evatt and Sugarmen's 'purpose and effect' analysis and Dixon's own reasoning on the 'rejected' or 'failed to pass' issue – is presented in distinctly circular terms:

> [B]efore one reaches the conclusion that the failure to fulfil the requirement of holding a free conference will result in the invalidity of the law if adopted, it is natural to treat the fact that the Legislative Council may decline a conference of managers as a reason to be added to the other considerations for holding that it is not a matter going to validity.[77]

This is then followed shortly afterwards by what seems to be an equally tautological 'conclusion':

> The real point sought to be made [by Clayton] is that a free conference is an essential condition of the ultimate validity of any statute enacted under s. 5B. To that the answer is that according to the principles governing the invalidation of statutes for deviation from the legis-

[72] *Clayton* (1960) 105 CLR 214, 246.
[73] ibid.
[74] The majority concluded without argument that a joint sitting had actually occurred; ibid 246.
[75] ibid 246.
[76] He returned to the point later in the judgment: "Is it possible to imagine a stronger case of inconvenience than the invalidation perhaps at some future time of a constitutional provision possessing all the outward appearances of a valid law on the ground that when it was made managers of the Council had not met managers of the Assembly before the members of the two Houses were required by the Governor to meet?"; ibid 247.
[77] ibid.

> lative procedure laid down by law no such invalidity should be held to ensue as a consequence of the lack of a meeting of managers in a free conference. Once that conclusion is reached there is an end of any contention that the proviso to s. 5 of the Colonial Laws Validity Act 1865 can apply; there is no imperative requirement. For the foregoing reasons, assuming that s. 5B possesses force and validity, there is no valid ground upon which it should be held that a fatal departure from its requirements has occurred justifying the intervention of the Court.[78]

This entire section of the judgment[79] has obvious shortcomings. Dixon does not invoke a single authority in support of his conclusion. This omission is ostensibly justified by the majority's observation that: "the decided cases illustrating the distinction relate to much humbler matters than the validity or invalidity of the constitution of the Legislature of a State".[80] Accepting that assertion to be accurate, one might suggest that the appropriate way for Dixon to have proceeded would be to identify decided cases which involved matters which were minimally less 'humble' than those raised here which had also concluded that procedural requirements were not 'imperative' and which therefore reinforced the assertion that s.5B provisos were not imperative either. The majority's failure to do so, coupled with the rather haphazard and partial way in which the opinion identifies and explains its reasons on this aspect of Clayton's case, creates the impression of a conclusion having been reached which is unencumbered by the anterior step of rigorous justification.

The problem is perhaps more one of presentation than substance. Viewed in the round, the majority opinion on the mandatory/directory point can perhaps be characterised as progressing through several logical steps. First, the individual elements of s.5B's text did not expressly confirm what legal consequences flowed from a failure to observe the various distinct procedural mechanisms which s.5B created. Second, the text *in toto* was drafted so imprecisely that it did not raise any strong implication as to whether particular procedural steps were mandatory or directory. Third, it was therefore appropriate to consider s.5B's underlying purpose to determine if that purpose could be seen as creating such an implication. Fourth, it could not be doubted that s.5B's underlying purpose was to ensure that a bill which enjoyed majority support in the Assembly but not in the Council would nonetheless be enacted if supported by a majority of voters in a referendum. Fifth, that underlying purpose raises a very strong presumption that any s.5B requirement dependent upon positive Council action could not be mandatory. Sixth, that strong presumption is reinforced rather than weakened by pertinent contextual considerations, notably the 'inconvenience' and 'jurisdiction' points which Dixon identified.

This is not to suggest that the majority's conclusion was not defensible (and obviously so). The point is rather that the legitimacy of that outcome could have been enhanced by more careful ordering of the reasons that underlay it.

The Dissenting Opinion

Fullagar found in the plaintiffs' favour, and did so in reliance on Dixon's opinion in *Trethowan*. In Fullagar's view, all the steps identified in s.5B were 'manner and form'

[78] ibid 248.
[79] ibid 246–48.
[80] ibid 247.

provisions per CLVA 1865 s.5[3]. *Trethowan* was also an authority that non-compliance with any step would mean any resultant 'Act' would be invalid, as Fullagar could see no basis for concluding that some of those steps were 'directory' rather than 'mandatory'. He referred to only one authority on the point (that being one more than the majority had done) and did not explain its pertinence to the matter before him.[81] Fullagar thought it clear that neither the free conference nor joint sitting conditions had been complied with, and did not accept that the Council's failure to engage with either step turned them into merely directory requirements. The consequence of this was not simply that any resultant (ie after approval at a referendum and the giving of the royal assent) 'Act' would be invalid, but also that an injunction should be granted to prevent a referendum being held at all.

There is a temptation to see Fullagar's judgment as elegantly straightforward in terms of its legal reasoning. That characterisation would have to rest, however, on an unwarranted presumption that s.5B was itself elegantly straightforward in terms of the law which it created. Since s.5B manifestly lacked that quality, Fullagar's opinion is perhaps better seen as simplistic rather than elegant, insofar as its effect was to lend s.5B's imprecise text a meaning which undermined rather than underlined the political purpose that prompted its enactment.

The Concurring Opinions

Kitto concurred in the result with the majority opinion. However, his reasoning rested on a different base. Like Fullagar, Kitto considered that all of the s.5B requirements were 'manner and form' provisos, and all were mandatory:

> Every step in the process is made conditional upon the completion of the preceding steps. The central feature of the constitutional amendment of which the enactment of s. 5B formed part was that the Legislative Council, as reformed, should remain as an integral part of the Legislature; and I find it impossible to read s. 5B without being impressed by the evident care that was employed to make certain that the Council's consent should continue to be indispensable for the enactment of a Bill, except where a defined course had been precisely followed.[82]

Kitto subsequently categorised s.5B as containing; "a most deliberate choice of words"[83] in order to achieve that result. That conclusion is hard to reconcile with the reality of the legislative debates on the bill;[84] but like the majority, Kitto did not consult that source. To this point, one might have expected Kitto to join Fullagar in dissent. However, it seemed that certain of these conditions were only *provisionally mandatory*. Kitto did not offer any legal authority to support the proposition that a mandatory requirement could

[81] The case being *Chanter v Blackwood (No 1)* [1904] HCA 2 (1904) 1 CLR 39, in which the Griffith court held (on a lengthy consideration of authorities) that a statutory requirement that a voter placed his cross on his ballot paper in the box alongside a candidate's name was not mandatory in the sense of invalidating a vote cast by putting the cross just outside the box.

[82] (1960) 105 CLR 214, 267.

[83] ibid 268.

[84] As is his later comment concerning what he ill-informedly portrayed as: "the anxiously contrived detail of the section"; ibid.

also be not mandatory. His reasoning rested on the premise that it was appropriate to read words into the text of s.5B in order to give effect to: "the nature and purpose of the section as a whole".[85] If that ('ultimate'?)[86] purpose was to deploy approval of a bill in a referendum as an alternative to the consent of the Council, then:

> The words in which a condition is stated, therefore, surely cannot mean that the very Chamber whose opposition to the Bill is to be prevented from proving a final obstacle to its enactment may, by refusing co-operation, make its opposition successful. For that reason, the assumption seems to me to be implicit that the Council is not unwilling to send managers to a free conference. If the Council is unwilling, the situation is one to which the reference to a free conference between managers is, in my opinion, by necessary implication inapplicable.[87]

Kitto held that this rationale would apply both to the Council's refusal to participate in a free conference and – if it did participate – to a subsequent refusal to hold a joint sitting.[88] In either circumstance, it was appropriate for the court to read s.5B as if it said that in the event of such a refusal the relevant condition became inapplicable. It may be that Kitto identified, but was not prepared to endorse, the obvious inadequacies in the majority's opinion on the mandatory/directory issue, but his own method is equally – if differently – unsatisfactory. To conclude without the support of authority that a breached proviso is both mandatory and non-mandatory is perhaps even less impressive as an exercise in judicial lawmaking than to conclude without authority – as did the majority – that the breached proviso is merely directory.

What Kitto was perhaps trying – and failing – to say[89] was that all of s.5B's procedural steps appeared, if construed in a narrowly literalistic fashion, to have a mandatory character. However, given the overall purpose of the section – namely, to remove the Council's power to prevent a measure being enacted – that literalistic reading became untenable in respect of the free conference. Had legislators wished that step to be mandatory, it would have been a simple matter for the bill's text to have been amended to put that consequence beyond doubt so that the 'necessary implication' could not be drawn.

Menzies reached the same conclusion as Kitto through essentially the same odd reasoning:

> I construe the section as providing a manner and form of legislating which must be followed for the making of a valid law in which each step not only follows that which precedes it but depends upon it. To put it in another way, I would say that unless laws not falling within s. 5A are made with the advice and consent of the Legislative Council and the Legislative Assembly, they can be made only by following the procedure laid down in s. 5B ... Moreover, when the law is a constitutional law to which s. 5 of the Colonial Laws Validity Act applies, as is the case here, that section itself treats adherence to requirements of manner and form as necessary for validity (Trethowan's Case (1932) AC, at p 541 (1932) 47 CLR, at p 106) so that once a requirement is seen as a matter of manner or form, it is not necessary to enquire whether the legislature that imposed it intended that a failure to observe it should result in invalidity.[90]

[85] ibid.
[86] The allusion is to Manning's second reading comment at *NSWLCD* 13 September 1932 p157 et seq; p 121 above.
[87] *Clayton* (1960) 105 CLR 214, 268.
[88] Although he considered that a joint sitting had occurred; ibid 265.
[89] As perhaps were Herron and McLelland in the court below.
[90] *Clayton* (1960) 105 CLR 214, 275.

But although this led Menzies to the conclusion that the free conference was 'imperative', it also led him to conclude that: "I do not construe the section as requiring a free conference in all circumstances."[91] He seemed not to appreciate the rather peculiar notion of a condition being both imperative and not required.

Menzies also resorted to s.5B's 'purpose' rather than its express wording to square this apparent circle. That purpose was that:

> [A] bill may become a law against the will of the Legislative Council … The overriding sense of the section is therefore that nothing that the Legislative Council does … can stop the process whereby a Bill will become law.[92]

The free conference provision was therefore mandatory only to the extent that the Council be offered the opportunity to participate in such a procedure, and if the Council refused so to do, the s.5 process could lawfully continue.

Conclusion

While one might perhaps exaggerate in attaching Birkenhead's 'embarrassing and even ridiculous' soubriquet[93] to some of the reasoning offered in the various High Court judgments in *Clayton*, they all compare poorly in terms of legal rigour and logical clarity with the stance adopted by Evatt and Sugerman in the State Supreme Court. The best that can be said of them perhaps – and especially of the majority opinion – is that they should be seen as an ungainly Australian manifestation of the 'statesman not jurist' approach to colonial constitutional law which Haldane had identified as the dominant (and, in his view, quite properly so) methodology followed by the Privy Council under Watson's leadership,[94] and to which Haldane in general as a Privy Council judge (and Birkenhead in *McCawley* and Sankey in *Trethowan* in particular) had also adhered.

It is certainly surprising – given that the Privy Council judgment in *McCawley* was invoked in all of the High Court opinions – that nothing at all was made by any of the judges of Birkenhead's 'meticulous precision' formula as an aid to determining the meaning and effect of the various procedural devices listed in s.5B. As noted above, any attempt to apply that label to s.5B does not withstand close examination.[95] Stevens' bill had upheld the long and not especially honourable colonial constitutional law tradition of drafting statutory provisions (be they Imperial or colonial in origin) in shabbily imprecise terms. There is an obvious attraction – from the perspective both of sparing courts in subsequent 'constitutional' litigation from having to resolve difficult questions of statutory interpretation which expose judges to accusations of improper political

[91] ibid 276.

[92] ibid 274. The "will" in that sentence should obviously be a "might", since s.5B envisaged that even after the Council's role had ended, the bill could not become a law unless: (i) the Assembly resolved to hold a referendum; (ii) the electorate approved the bill; (iii) the Assembly presented it for assent; and (iv) the Governor (or, if required, the King) gave assent.

[93] Vol 1 p 310.

[94] (1899) 'Lord Watson' *Juridical Review* 278; vol 1 pp 177–79.

[95] Pp 119–25 above.

interference by the losing party and of motivating legislators to be much more precise in drafting statutory texts – in a principle which provides that if breaching procedural requirements which depart from the 'ordinary way' of legislating are to have the effect of invalidating a 'statute'[96] then those requirements must be 'meticulously precise' as to both their content and the legal consequences of their breach.

The judgment did not excite any great public controversy in the popular press, perhaps because of a widespread perception that the government's bill was unlikely to be approved in a referendum. Any such presumption was well founded. The referendum was subsequently held in April 1961. As in Queensland in 1917, the abolition cause was lost by a comfortable margin, 882,512 to 1,089,193. Again as in Queensland in 1917, the defeat had no obviously deleterious impact on Labour's electability: Heffron led the party to an increased majority at the March 1962 election.

While many observers might have expected Lang by this point to have disappeared into political irrelevance and personal ignominy, his reputation and public profile enjoyed a remarkable resurgence in the mid-1960s and on into the 1970s. The man and his political record were embraced particularly fondly among politically active and left-leaning students. He was (once again) readmitted to the Labour Party in 1971,[97] and lived on, in robust physical and mental health,[98] until 1975.[99]

Lang did not quite manage to outlive Steven's 'reformed' Legislative Council. A Labour government bill put forward in 1976 to alter the Council's 'electoral system' to direct popular election, after having twice failed to pass the Council, was eventually agreed upon at a s.5B free conference between the two houses. The bill was subsequently approved by an overwhelming referendum majority and came into force as the Constitution and Parliamentary Electorates and Elections (Amendment) Act 1978.[100]

Lang would likely have been not much impressed by this reform. He would surely, however, have been greatly surprised by the prominence that *Trethowan* has subsequently enjoyed in British and Commonwealth law and legal theory in consequence of his decision to pursue appeals in the case before both the High Court and Privy Council.

[96] Or founding a basis for the grant of pre-enactment injunctive remedies.

[97] *Canberra Times* 29 June 1971 p2, https://trove.nla.gov.au/newspaper/article/131814562; Nairn (1995) op cit pp 314–17.

[98] Morrison (1976) op cit notes that Lang, while in his mid-90s, had vigorously contributed his own recollections to Morrison's research.

[99] The *SMH* offered benign, almost benevolent reviews of Lang's life and career; see especially 28 September 1975 p49 – 'Jack Lang's turbulent years'; 1 October 1975 p3. (Post-1955 editions of the *SMH* are not available on the Trove database). For the then fiercely critical view taken of Lang by some factions on the (far) political left, see *Tribune* 1 October 1975 p2, https://trove.nla.gov.au/newspaper/article/236922324.

[100] For a description of the Act's passage, see Evans and Lovelock op cit ch 2.

8

Uses – and Abuses – of the *Trethowan* Principle

> 163. If the sovereign Parliament can redefine itself downwards, to remove or modify the requirement for the consent of the Upper House, it may very well be that it can also re-define itself upwards, to require a particular Parliamentary majority or a popular referendum for particular types of measure. In each case, the courts would be respecting the will of the sovereign Parliament as constituted when that will had been expressed. But that is for another day.
>
> Baroness Hale in *R (Jackson) v Attorney-General* [2005] UKHL 56, [2006] 1 AC 262.

My original purpose in setting off down the path of writing this book was to explore what insights a detailed study of *Trethowan* might afford to arguments in the UK concerning the legal enforceability and political legitimacy of legislative attempts to lend some kind of entrenched status to particular moral values within our constitutional order. In that respect, this project mirrors my previous study of the trilogy of *Harris* cases decided in South Africa in the 1950s.[1] *Trethowan* and *Harris* have long been staple ingredients of LLB and GDL curricula in public law classes in British law schools in relation to students' exploration of 'manner and form' challenges to orthodox understandings of the doctrine of parliamentary sovereignty. (A third case, from what was Ceylon in the 1960s – *Bribery Commissioner v Ranasinghe*[2] – features less often.) It is a likely unavoidable consequence of the ever-increasing amount of material that is potentially relevant to such classes in UK universities that the cases are rarely explored in any great depth in terms of their respective political contexts, nor with any great sophistication in terms of their juridic implications.

There is also a substantial body of literature published in academic books and journals addressing *Trethowan* and *Harris* – sometime singly and sometimes together – much of which meets the second (if not so often the first) of those shortcomings.[3]

[1] Loveland (1999) *By due process of law? Racial discrimination and the right to vote in South Africa 1850–1960*. The cases are *Harris and others v Donges (Minister of Interior)* (1952) 1 TLR 1245; *Harris and others v Donges (Minister of Interior) (No 2)* (1952) 4 SA 769 (A); *Collins v Donges (Minister of Interior)* (1957) 1 SA 552 (A); considered in Loveland (2018) op cit pp 33–35, 48–49.

[2] [1965] AC 172; discussed briefly in Loveland (2018) op cit pp 35–36.

[3] On *Trethowan*, see especially Goldsworthy (2007) op cit; Friedmann (1950) 'Trethowan's case, parliamentary sovereignty and the limits of legal change' *Australian LJ* 103; Dixon (first published 1935) 'The law and the constitution' in Dixon (1965) *Jesting Pilate*. On *Harris* – where the focus is often just on *No 1* rather than *No 2* and *Collins* – see Griswold (1952) 'The "coloured vote case" in South Africa' *Harvard LR* 1361; Cowen (1952) and (1953) 'Legislature and judiciary: part 1 and 2' *MLR* 282 and 273; Lewin (1956) 'The struggle for law in South Africa' *Political Quarterly* 176. Both *Trethowan* and *Harris No 1* are drawn on extensively in Wade (1955) 'The basis of legal sovereignty' *Cambridge LJ* 172; Jennings (1959 5th edn) *The law and the constitution* ch IV.

Many, but certainly not all, of those analyses presumably share my view that our Constitution's acceptance as a foundational principle that Parliament can in the 'ordinary way' enact laws on any subject has – and has long had – profoundly unsatisfactory political consequences.[4]

As anyone who has read the previous chapters of both volumes of this project will appreciate, that original interest was somewhat overtaken by events. I had very little knowledge of New South Wales's constitutional and political history when I began this study and even less relating to Queensland; really no more than a familiarity with the High Court and Privy Council judgments in *Trethowan* and a vague (and erroneous) recall of the Privy Council's decision in *McCawley*. It soon became apparent that the legal and political seams to be mined in respect of both cases were remarkably rich[5] – I had originally thought *McCawley* could be dealt with in a single chapter and then I met Tom Ryan, Ted Theodore and Pope Cooper – with the result that the project's scope grew much beyond what I had initially envisaged, and focused much more than I had expected on the intricacies of Australian constitutional developments. There are many fascinating stories to be told about the interconnections between law and politics in those historical contexts, and to a large extent these two books have turned into an exercise in such storytelling.

I nonetheless remain very conscious of my position as a novice and outsider with respect to Australian constitutional matters. I perhaps now know enough to realise how much I do not know. Consequently, I will not presume in this final chapter to suggest what lessons (my particular portrayal of) the *McCawley/Trethowan* saga(s) might have in that context. There are many Australian scholars far better placed to perform that task than I am. I hope I may be forgiven, then, for returning in this chapter to my original UK-centric concern and using it in a fashion which presumes on the reader's part a fair degree of familiarity with UK constitutional theory and practice.

As a teacher, I have never been much interested in setting my students exams or term papers based on 'problem questions'. I have always found the construction of overarching narratives a much more stimulating (manner and) form of assessment. But, of course, overarching narratives are frequently the aggregation of analysis of lots of small problems, and so, somewhat unusually perhaps, I propose to end this book by posing – and then offering some answers to – a hypothetical problem.[6]

I. An Entrenchment Problem

By the winter of 2023, the Labour Party led by Sir Keir Starmer QC held a consistent but small lead over the Conservative Party in national opinion polls. Starmer had also succeeded in negotiating electoral pacts with the Scots Nationalist and Liberal parties in which the parties agreed to give the other two parties a clear run against the

[4] One of the most helpful overviews of the entrenchment debate published in recent years is Barber (2016) 'Why entrench?' *International Journal of Constitutional Law* 325.

[5] And the interweaving of 'politics' and 'law' was so tight and so elaborate.

[6] Bearing in mind William Wade's comment: "All writers on sovereignty are bound to deal in improbable examples"; (1955) op cit p173. As of late 2020, my example does not seem as improbable as one might hope.

Conservatives in some 50 seats. In the context of severe economic difficulties caused by the withdrawal of the UK from the European Union and the lingering effects of the COVID-19 pandemic, the Labour, Scots Nationalist and Liberal parties also agreed that they would all campaign in the May 2024 election on the principal basis that the UK should rejoin the European Union if the EU Member States were willing to allow it to do so. That commitment seemed to have no adverse effect on the parties' electoral support; opinion pollsters were predicting that the Conservative Commons majority would turn into a hung parliament, with a plurality of Labour MPs and a significant numbers of Scots Nationalist and Liberal MPs after the election.

Early in 2024, the Johnson government promoted a bill entitled The United Kingdom Safeguarding of National Sovereignty Act 2024. The bill was pressed in less than a week through the House of Commons, where (with all 650 members voting) it secured a majority of 60 at second reading and 50 at third reading. In the House of Lords, the bill passed all its stages with small majorities. The bill was given the royal assent by King Charles in March 2024.

The bill had been denounced by opposition politicians both as a monstrous attempt to bind the hands of future parliaments and as a measure which was legally futile. Prime Minister Johnson had defended it as a necessary means to ensure that such a momentous decision as the UK rejoining the European Union should only be made on the basis of a carefully conducted lawmaking process which attracted very high levels of political support. The entire text of the Act is reproduced below.

The United Kingdom Safeguarding of National Sovereignty Act 2024

An Act to entrench the United Kingdom's freedom from loss of its sovereignty to the European Union

Whereas the sovereignty of a country's people is their most precious political and legal right, and Whereas the people of the United Kingdom in 2016 chose to reclaim their sovereignty from the European Union, and Whereas that decision is properly regarded as the ultimate political fact underlying the United Kingdom's constitution, and Whereas such sovereignty of the people should be and on the coming into force of this Act shall be an entrenched characteristic of the United Kingdom's constitution, and Whereas to surrender that sovereignty at any point in the future is so momentous a political change as to demand approval by an unusual form of lawmaking, and Whereas the orthodox presumption is that Parliament may enact any law by a simple majority in both Houses plus the Royal Assent, and Whereas by a majority of fifty at third reading this measure was approved in the House of Commons, and Whereas the said majority of members in the House of Commons intends that this measure shall in future prevent Parliament by the orthodox process from repealing this Act, and Whereas the said majority of members in the House of Commons accepts that any such unusual manner and form of lawmaking must be defined with meticulous precision if it is to be recognised and enforced by the courts in the face of an attempt by a future Parliament to repeal or amend such entrenchment by a law passed in the orthodox manner and form;

Be it enacted by the King's most Excellent Majesty, by and with the advice and consent of the Lords Spiritual and Temporal, and Commons, in this present Parliament assembled, and by the authority of the same, as follows:–

1. Control of the prerogative power to sign treaties

(1) Neither His Majesty the King nor any of his heirs or successors may exercise the prerogative power to ratify treaties in respect of any Treaty concerning the

accession of the United Kingdom to the European Union until such time as this Act has been repealed in express terms and in accordance with the manner and form of legislating herein created.

(2) For the purposes of this Act 'European Union' shall include any successor body to the European Union.

2. Control of Parliament's power to control His Majesty's prerogative power to sign treaties

(1) The Parliament of the United Kingdom shall not enact any legislation removing or transferring to any other person or body of persons His Majesty's prerogative power to ratify treaties in respect of any Treaty concerning the accession of the United Kingdom to the European Union until such time as this Act has been repealed in express terms and in accordance with the manner and form of legislating herein created.

3. Control of Parliament's power to give domestic effect to European Union law

(1) The Parliament of the United Kingdom shall not enact any legislation giving effect to or purporting to give effect in United Kingdom law to any provision of European Union law created after the coming into force of this Act until such time as this Act has been repealed in express terms and in accordance with the manner and form of legislating herein created.

4. Compliance with specified manner and form of legislating required to repeal this Act

(1) No Act of the United Kingdom Parliament which repeals or purports to repeal this Act shall be recognised by any court in the United Kingdom as having any legal effect unless such Act is passed in the manner and form herein specified.

5. Requisite manner and form – express repeal

(1) For the purposes of this Act, 'express terms' means that no Act purporting to repeal The United Kingdom Safeguarding of National Sovereignty Act 2024 shall be valid unless:

(a) The title of such Act is The United Kingdom Surrender of National Sovereignty Act [plus year of enactment]; and

(b) Such Act shall have only one section, which section shall state verbatim and only: 'The United Kingdom Safeguarding of National Sovereignty Act 2024 is hereby repealed and the sovereignty of the people of the United Kingdom is hereby made vulnerable to surrender to the European Union'.

6. Requisite manner and form – the lawmaking process

(1) Any bill purporting to repeal this Act shall originate in the House of Commons and:

(a) Any such bill shall be entitled The United Kingdom Surrender of National Sovereignty Bill; and

(b) Clause 1 of such bill shall state verbatim and only: 'The United Kingdom Safeguarding of National Sovereignty Act 2024 is hereby repealed and the sovereignty of the people of the United Kingdom is hereby made vulnerable to surrender to the European Union'.

(c) The House of Commons may at any stage of proceedings reject such bill by a simple majority of members voting.

(d) The House of Commons may not at any stage of proceedings amend such bill in any fashion.

(2) A period of at least eight weeks shall elapse between the conclusion of such bill's second reading in the House of Commons and the commencement of the bill's third reading in the House of Commons.

(3) Any such bill may not be sent from the House of Commons to the House of Lords unless such bill shall have been approved by no fewer than 400 members of the House of Commons at third reading.

(4) In the eventuality that the number of members of the House of Commons shall at some future date or dates be increased or decreased then the number specified in s.6(3) above shall increase or decrease accordingly in proportion to the increase or decrease of the number of members of the House of Commons.

    (a) Any fractional number resulting from such increase or decrease shall be rounded upwards.

(5) If any such bill is approved in accordance with s.6(2) and s.6(3) above, such bill may not be sent to the House of Lords for passage in that House until at least eight weeks have passed since the third reading vote in the House of Commons.

    (a) The House of Lords may at any stage of proceedings reject such bill by a simple majority of members voting.
    (b) The House of Lords may not at any stage of proceedings amend such bill in any fashion.

(6) If any such bill is thereafter passed in the House of Lords, it shall not be presented to His Majesty for the Royal Assent until the conditions specified in s.6(8)–(11) herein have been satisfied.

(7) If, notwithstanding the proviso in s.6(6) above, any such bill is presented to His Majesty for assent when the conditions specified in s.6(8)–(11) herein have not been satisfied, His Majesty shall not give assent until the conditions specified in s.6(8)–(11) herein have been satisfied.

(8) On completion of any such bill's passage through the House of Lords, then:

    (a) The Electoral Commission shall make arrangements in accordance with its powers under the Political Parties, Elections and Referendum Act 2000 for the holding of a referendum at a date no earlier than twelve weeks and no later than twenty-six weeks after the bill has completed its passage in the House of Lords.
    (b) In such referendum the question shall be:
        Do you wish The United Kingdom Safeguarding of National Sovereignty Against the European Union Act 2024 to be repealed?
        Yes
        No
    (c) The Electoral Commission shall have no role in approving or amending the question identified in s.6(8)(b) herein.

(9) If fewer than three quarters of registered voters vote in the referendum held in accordance with s.6(6) the bill shall immediately lapse.

    (a) For the purposes of this section a blank ballot paper or a spoiled ballot paper shall not be counted as a vote.

(10) If fewer than 53% of the votes cast in the referendum held in accordance with s.6(6) are 'Yes' votes the bill shall immediately lapse.

(11) If 53% or more of the votes cast in the referendum held in accordance with s.6(6) are 'Yes' votes the bill shall be presented to His Majesty by the Speaker of the House of Commons for his assent no earlier than seven days after the publication of the report specified in s.6(12) below.

(12) The Chair for the time being of the Electoral Commission shall within seven days of the conduct of the referendum publish a report certifying the turnout in and result of the referendum.

7. Sections 5 and 6 create mandatory requirements

(1) The various provisos identified in s.5 and s.6 are mandatory requirements.

8. Enforcement of s.5 and s.6 – competent tribunal

(1) Any claim brought under this Act shall be heard by a panel of no fewer than seven members of the Supreme Court save that;

(a) For the purposes of the grant of interim relief under s.10 and s.12 herein, any application shall be heard by a panel of three members of the Supreme Court.

(2) In any such claim, the Supreme Court shall exercise original jurisdiction.

(3) In any such claim the Supreme Court shall make such arrangements concerning the conduct of proceedings, including but not limited to the giving of oral evidence and the cross-examination of witnesses, as it thinks fit.

9. Enforcement of s.5 and s.6 – locus standi requirements

(1) The provisions of this Act may be enforced in the following fashion.

(2) The only claimants who shall have standing to seek a remedy under this Act are:

(a) The Leader of His Majesty's opposition for the time being;

(b) The First Minister of Scotland, or Wales, or Northern Ireland for the time being;

(c) Any group of twenty or more members of the House of Commons for the time being;

10. Enforcement of s.5 and s.6 – the defendant

(1) In respect of any claim brought under this Act, the defendant shall be the Prime Minister for the time being.

11. Enforcement of s.5 and s.6 – remedies prior to 'enactment' – interim relief

(1) If, prior to the giving of the royal assent to the bill in issue, in the opinion of the Court the claimant(s) has(have) demonstrated a credible case that one or more of the mandatory requirements specified in s.5 and/or s.6(1)–(10) herein has not been complied with, then;

(a) The Court shall order that the passage of the bill in issue shall be immediately suspended until the claim has been finally heard and decided.

(2) Any such claim must be issued within 14 days of the alleged non-compliance with the relevant mandatory requirement(s).

(3) In granting an interim remedy under this section the Court may injunct any person or persons including His Majesty from taking any step which in the opinion of the court would have the effect of continuing the passage of the bill in issue.

(4) For the purposes of this section, the Court may issue such an injunction against:

(a) Any named persons or persons; and/or

(b) Any person without specifying the name of such person or persons.

12. Enforcement of s.5 and s.6 – remedies prior to 'enactment' – final relief

(1) If, prior to the giving of the royal assent to the bill in issue, in the opinion of the Court the claimant(s) has(have) demonstrated that one or more of the mandatory requirements specified in s.5 and/or s.6 herein has not been complied with, then;

(a) The Court shall order that the passage of the bill in issue shall be immediately ended.

(2) In granting a remedy under this section the Court may injunct any person or persons including His Majesty from taking any step which in the opinion of the court would have the effect of continuing the passage of the bill in issue.

(3) For the purposes of this section, the Court may issue such an injunction against:

(a) Any named persons or persons; and/or

(b) Any person without specifying the name of such person or persons.

13. Enforcement of s.5 and s.6 – remedies subsequent to 'enactment' – interim relief

(1) If, subsequent to the giving of the royal assent to the bill in issue, in the opinion of the Court the claimant(s) has(have) demonstrated a credible case that one or more of the mandatory requirements specified in s.5 and/or s.6(1)–(10) herein has not been complied with, then;

(a) The Court shall order:

(i) That His Majesty shall not exercise the prerogative power to ratify treaties in respect of any Treaty concerning the Accession of the United Kingdom to the European Union until such time as this matter has been finally heard and decided; and

(ii) Any statutory provision or provisions passed after 1 May 2024 purporting to make the United Kingdom a member of the European Union or purporting to give effect in United Kingdom law to any provision of European Union law shall be of no force or effect pending this matter being finally heard and decided.

(2) Any such claim must be issued within 14 days of the granting of the Royal Assent.

14. Enforcement of s.5 and s.6 – remedies subsequent to 'enactment' – final relief

(1) If, subsequent to the giving of the royal assent to the bill in issue, in the opinion of the Court the claimant(s) has(have) demonstrated that one or more of the mandatory requirements specified in s.5 and/or s.6(1)–(10) herein has not been complied with, then;

(a) The Court shall order that:

(i) The Act in issue is invalid ab initio and;

(ii) The United Kingdom Safeguarding of National Sovereignty Against the European Union Act 2024 retains its full force and effect; and

(iii) Any statutory provision or provisions passed after 1 May 2024 purporting to make the United Kingdom a member of the European Union or purporting to give effect in United Kingdom law to any provision of European Union law are of no force or effect.

15. Jurisdiction of the court – further matters

(1) In finally deciding any claim brought under this Act seeking prior to enactment relief within s.13 herein;

(a) The Court shall also issue a declaratory judgment in accordance with s.15 as if the bill in issue had already been purportedly enacted notwithstanding any failure of compliance with any manner and form requirement specified in s.5 and s.6 herein; and

(b) Any such declaratory judgment shall bind any tribunal or court in the United Kingdom including the Supreme Court.

16. Article 9 of the Bill of Rights and parliamentary privilege disapplied

(1) Article 9 of the Bill of Rights is disapplied for the purposes of the conduct of any proceedings and/or the grant of any remedy sought by any person or persons under this Act.

(2) No provision of parliamentary privilege shall be applicable to prevent or restrict in any fashion the conduct of any proceedings and/or the grant of any remedy sought by any person or persons under this Act.

17. Evidence

(1) For the purposes of s.5 and s.6(1)–(6) herein, the official reports of the House of Commons and House of Lords in Hansard shall be taken as prima facie evidence as to the satisfaction or otherwise of the relevant mandatory provisions; but

(a) Any party may lead such evidence as the Court thinks fit in rebuttal of that prima facie presumption.

(2) For the purposes s.6(7)–(10) herein, the report of the Chair of the Electoral Commission required by s.6(11) herein shall be taken as prima facie evidence as to the satisfaction or otherwise of the relevant mandatory provisions; but

(a) Any party may lead such evidence as the Court thinks fit in rebuttal of that prima facie presumption.

18. Interveners

(1) The Supreme Court shall admit as interveners any such person or persons identified in s.9 above who is or are not the claimant who wish to be so admitted.

19. Commencement and short title

(1) This Act shall come into force immediately upon the bill receiving the royal assent.
(2) This Act may be cited as The Safeguarding of Sovereignty Act 2024.

During the May 2024 general election campaign, the Labour, Scots Nationalist and Liberal parties all repeatedly emphasised that they wished to see The United Kingdom Safeguarding of National Sovereignty Against the European Union Act 2024 repealed and maintained consistently that the Act's entrenchment provisions were not legally effective and could be repealed by any subsequently enacted statute passed in the ordinary way. The election results were as charted in Table 8.1 below.

Sir Keir Starmer subsequently formed a minority Labour government, which attracted support from the Scots Nationalist and Liberals and some of the small parties on the basis that the government would immediately promote a bill to repeal The United Kingdom Safeguarding of National Sovereignty Against the European Union Act 2024.

Table 8.1 UK general election, 1924 (2 May 1924)

Party	% of vote	Seats won	Change
Labour	33.5	285	+83
Conservative	36.0	275	–90
Scots Nationalist	4.8	45	–3
Liberal	13.2	15	+4
Sinn Fein	1.1	10	+3
Democratic Unionists	0.9	8	–
United Kingdom Independence	7.8	4	+4
Others	3.7	8	–1

The bill, entitled The European Union (Preparation for Re-entry) Bill, was introduced into the Commons early in July 2024. It had just one section, which read: 'The United Kingdom Safeguarding of National Sovereignty Against the European Union Act 2024 is hereby repealed.' Prior to the bill beginning its parliamentary passage,

Prime Minister Starmer announced that he considered – as the Labour Party had maintained during the election campaign – that The United Kingdom Safeguarding of National Sovereignty Against the European Union Act 2024 could be repealed by any statute passed in the ordinary way.

The bill passed its second reading in the House of Commons, with some 340 members voting in favour on 8 July. The House thereupon suspended its usual standing orders and, by a majority of 20, voted to take the bill's committee, report and third reading stages in a single six-hour session on 9 July. No amendments were made to the bill at the committee or third reading stage, and the bill passed third reading, with some 335 members voting in favour.

On 10 July, the Leader of the Opposition – the Right Honourable Boris Johnson MP – issued a claim in the Supreme Court under s.12 and s.13 of The United Kingdom Safeguarding of National Sovereignty Against the European Union Act 2024. The Prime Minister promptly undertook that no further steps would be taken to progress the bill until such time as the Supreme Court had finally heard and decided the matter. Interim relief was therefore not granted, and the matter was set down for hearing in September 2024.

II. Entrenchment in the UK Context: Presumptions – Orthodox and Unorthodox – On Legal Enforceability

Quite how the Supreme Court might resolve such litigation is a matter I currently propose to pursue elsewhere.[7] In the remainder of this chapter, I will simply sketch out in broad terms how lessons drawn from a close examination of *McCawley* and *Trethowan* might impact upon the contemporary viewpoint as to how the problem might be approached. Before broaching that issue, it may be helpful to identify related issues about the nature of Parliament's sovereignty which – while fascinating jurisprudentially and important politically – are tangential to the question considered here.

Common Law Constitutionalism as an 'Entrenchment' Device

The concern in the problem outlined above is not with what is now sometimes referred to as 'common law constitutionalism' or 'the principle of legality' as a source of constraints on legislative competence.[8] The paradigmatic example of that concept examined in earlier chapters is Pope Cooper's claim in *Cooper* and its subsequent endorsement by the State

[7] I have written several flaws into the text of my hypothetical Act and deliberately omitted other pertinent matters, and one lesson that writing this book and the *Harris* study has imparted is that I have very likely overlooked (many) other weaknesses in my Act's provisions.

[8] Nor am I considering circumstances in which Parliament's capacity to make law in the 'ordinary way' is removed by the oblique expedient of Parliament, with its last act (or Act), abolishing itself and promulgating a wholly new constitutional order in which lawmaking powers are allocated to one or more new legislative bodies in a fashion which precludes reinstatement of the abolishing legislature (whether at all or only at the initiative of a newly defined sovereign lawmaker). Similarly, I am bypassing any assessment of the force of contention that the Treaty of Union 1701 between Scotland and England and the respective Acts of Union

Supreme Court and High Court in *McCawley*.[9] The *Cooper* constraint was not onerous in terms of political achievability; bicameral bare majorities approving express provisions in two separate Acts (a separation that could – perhaps – be mere seconds) was all that was required. Nonetheless, that judicially engineered departure from the 'ordinary way' of legislating was of course dismissed as 'embarrassing and even ridiculous' in the Privy Council in *McCawley*,[10] the dismissal being rooted in Feez and Stumm's inability to identify any explicit legislative source for 'Two Act entrenchment'. The promulgation by the High Court in *Cooper* of Two Act entrenchment as a legally enforceable characteristic of Queensland's Constitution – and the High Court's endorsement of that principle in *McCawley* – could not in themselves, in the Privy Council's view, provide the principle with a legal base. That base could only be found in the most explicit ('with meticulous precision') of legislative provisos, be they Queensland or Imperial in origin.

In the modern UK context, the notion of common law constitutionalism or the principle of legality[11] as an entrenchment device has been expressed in various contexts as a means to require that there be express rather than implied repeal of certain statutes or statutory provisions. The 'modern' origins of the idea can be traced to a series of judgments identifying certain 'basic rights' with which statutory provisions could interfere only if stated to do so in express terms or – an addendum rather weakening the force of the principle – by necessary implication.[12] The most obvious and oft-cited exemplar of the idea is Lord Hoffmann's comment in *R v Secretary of State for the Home Department, ex parte Simms*:[13]

> Parliamentary sovereignty means that Parliament can, if it chooses, legislate contrary to fundamental principles of human rights. The Human Rights Act 1998 will not detract from this power. The constraints upon its exercise by Parliament are ultimately political, not legal. But the principle of legality means that Parliament must squarely confront what it is doing and accept the political cost. Fundamental rights cannot be overridden by general or ambiguous words. This is because there is too great a risk that the full implications of their unqualified meaning may have passed unnoticed in the democratic process.[14]

Lord Hoffmann developed the theoretical foundations of this concept in a lecture delivered two years later.[15] Hoffmann's rationale for the legality principle – 'that Parliament must squarely confront …' – is essentially on all fours with the political premise

passed by the Scots and English Parliaments created a new nation with a Parliament of limited competence; on which point, see especially the insightful critiques by Smith (1957) 'The Union of 1707 as fundamental law' *Public Law* 99; MacCormick (1978) 'Does the United Kingdom have a constitution? *Northern Ireland Law Quarterly* 1; Upton (1989) 'Marriage vows of the elephant: the constitution of 1707' *LQR* 79; Wickes (2001) 'A new constitution for a new state: the 1707 Union of England and Scotland' *LQR* 109.

[9] Vol 1 pp 221–28 respectively. I regard the suggestion (vol 1 p 284) that Two Act entrenchment had a statutory root in s.106 of the Commonwealth Constitution Act 1900 as untenable.

[10] Vol 1 p 310.

[11] See especially Poole (2003) 'Back to the future? Unearthing the theory of common law constitutionalism' *OJLS* 435; Jowell (2006) 'Parliamentary sovereignty under the new constitutional hypothesis' *Public Law* 562; Steyn (2006) 'Democracy, the rule of law and the role of the judges' *EHRLR* 243; Young (2020) 'Fundamental common law rights and legislation' in Elliot and Hughes (eds) *Common law constitutional rights.*

[12] See eg *R & W Paul Ltd v Wheat Commission* [1937] AC 139; *Raymond v Honey* [1983] 1 AC 1. For a discussion of these and similar cases, see Browne Wilkinson (1992) 'The infiltration of a Bill of Rights' *Public Law* 397.

[13] [2000] 2 AC 115.

[14] ibid 131; emphasis added.

[15] (2002) 'Democracy through law' *European Human Rights LR* 723. The lecture offers a forceful counterpoint to suggestions that judicial lawmaking is 'undemocratic'.

underlying Pope Cooper's Two Act entrenchment device.[16] Reduced to essentials, that rationale is that if the legislature wishes to enact what judges regard as morally unpalatable laws, then the (almost certainly) government proponents of such laws must – by being candid as to the effect of the proposed laws – render themselves accountable during the enactment process to questioning and criticism from either house, in the press or from the public. It takes but little reflection to see that this principle interferes with Parliament's lawmaking process – as well as subjecting the outcome of that process to an unusual interpretive paradigm – in the limited sense that the relevant express terms the court requires in the Act must have been laid out in the text of the bill at some point during its enactment (at least at the final stage of the bill's passage).

It is obviously easy to suggest that the principle is 'undemocratic', both because the list of 'rights' which merit protection against implied repeal are a judicial rather than statutory creation and because of the judiciary's unelected status. But this – equally obviously – is to take a rather simplistic view of what democratic lawmaking might entail.[17] A recurrent theme of the events studied in this book is the frequent non-engagement of legislators with the measures being enacted, and the frequent incompetence of their participation when they do try to engage with bill's texts. This is not to suggest that such failings are a ubiquitous feature of Parliament's lawmaking in the modern era; it is merely to note that if one equates 'democratic' legislative lawmaking with careful, thorough and expert evaluation of bills then the 'democratic' credentials of much contemporary legislation may be rather wanting. Analytical rigour is perhaps a more common element of the judicial than of the legislative process.[18]

The boundary lines of the common law legality principle are blurred by its intermingling with developments consequent upon the UK's accession to the European Economic Community and the passage of the European Communities Act 1972. The initial source of this evident innovation is the House of Lords' 1991 judgment in *Factortame (No 2)*,[19] and in particular a passage in the judgment of Lord Bridge:

> If the supremacy within the European Community of Community law over the national law of member states was not always inherent in the E.E.C. Treaty (Cmnd. 5179-II) it was certainly well established in the jurisprudence of the European Court of Justice long before the United Kingdom joined the Community. Thus, whatever limitation of its sovereignty Parliament accepted when it enacted the European Communities Act 1972 was entirely voluntary. Under the terms of the Act of 1972 it has always been clear that it was the duty of a United Kingdom court, when delivering final judgment, to override any rule of national law found to be in conflict with any directly enforceable rule of Community law.

Quite how that 'limitation' had been achieved was unfortunately not something that the House of Lords explained. The judgment did not endorse the position

[16] Vol 1 p 216.

[17] For a very clearly 'undemocratic' – and often overlooked – early application of the principle, see both *Chortlton v Lings* (1868) LR 4 CP 374 and *Nairn v University of St Andrews* [1909] AC 147, in which the courts (the House of Lords in *Nairn*) held that Parliament could not effect so momentous a constitutional change as enfranchising women by anything other than the most explicit of textual formulae.

[18] Such criticism of judicial lawmaking may also ignore questions relating to the 'democratic' credentials of laws governing a legislature's composition: appointive and hereditary rather than elective in the Lords, and national governments formed within the Commons on the basis of minority electoral support.

[19] *R v Secretary of State for Transport, ex parte Factortame (No 2)* [1991] 1 AC 603.

taken by the European Court of Justice (ECJ) in *Van Gend*, *Costa* and *Internationale Handelsgesellchaft*[20] that community law had an inherent capacity to – to use a generic term – 'override' provisions of national law, whatever the respective normative status of the domestic and community law measures in issue. From that perspective, the terms of any domestic legal provision would be an unnecessary irrelevance to the status of community law in the domestic legal order.[21]

There was obviously no proviso in the European Communities Act 1972 that (expressly) sought to safeguard the legal effect of any of its provisions against implied repeal. The best that can be said in defence of the assertion that the House of Lords' *Factortame* innovation had a base in the 1972 Act is – with some irony – that it was *implied* in s.2's tortuously worded proviso that domestic courts construe and apply statutory provisions – whether pre- or post-dating the 1972 Act coming into force – in a fashion which gave force to directly effective community law; and in s.3's requirement that UK courts had to follow the ECJ's case law in respect of the meaning and effect of any community law provision.[22]

Factortame entrenchment was likely a politically feeble creature, being purely linguistic in nature and lacking even the Two Act formality of Pope Cooper's entrenchment device.[23] Nonetheless, in holding that directly effective community law could not be impliedly repealed by domestic legislation, the House of Lords was proposing a distinct departure from orthodox constitutional theories.

Whether *Factortame* entrenchment was also a judicially engineered stepping stone towards a more significant departure from the 'ordinary way' of legislating was – unfortunately perhaps – never put to a legal test. The third Thatcher government and the subsequent Major administrations lacked the political inclination or courage to promote a new merchant shipping bill which expressly provided that domestic courts were to apply the terms of the Act – if enacted – irrespective of any inconsistency between those terms and any directly effective provision of community law.

The weak nature of *Factortame* entrenchment as a constraint on bicameral[24] bare majoritarian lawmaking may in part explain the readiness of some UK judges – both in court and in the academic press – to suggest that *Factortame*'s express repeal principle can properly be applied as a defence protecting some other statutory provisions against implied repeal. Such reasoning lacks even the flimsy fig leaf of a statutory source to

[20] Respectively Case 26/62 *Van Gen den Loos v Nederlandse Administratie der Belastingen* [1963] ECR 1; Case 6/64 *Costa v ENEL* [1964] CMLR 425; Case 11/70 *Internationale Handelsgesellsshaft v Einfuhr- und Vorratsstelle für Getreide und Futtermitte* [1970] ECR 1125.

[21] For various explanations, see especially Allan (1997) 'Parliamentary sovereignty: law politics and revolution' *LQR* 433; Wade (1996) 'Sovereignty – revolution or evolution' *LQR* 568; Craig (1991) 'Sovereignty of the United Kingdom Parliament after *Factortame*' *Yearbook of European Law* 221. Nor did *Factortame (No 2)* endorse the ECJ's position that a country, on acceding to the Community, had limited its national sovereignty; ie, in the UK context, it would be the Queen's exercise of her prerogative power to sign the Treaty of Accession, not the 1972 Act, that was legally significant. This point was grasped by Raymond Blackburn – if by few others in the United Kingdom – in *Blackburn v Attorney-General* [1971] 1 WLR 1037.

[22] There is no verbatim reference to the 'supremacy' or 'precedence' (or, indeed, direct effect) of community law in s.2 or s.3.

[23] The 'likely' caveat acknowledges the point that the 'express repeal' case law does not tell us just how 'express' express repeal might have to be in order to be recognised by the courts as legally effective.

[24] Constitutional theorists with too much time on their hands might wonder if a 'statute' which made provision for express disapplication of some directly effective European Union law would have been recognised as valid by UK courts if enacted under the Parliament Act procedure.

which *Factortame* entrenchment might lay claim and can only be rooted in variations on the theme of the common law principle of legality.

We nonetheless find ourselves, some 30 years after *Factortame (No 2)*, roaming a constitutional landscape in which several (if not quite many) statutory provisions, whether of recent vintage (eg the Human Rights Act and the devolution legislation) or much more historically remote (eg Magna Carta and the Bill of Rights), have also been pronounced by the senior courts to be immune to implied repeal. It is now not unusual to see the notion of the 'constitutional' status of a statutory provision being invoked by the courts as a justification to engage in all manner of weird and wonderful interpretive techniques to sustain a conclusion that although s.*x* of statute *y* does appear on first (or even second and third) reading to breach some or all provisions of 'constitutional statute' *z*, Parliament could not possibly have intended to produce that effect and therefore s.*x* must mean something other than what its plain words obviously require.

The concept of the 'constitutional statute' will likely be Sir John Laws's primary contribution to our public law jurisprudence. The idea was sketched out in a series of academic articles in the 1990s,[25] and then applied in obiter comments within his judgment in *Thoburn v Sunderland City Council*:[26]

> We should recognise a hierarchy of Acts of Parliament: as it were 'ordinary' statutes and 'constitutional' statutes. The two categories must be distinguished on a principled basis. In my opinion a constitutional statute is one which (a) conditions the legal relationship between citizen and State in some general, overarching manner, or (b) enlarges or diminishes the scope of what we would now regard as fundamental constitutional rights … Examples are the Magna Carta, the Bill of Rights 1688, the Act of Union, the Reform Acts which distributed and enlarged the franchise, the HRA, the Scotland Act 1998 and the Government of Wales Act 1998. The ECA clearly belongs in this family.[27]

Sir John's justification for affording these 'fundamental (statutory) constitutional rights' protection against implicit alteration or repeal overlaps substantially with Lord Hoffmann's analysis in *Simms*. The rationale, in essence, is that certain moral values – whether found in common law (*Simms*) or statute (*Thoburn*) – are too important to be left at the mercy of mendaciously or incompetently enacted legislation.

Thoburn itself was not appealed to a higher court. However, in subsequent judgments, the House of Lords/Supreme Court has given a clear imprimatur to John Laws' analysis; the best illustration is perhaps a passage in the Supreme Court's decision in *R (HS2 Action Alliance Ltd) v Secretary of State for Transport*:[28]

> 207. The United Kingdom has no written constitution, but we have a number of constitutional instruments. They include Magna Carta, the Petition of Right 1628, the Bill of Rights and (in Scotland) the Claim of Rights Act 1689, the Act of Settlement 1701 and the Act of Union 1707. The European Communities Act 1972, the Human Rights Act 1998 and the Constitutional Reform Act 2005 may now be added to this list. The common law itself also recognises certain principles as fundamental to the rule of law.

[25] Laws (1993) 'Is the High Court the guardian of fundamental constitutional rights?' *Public Law* 59; (1995) 'Law and democracy' *Public Law* 72; (1998) 'The limitations of human rights' *Public Law* 254.

[26] [2002] 1 CLMR 1461.

[27] ibid para 62.

[28] [2014] UKSC 3, [2014] 1 WLR 324.

Lord Hoffmann's principle of legality in relation to common law principles has also enjoyed continued judicial endorsement, culminating most recently in the majority Supreme Court opinion in *R (Privacy International) v Investigatory Powers Tribunal*,[29] which, in addition to engaging in some distinctly unconvincing interpretive adventures to neuter a statutory ouster clause, made speculative comments about the Court's potential willingness to refuse to apply statutory provisions which were inconsistent with judicial understandings of 'the rule of law'.

These developments have, of course, stimulated a great outpouring of fascinating academic literature assessing the legality and legitimacy of judicially created[30] and enforced limits to Parliament's lawmaking powers.[31] I do not propose to add here to that particular debate. My interest is in the rather narrower question of how the courts would respond to Parliament's explicit attempt – enacted with the most 'meticulous precision' – to constrain its own future legislative power in circumstances where a court could not credibly dress up resistance to the government that had successfully promoted such an Act in terms of interpretive innovation. No government has yet sought to promote a bill which – if enacted – would put this question to the test.

Orthodox Views on the Legal Enforceability of a Statutory Entrenchment Device …

Should a lame duck Johnson government – as outlined above – succumb to the temptation to do so, the 'orthodox' position in respect of my imaginary problem is that Prime Minister Starmer (channelling his inner – if hitherto unknown – Tom Ryan and appearing as defendant's leading counsel as well as defendant)[32] would succeed in persuading the Supreme Court that the legislative 'rigmarole' and 'malarkey' embarked upon by the Commons and Lords at the Johnson administration's behest – while a fascinating topic for academic discussion – simply could not empower the Court to prevent Parliament from repealing The United Kingdom Safeguarding of National Sovereignty Against the European Union Act 2024 in the ordinary way, and nor could the House of Commons, the House of Lords and the Monarch be prevented by the Court from exercising their usual legislative functions in the 'ordinary way'. Sir Keir might even suggest – before turning to domestic legal authority – that Mr Johnson's statute has no more constitutional significance than a Dog Act.[33] The question is simple: 'Can Parliament bind its successors?' The answer is similarly simple: 'No.'[34]

[29] [2020] AC 491. For early comment, see Ong (2020) 'The ouster of parliamentary sovereignty' *Public Law* 41; Elliot and Young (2019) '*Privacy International* in the Supreme Court: jurisdiction, the rule of law and parliamentary sovereignty' *Cambridge LJ* 490.

[30] For present purposes, I regard *Factortame* entrenchment as a judicial 'creation', given the lack of any meticulously precise enunciation of the principle in the European Communities Act 1972.

[31] Among the most thought-provoking of which are Elliot (2003) 'Embracing constitutional legislation: towards fundamental law' *NILQ* 25; (2017) 'Judicial power and the United Kingdom's changing constitution' *Queensland LJ* 274; Young (2020) 'Fundamental common law rights and legislation' in Elliot and Hughes (eds) *Common law constitutional rights*; Allan (2011) 'Questions of legality and legitimacy: form and substance in British constitutionalism' *International Journal of Constitutional Law* 155; Ahmed and Parry (2017) 'Constitutional statutes' *OJLS* 461; Craig (2014) 'Constitutionalising constitutional law' *Public Law* 373.

[32] Vol 1 pp 280–82 and 307.

[33] Unlike Lord Birkenhead in *McCawley*, Sir Keir would understand Higgins's observation; vol 1 p 309.

[34] For reasons of dramatic licence, I assume the Court would, in exercising its power under s.8(3), inter alia ask the defendant to make submissions first.

The Enrolled Bill Rule Cases

One supposed pillar of the immortality of the 'ordinary way' of legislating is the cluster of so-called enrolled bill rule cases, notably *Edinburgh and Dalkeith Railway v Wauchope*, *Lee v Bude and Torrington Railway* and the modern treatment of the question by the House of Lords in *Pickin v British Rail.*[35] The point raised initially in *Wauchope* – although not actually pursued in the House of Lords – was that a (private) Act of Parliament would be void if its process of enactment did not comply with House of Commons standing orders.[36] Viewed in isolation, statements of several members of the Court suggest that any statutory attempt to control the 'manner and form' of Parliament's lawmaking process would be futile:

> I will only add one word on a point which has been abandoned at this Bar, but an idea of the value of which seems to have prevailed in the Court below; namely, that the want of notice in one of the preliminary stages of an Act of Parliament, operates to prevent that Act from affecting the rights of the parties to whom such notice ought to have been given. Such a doctrine is wholly without justification.[37] …
>
> There is no foundation for such an idea; but such an impression appears to have existed in Scotland, and I express my clear opinion upon it, that no such erroneous idea may exist in future.[38] …
>
> I cannot but express my surprise that such a notion should ever have prevailed. There is no foundation whatever for it. All that a Court of Justice can do is to look to the Parliamentary roll: if from that it should appear that a bill has passed both Houses and received the Royal assent, no Court of Justice can inquire into the mode in which it was introduced into Parliament, nor into what was done previous to its introduction, or what passed in Parliament during its progress in its various stages through both Houses.[39]

The issue in *Lee* was alleged fraud on the part of the relevant Act's promoters, but that was an allegation the court considered it had no competence to investigate:

> We sit here as servants of the Queen and the legislature. Are we to act as regents over what is done by parliament with the consent of the Queen, lords, and commons? I deny that any such authority exists. If an Act of Parliament has been obtained improperly, it is for the legislature to correct it by repealing it: but, so long as it exists as law, the Courts are bound to obey it. The proceedings here are judicial, not autocratic, which they would be if we could make laws instead of administering them.[40]

The (near) modern era House of Lords judgment in *Pickin*[41] (also concerned with alleged fraud in a bill's promotion) firmly approved the conclusion reached in

[35] Respectively *Wauchope* (1842) 8 Cl and Fin 710; 8 ER 279 (HL); *Lee* (1871) LR 6 CP 576; *Pickin* [1974] AC 765 (HL).

[36] The relevant standing order here being that the person affected by the bill, if enacted, be given notice of its passage so that they could make representations as to its contents if they wished to do so.

[37] *Wauchope* (1842) 8 Cl and Fin 710, 720 (Lord Brougham).

[38] ibid (Lord Cottenham).

[39] ibid 725 (Lord Campbell).

[40] *Lee* (1871) LR 6 CP 576, 582 (Willes J). The judgment was a first instance decision of the Court of Common Pleas.

[41] [1974] AC 765 (HL).

Wauchope and *Lee* and contains similarly forceful statements of the Court's incapacity to interrogate the conduct of the legislative process, particularly per Lord Morris:

> The question of fundamental importance which arises is whether the court should entertain the proposition that an Act of Parliament can so be assailed in the courts that matters should proceed as though the Act or some part of it had never been passed. I consider that such doctrine would be dangerous and impermissible. It is the function of the courts to administer the laws which Parliament has enacted. In the processes of Parliament there will be much consideration whether a Bill should or should not in one form or another become an enactment. When an enactment is passed there is finality unless and until it is amended or repealed by Parliament.[42]

Lord Wilberforce added a pragmatic – evidential – justification for that legal principle:

> I do not understand how the courts can inquire whether Parliament was misled by this recital into enacting section 18. How can we know how Parliament understood the recital – who is 'Parliament' for this purpose – the members of both Houses or of either House – the members of the committee on private Bills – the counsel who advise the chairmen of these committees – the officials whose business it is to look at recitals and at the Bill? We know nothing, and by no process short of summoning some or all of these persons and examining their records can we find out on what view of the facts or on what consideration of policy section 18 was enacted …[43]

The government's submission would surely be that if: "no Court of Justice can inquire into the mode in which [a bill] was introduced into Parliament, nor into what was done previous to its introduction, or what passed in Parliament during its progress in its various stages through both Houses", then the undisputed facts that s.6(2) and (3)[44] had not been complied with are irrelevant in this litigation, as they would be had the bill completed its passage in the orthodox fashion. The Prime Minister would obviously have to concede that *Wauchope* et al *sensu stricto* address only circumstances in which an 'Act' has indeed been 'enacted'. None of the claimants in those cases had sought to injunct the continued passage of the relevant bill prior to its enactment, as is the situation in this case. But what is prohibited to the courts by *Wauchope*, *Lee* and *Pickin* is intrusion into the parliamentary lawmaking process, and such forbidden intrusion is manifestly what Mr Johnson is asking the Court to undertake.

The Implied Repeal Cases

Sir Keir might also invoke the much-cited 1934 judgment of the Court of Appeal in *Ellen Street Estates v Minister of Health*[45] to sustain the proposition that were Parliament to enact a statutory provision in respect of matter A, B or C ordering the courts not to

[42] ibid 788–89: exhibiting (a point Mr Starmer would diplomatically not allude to) a splendid ignorance of or indifference to the empirical reality of some (much?) legislative lawmaking; vol 1 pp 44–52 and 105–114.

[43] ibid 796. The evidential task in *Wauchope* – relating just to the giving of notice – would have been much less onerous. See also Lord Simon (ibid 799), offering the more dramatic pragmatic reason of avoiding 'dangerous strains' between the law courts and Parliament.

[44] At least eight weeks between Commons second and third reading and approval by at least 400 members at Commons third reading respectively.

[45] [1934] 1 KB 590.

recognise as valid any subsequent statutory provision affecting matter A, B or C unless that subsequent provision identified its proposed effect on matter A, B or C in terms specified by the initial Act, the courts would nevertheless be bound to apply any subsequent statutory provision which did affect matters A, B or C irrespective of whether or not that provision did use the express form of words required by the original Act. The Supreme Court would surely be taken to several passages in *Ellen Street* rejecting the proposition that Parliament could require the courts only to recognise *express* repeal (or amendment) of particular legislative provisions.

For Scrutton LJ, the suggestion that Parliament could do so was:

> [A]bsolutely contrary to the constitutional position that Parliament can alter an Act previously passed, and it can do so by repealing in terms the previous Act – Mr. Hill agrees that it may do so – and it can do it also in another way – namely, by enacting a provision which is clearly inconsistent with the previous Act.[46]

And per Maugham LJ – his legal career not having been handicapped, it seems, by the dismissive treatment accorded to his submissions in *McCawley* before the Privy Council:[47]

> The Legislature cannot, according to our constitution, bind itself as to the form of subsequent legislation, and it is impossible for Parliament to enact that in a subsequent statute dealing with the same subject-matter there can be no implied repeal. If in a subsequent Act Parliament chooses to make it plain that the earlier statute is being to some extent repealed, effect must be given to that intention just because it is the will of the Legislature.[48]

The Wade Analysis

The Supreme Court has latterly become much more willing to accept that academic analyses may have something of value to say in litigation concerning basic constitutional principles. Any advocate of orthodoxy would likely focus primarily, however, on William Wade's much cited and evidently very influential paper in the 1955 *Cambridge Law Journal* – 'The basis of legal sovereignty'. Wade's analysis is too well known to require extensive recitation here. Its central proposition for current purposes is that the orthodox understanding of Parliament's sovereignty is not a legal concept at all – and hence not amenable to change through any legal process – but an 'ultimate political fact' consequent on the outcome of the 1688 revolution, and therefore alterable only through a subsequent revolution which created a new (set of) ultimate political fact(s). In Wade's view, *Trethowan* (and *Harris*) can provide no support for 'manner and form' entrenchment being effective in the UK context, since the powers of both legislatures – and, indeed, the legislatures themselves – derived not from 'ultimate political facts', but from a UK statute, a legal source which in the *Trethowan* scenario permitted the legislature acting in the ordinary way to create such entrenchment and which in *Harris* imposed such entrenchment ab initio.

[46] ibid 595–96.
[47] Vol 1 pp 307 and 310.
[48] *Ellen Street* [1934] 1 KB 590, 597.

Prime Minister Starmer might happily concede – as did Professor Wade some 40 years on from publication of his seminal paper[49] – that *Factortame* entrenchment can be explained as a (thus far) *sui generis* instance of such a 'revolution' having occurred when Parliament enacted the European Communities Act 1972. It is – if one were to adopt (as the Prime Minister's opponent no doubt would) a nonsensical cliché – the exception that proves the rule. Sir Keir might indeed readily go further and concede with similar good grace that the notion of 'constitutional statutes', despite the imprecision of its juridic origins, has become a sound one within the UK's constitutional law. And he could readily accept that both the 2024 Act and the Starmer bill (if enacted) should properly be regarded as 'constitutional statutes'. But – he might continue – those concessions take Mr Johnson only so far – and not far enough to win the argument.

The concession the Prime Minister presumably would not and could not make is that the requirement for *express repeal* of 'constitutional statutes' – which must, given the repeal of the European Communities Act 1972, exist (in 2024) solely as a matter of common law – does not extend so far as to require the courts to apply entrenching legislation in which Parliament has specified exactly what form of words is required in a subsequent Act's title and content. The contention would surely be that the meaning of 'express repeal' is a matter for the court to determine and that the Starmer bill (if enacted) is cast in terms which manifestly have that effect in respect of the 2024 Act.

The Relevance of Miller (No 2)

The government's submissions would likely also be rooted in some of the observations made by the Supreme Court in *Miller v The Prime Minister* (hereafter *Miller (No 2)*).[50] Baroness Hale had perhaps made that judgment something of a hostage to fortune by suggesting that it was a "one-off".[51] It should not come as a surprise to any informed political observer that a government which would try to close 'Parliament' down temporarily to prevent questioning of its primary policy agenda would also be willing to try to prevent 'Parliament' addressing that matter at all in future. *Miller (No 2)*'s ratio is, of course, restricted to judicial control of the prerogative power of prorogation; but the reasoning underlying the ratio may lend itself to rather broader application. The unappreciated consequences of *Miller (No 2)* for our hypothetical entrenchment litigation are not difficult to discern. They are found in part at paras 38–40 of the judgment:

> 39 … ["The Constitution"] includes numerous principles of law, which are enforceable by the courts in the same way as other legal principles. In giving them effect, the courts have the responsibility of upholding the values and principles of our constitution and making them effective. It is their particular responsibility to determine the legal limits of the powers conferred on each branch of government, and to decide whether any exercise of power has transgressed those limits. The courts cannot shirk that responsibility merely on the ground that the question raised is political in tone or context.

[49] (1996) 'Sovereignty – revolution or evolution?' *LQR* 568.
[50] [2019] UKSC 41, [2020] AC 373.
[51] ibid para 1.

> 40. The legal principles of the constitution are not confined … include … principle of the separation of powers between the executive, Parliament and the courts:
>
> 41. Two fundamental principles of our constitutional law are relevant to the present case. The first is the principle of Parliamentary sovereignty: that laws enacted by the Crown in Parliament are the supreme form of law in our legal system, with which everyone, including the government, must comply …

'The Crown in Parliament' qua legislative 'sovereign', Sir Keir would submit, has since 1688 been recognised as expressing itself through a bare majority in each House followed by the royal assent. That is a constitutional principle with which everyone – which 'everyone' includes obviously the Supreme Court – 'must comply'. But for the Court to enforce the 2024 Act would be to prevent 'the Crown in Parliament' from exercising its sovereign power; in doing so, the Court would be 'transgressing the limits' of its own powers according to our accepted 'constitutional principles'; it would be undermining the principle of the separation of powers by turning the 'Crown in Parliament' into a legislature of limited competence. If the Court in these circumstances applied the 2024 Act's requirements for an enhanced Commons majority and a referendum to any measure effecting its (express) repeal, the Court would be 'shirking the responsibility … of upholding the values and principles of our constitution and making them effective'.[52]

Adapting the analysis offered in *Miller (No 2)* to fit the scenario currently before the Court, Sir Keir might then turn to para 49 of the judgment:

> [I]t is of some assistance to consider how the courts have dealt with situations where the exercise of a power conferred by statute, rather than one arising under the prerogative, was liable to affect the operation of a constitutional principle. The approach which they have adopted has concentrated on the effect of the exercise of the power upon the operation of the relevant constitutional principle. Unless the terms of the statute indicate a contrary intention, the courts have set a limit to the lawful exercise of the power by holding that the extent to which the measure impedes or frustrates the operation of the relevant principle must have a reasonable justification.

The 'power conferred' here, of course, is conferred on the Court rather than on the Executive, that power prima facie being – to move to para 50 of *Miller (No 2)* – to: "prevent or frustrate the ability of Parliament to carry out its constitutional functions as a legislature". The 2024 Act in effect does not just 'impede or frustrate' the operation of a constitutional principle; it obliterates that principle entirely. Any justification for it would have to be similarly extreme. Absent such justification, the (purported) power conferred on the Court is not a valid power at all.[53]

Submissions might end – blending the legal and political – by invoking Birkenhead's 'shackles' metaphor from *McCawley*:[54]

> Some communities, and notably Great Britain, have not in the framing of constitutions felt it necessary, or thought it useful, to shackle the complete independence of their successors.

[52] One could concede that express repeal is not inconsistent with the principle of bare majoritarianism.

[53] One might expect here that the government would meet the 'contrary intention' caveat by – with delicious irony – submitting that such intention to be effective would have had to be expressed in the 2024 Act in the most explicit of terms, ie a s.1 which stated: "The powers conferred on the Supreme Court by this Act are intended to amend and restrict the constitutional principle that the Crown in Parliament acting through bicameral simple majority and the grant of the royal assent may enact legislation on any subject whatsoever …"

[54] Vol 1 p 308.

> They have shrunk from the assumption that a degree of wisdom and foresight has been conceded to their generation which will be or may be wanting to their successors, in spite of the fact that those successors will possess more experience of the circumstances and necessities amid which their lives are lived …[55]

Sir Keir would finally conclude with a *McCawley*-inspired rhetorical flourish that the 2024 Act denigrates and seeks to destroy the "spirt and genius"[56] of the UK's Constitution, a project to which the Supreme Court should not be a party; or perhaps – reaching further back into our constitutional history and citing a rather more distinguished jurist than Birkenhead – it would assert that the 2024 Act seeks: "to set the judicial power above that of the legislature, which would be subversive of all government".[57]

And Unorthodox Views on the Legal Enforceability of a Statutory Entrenchment Device …

If one is to use *Trethowan* as a springboard from which to assail orthodox theories, the obvious jump-off point is a passage in Dixon's High Court judgment. Having explained that drawing an analogy with the power of the UK's Parliament is of no assistance in determining s.7A's legal effect – since the UK's Parliament is 'sovereign' while the legislature of New South Wales is not – Dixon then observed:

> It must not be supposed, however, that all difficulties would vanish if the full doctrine of parliamentary supremacy could be invoked. An Act of the British Parliament which contained a provision that no Bill repealing any part of the Act including the part so restraining its own repeal should be presented for the royal assent unless the Bill were first approved by the electors, would have the force of law until the Sovereign actually did assent to a Bill for its repeal. In strictness it would be an unlawful proceeding to present such a Bill for the royal assent before it had been approved by the electors. If, before the Bill received the assent of the Crown, it was found possible, as appears to have been done in this appeal, to raise for judicial decision the question whether it was lawful to present the Bill for that assent, the Courts would be bound to pronounce it unlawful to do so.
>
> Moreover, if it happened that, notwithstanding the statutory inhibition, the Bill did receive the royal assent although it was not submitted to the electors, the Courts might be called upon to consider whether the supreme legislative power in respect of the matter had in truth been exercised in the manner required for its authentic expression and by the elements in which it had come to reside.[58]

That sentiment is echoed in Baroness Hale's recent musing in *R (Jackson) v Attorney-General*[59] about Parliament's capacity to 'redefine itself':

> 163. If the sovereign Parliament can redefine itself downwards, to remove or modify the requirement for the consent of the Upper House, it may very well be that it can also re-define

[55] [1920] AC 691, 703.

[56] ibid.

[57] The quote is from Blackstone (1765) *Commentaries on the Laws of England* p62.

[58] (1931) 44 CLR 394, 426. Dixon subsequently developed these ideas in several academic articles and lectures: (1935), (1955), (1957) op cit.

[59] [2005] UKHL 56, [2006] 1 AC 262. In this judgment, the House of Lords – rather surprisingly – held that the legislatures created by the Parliament Act 1911 (ie a bare majority in the Commons plus the Monarch after

> itself upwards, to require a particular Parliamentary majority or a popular referendum for particular types of measure. In each case, the courts would be respecting the will of the sovereign Parliament as constituted when that will had been expressed. But that is for another day.

That 'other day' now having arrived, Mr Johnson's counsel would likely begin by submitting that the Court was now faced with a question it has never before been asked to answer, and had been presented by Mr Starmer with judicial and academic authorities which were really not at all on point, and with a stage-setting question that was 'simple' not in the sense of being straightforward, but of lacking subtlety and sophistication. Better 'simple' questions might be:

1. Will the courts enforce statutory provisions which alter the respective constitutions (in the sense of composition)[60] of the House of Commons and/or the House of Lords?
2. Will the courts enforce statutory provisions which alter the respective powers of the House of Commons and/or the House of Lords?
3. Will the courts enforce statutory provisions which alter the respective privileges of the House of Commons and/or the House of Lords?
4. Will the courts enforce statutory provisions which alter the lawmaking procedures of the House of Commons and/or the House of Lords?

The answer to the first three questions is manifestly 'Yes'. Why, then, is the answer to the fourth question 'No'? It is surely not – Johnson's counsel would suggest – because of the authorities relied upon by the Prime Minister.

The Enrolled Bill Rule Cases

None of the judges who sat in *Wauchope* or *Lee* troubled themselves with explaining the legal basis of their conclusions. That basis must, however, have lain in common law presumptions as to the scope of parliamentary privilege and/or a simple application of Article 9 of the Bill of Rights. Of the five Law Lords who sat in *Pickin*, Lords Reid, Wilberforce, Cross and Morris also skipped over that issue, contenting themselves with approving the judgments reached in *Wauchope*, *Lee* and several other like cases. Only Lord Simon addressed the question directly, suggesting that both sources were applicable and led to the same conclusion.

No particular subtlety underlies the argument that the conclusions reached in the enrolled bill rule cases rest entirely on the basis that the judicial intervention being sought did not have a *statutory* source at all. That intervention could at most – in a normative sense – have been rooted in the common law on the intertwined assumption that the privilege in issue did not fall within Article 9. But unless we were suddenly to

a bill passed in the Commons has been rejected three times in the Lords) and by the Parliament Act 1949 (ie a bare majority in the Commons plus the Monarch after a bill passed in the Commons has been rejected twice times in the Lords) is as much a sovereign legislature as Parliament in its orthodox bicameral bar majority plus royal assent form.

[60] ie inter alia how many members each house has; how those members are chosen; and the qualifications for membership.

accept the patently absurd proposition that parliamentary privilege – independently of Article 9 – has a normatively superior status to statute, such judicial non-intervention could not stand in the face of an express statutory command that the courts must accept jurisdiction to interfere. Accepting Article 9 to be a 'constitutional' statutory provision[61] – and so immune to implied alteration or repeal – Article 9 has in this matter been expressly disapplied by s.16 of the 2024 Act. The Court could not credibly refuse to intervene here on the basis simply of following *Wauchope* and *Pickin*: to do so, it would have to make new law;[62] and such new law would be in substance not evolutionary but revolutionary.[63]

The Implied Repeal Cases

Mr Johnson's counsel would make similarly short work of *Ellen Street Estates*. The textual basis for the claimant's argument in *Ellen Street Estates* is, frankly, risible – the product perhaps of counsels' overactive imaginations[64] and an unscrupulous slum landlord's financial desperation; a combination not well placed to advance the cause of radical constitutional reform. All one finds in s.7 of the Acquisition of Land (Assessment of Compensation) Act 1919 supporting the claim of a prohibition on implied repeal is this:

> s.7(1) The provisions of the Act or order by which land is authorised to be acquired, or of any Act incorporated therewith, shall, in relation to matters dealt with in this Act, have effect subject to this Act, and so far as inconsistent with this Act shall cease to have or shall not have effect.

The claimant's argument hinged entirely on the 'or shall not have' phrase, the meaning of which is at best obscure.[65] There is no obvious basis for treating the ratio of the judgment as being that a statutory provision (A) which in express terms identifies itself and/or other statutory provisions (B, C etc) as amenable to repeal or amendment only by a future statutory provision which expressly identifies provision A, B or C as being repealed or amended has no legal effect as a means to prevent provision A, B or C being impliedly repealed or amended by subsequent legislation. The judges in the Court of Appeal certainly offered blunt statements as to constitutional orthodoxy – but in doing

[61] Mr Johnson – at least in this case – would surely accept this to be correct, as it provides a departure – albeit a modest one – from the orthodox position which his Act attacks in much more immodest terms.

[62] Any judicial reluctance to examine the parliamentary process based on evidential questions is also a matter which the 2024 Act has explicitly addressed. The Court is also spared – at least for the moment – the 'dangerous strains' to which Lord Simon alluded in *Pickin* (n 35 above) – by the Prime Minister's readiness to pause the bill pending judgment being issued.

[63] The drafting of the 2024 Act also meets the disquiet shown by the Australian Hight Court in *Trethowan* and *Clayton* about assuming an implied jurisdiction to provide a remedy preventing the enactment of an 'Act' rather than invalidating such an 'Act' once passed; pp 80–86 and 141–47 above.

[64] Lead counsel was – I assume – the HA Hill who subsequently authored a guide to the Town and Country Planning Act 1947, and who, despite the rejection of his legal argument in *Ellen Street*, evidently continued – according to an editorial in the *Municipal Journal and Public Works Engineer* of 3 January 1936 – to feel that his client's substantive moral argument was well founded. Junior counsel, AW Nicholls, subsequently wrote a guide to compulsory acquisition of land laws.

[65] Scrutton LJ characterised the argument as 'even more impossible' than the claimant's more technical submission as to the Act's meaning, which submission Scrutton had previously damned as an argument he could not follow; *Ellen Street* [1934] 1 KB 590, 594–95.

so they were not actually confronted with the problem that those statements have subsequently often been taken to have addressed.

Further, if, as appears to be broadly accepted, the requirement of express repeal in respect of constitutional statutes must be – now that the European Communities Act 1972 has been repealed – a requirement that arises at common law, and if, as is even more broadly accepted, Parliament has the capacity to amend or abolish any provision of the common law, it must follow that Parliament can specify what 'express repeal' shall mean in particular circumstances. That matter remains at large for a court to determine only when – as is manifestly not the case here – Parliament has not 'expressly' addressed the issue.

The Jennings (and Wade) Analyses

Mr Johnson's counterweight to Professor Wade's 'ultimate political fact' thesis would likely be rooted largely in Sir Ivor Jennings's promulgation of a 'manner and form' entrenchment theory in the 1950s. Those ideas have latterly been lent a renewed topicality by Michael Gordon's forceful reassertion of their cogency.[66]

The relevant passages in the fifth (1959) edition of Jennings's *The law and the constitution* display – Mr Johnson's counsel would submit – a compelling logic both in their structure and in their substance. Jennings had observed in 1959 – and the observation remains relevant in 2024 – that the courts had yet to face the question of the enforceability of an explicit 'manner and form' entrenching statute. There is no authority in the core sense of that term for the court to invoke. The substantive logic which Jennings propounds rests on the inherent paradox informing the orthodox position that a legally sovereign lawmaker cannot divest itself of its legal sovereignty: that it is simultaneously both legally sovereign and not. In Jennings's view, the notion of sovereignty must encompass the sovereign's power to change its own identity for some purposes or all:

> "Legal sovereignty" is merely a name indicating that the legislature has for the time being power to make laws of any kind in the manner required by law … If this is so, the "legal sovereign" may impose legal limitations upon itself because its power to change the law includes the power to change the law affecting itself.[67]

Jennings, of course, invokes both *Trethowan* and *Harris* to support his argument, but does so in qualified terms.[68] *Harris* may provide a more readily applicable illustration than *Trethowan* of a legally sovereign Parliament having more than one identity, as the South African Parliament's two manifestations at any given time involved only different combinations of the same legislators, sitting (albeit more snugly in joint session) in the same buildings and deliberating in the same way. In adding an external element to the

[66] Gordon (2009) 'The conceptual foundations of parliamentary sovereignty: reconsidering Jennings and Wade' *Public Law* 519.

[67] Jennings (1959) op cit pp 152–53.

[68] "It is not suggested that these decisions determine the law as it applies in the United Kingdom. They simply illustrate the point that the power of a legislature derives from the law by which it is established"; ibid p156.

legislative process, Peden's s.7A lent an additional complication to any attempt to justify an entrenchment provision on the basis that Parliament has merely subdivided or redefined *itself* for lawmaking purposes.

The 2024 Act, adopting perhaps a 'belt and braces' approach to entrenchment,[69] both alters the internal identity of the 'ordinary' legislature and integrates it with an additional, external component. It might be suggested that in fusing the *Trethowan* and *Harris* entrenchment techniques, the 2024 Act has overreached the type of limitation that Jennings had in mind. That assertion is in (large) part belied by Jennings's reliance on *Trethowan* as an illustration of his principle being given effect. But Mr Johnson additionally has a doctrinal benefit that was not available to Ivor Jennings. In endorsing the assertion that the Parliament Act legislature is an alter ego rather than delegate of the tricameral Parliament, and that the Commons plus Monarch 'Parliament' produces 'Acts' rather than delegated legislation (and does so because s.1 and s.2 of the Parliament Act 1911 say that it does so), *Jackson* takes us on several long strides towards acceptance of the Jennings thesis. Where is the constitutional logic in accepting – as *Jackson* does – that Parliament can redefine itself 'downwards' but in refusing to accept here that Parliament cannot redefine itself 'upwards'?[70]

The claimant might also reformulate the Jennings thesis in a somewhat different fashion by suggesting that what Jennings was in fact propounding but not expressly acknowledging was that Parliament 'in the ordinary way' can enact legislation controlling the powers or altering the identity for one purpose, some purposes or all purposes, not of *itself* but of its component parts. So s.6(3) simply prevents the Commons from performing a particular legislative task unless a precisely defined number of its members agree to do so, while s.6(6) and s.6(7) place related constraints on the powers of the House of Lords and the Monarch respectively. In providing the remedies created by the 2024 Act, the Court would not be restricting the powers of 'Parliament' at all, but rather the powers of its component – and normatively subordinate – institutions.

Inviting reliance on Jennings would necessitate some rebuttal of Wade's earlier critique. That might entail in part the submission that Wade's analysis of the status of 'the Parliament Act Parliament' as an institution normatively inferior to the (tri) bicameral Parliament and of Parliament Act measures as delegated legislation has been rejected by the House of Lords in *Jackson*. Having been 'wrong' on this point,[71] Wade was also likely wrong in 1955 in propounding his 'ultimate political fact' and revolution thesis, and that 'meticulously precise' statutory redefinition of Parliament's identity for particular lawmaking purposes has always been something that courts would uphold. An alternative and perhaps less attractive submission would be that Professor Wade was wrong about the Parliament Acts but right about the need for revolution, and that the passage of the 2024 Act was as much a moment of revolution as the passage of the European Communities Act 1972 itself.

[69] Or – if one sticks with the *Trethowan* theme – a 'two padlocks rather than one' strategy; see p 43 above.
[70] Such logic is not hard to find, but that is another argument I currently propose to pursue elsewhere.
[71] I have noted elsewhere that Wade's analysis is surely 'right'; (2018) op cit pp 165–68.

The (ir)relevance of Miller (No 2)

The Leader of His Majesty's Loyal Opposition would presumably suggest that the defendant's invocation of *Miller (No 2)* to buttress the government's case is – if not designedly disingenuous – then at least sadly misconceived. The obvious basis for that contention is that *Miller (No 2)* was concerned solely with the relationship between 'Parliament' and the Crown (both in the narrow sense of Parliament as the creator of legislation which is normatively superior to actions taken under the prerogative and in the broader sense of an institution functioning to hold the Crown to effective account). The Prime Minister, it would be asserted, has in a not very subtle sleight of hand tried to equate the Court's long-established constitutional role in enforcing limits to the powers of the Crown with a wholly novel constitutional role in enforcing limits to the power of Parliament.

Had Parliament, prior to *Miller (No 2)* being decided, enacted a statutory provision which permitted the Crown to prorogue Parliament for any such period up to eight weeks as the Prime Minister might think fit, then Ms Miller (likely) would not have succeeded.[72] And she would not have succeeded because the courts would have given effect to clearly expressed statutory provisions. And that is just what Mr Johnson is asking the Court to do in this case.

However, should the Court consider that there is indeed some traction in the Prime Minister's submissions on this point, the 'justification' for the reform introduced by the 2024 Act is both self-evident and compelling. The theme is obviously well caught by Rich's observation in the High Court in *Trethowan*: "There is no reason why a Parliament representing the people should be powerless to determine whether the constitutional salvation of the state is to be reached by cautious and well considered steps rather than by rash and ill-considered measures."[73]

The former Prime Minister would likely have invoked such sentiments during the Act's parliamentary passage, asserting that giving free rein to bare legislative majorities on so momentous a political question as surrendering national sovereignty proved a recipe for political chaos between 2016 and 2021, and such chaos should be avoided going forward. Many Conservative MPs would no doubt have lined up to offer similar sentiments during the legislative debate, informing the Commons that their constituents were sick and tired of the constant uncertainty occasioned by pro-Remain political agitators. The then government's position would surely have been that enacting the bill would simply mean that the UK had embraced on this one matter an understanding of democratic governance that is adopted in most countries in the Western world – that some political questions are simply too important to be left to the ordinary political process. Mr Johnson might even have drawn support – with opportunistic cynicism and selective misquotation – from distinguished former members of the senior judiciary, alighting perhaps on Baroness Hale's comment in *R (Chester) v Secretary of State for Justice* that: "Democracy is about more than respecting the views of the majority"[74]

[72] 'Likely' because one cannot exclude the possibility that Ms Miller might have persuaded the courts that Johnson was acting in bad faith, an enterprise in which she would 'likely' have been assisted by Johnson's unwillingness to provide any evidence as to his good faith.

[73] (1931) 44 CLR 394, 420.

[74] [2013] UKSC 63, [2014] AC 271 [88].

and also citing Lord Sumption's approval of that sentiment: "Of course as Baroness Hale has pointed out, it does not follow that a democracy can properly do whatever it likes, simply by virtue of the democratic mandate for its acts."[75]

On Symmetry and Asymmetry in Entrenchment Devices

Miller (No 2) can certainly be read as having hung a welcome sign over the public law door to arguments that seek to extend the range of 'political' matters that may properly be weighted in the judicial balance in resolving 'legal' disputes. In my hypothetical scenario, Sir Keir – faced as he is with a second 'one-off' constitutional moment – might ask the Court, in rebuttal of the claimant's 'justification', to invite a further 'political' consideration into the judicial arena. In broad terms, the suggestion would be that the Court's reasoning in *Miller (No 2)* indicates that considerations as to the legitimacy of the 2024 Act (may) have become justiciable matters which should shape the Court's response as to the Act's legal enforceability.

One might readily suggest that Bavin and Pedden's entrenchment device prima facie lacked moral legitimacy because of its *essentially asymmetrical character*, in the senses of what we might term both '*transactional symmetry*' and '*contextual symmetry*'. Neither matter was broached in any shape or form in any court during the *Trethowan* litigation, presumably because in that era presumptions as to the proper focus of judicial attention were limited to matters of legality rather than (also) legitimacy. Those presumptions would perhaps hold (very much) less force in the UK in 2024.

Transactional Symmetry

By 'transactional symmetry', I mean simply: 'Was the degree of entrenchment provided for in the entrenching device matched or exceeded by the lawmaking process through which the device was introduced?'[76] The *Trethowan* entrenching device was bicameral bare majoritarianism plus referendum plus royal (reserved) assent. Its introduction was effected by a less exacting lawmaking process: bicameral bare majoritarianism plus royal (reserved) assent. Transactional symmetry would be achieved in circumstances where – to use the obvious familiar term – the 'manner and form' of lawmaking used to create the entrenching device precisely matched the 'manner and form' of the entrenching device itself. Had Bavin's government yielded to the suggestions of some Labour Assembly members that s.7A not be enacted unless approved by a bare majoritarian referendum as well as bare majoritarian votes in the Assembly and Council and had been reserved for royal assent, s.7A would have been – if so enacted – a transactionally symmetrical entrenchment device.[77]

[75] ibid [112].

[76] Some time after thinking of this issue and label, I came across a fascinating paper (considering recent Australian developments) which had previously used the asymmetric/symmetric dichotomy and found it a helpful source to develop my ideas; Rozkowski and Goldsworthy (2012) 'Symmetric entrenchment of manner and form requirements' *Public Law Review* 216.

[77] I am assuming symmetry of form as well as substance, ie that the referendum would precede assent. A proviso in a bill enacted in the 'ordinary way' that the Act would not come into force unless it attracted a

As enacted, s.7A can be characterised as having '*negative* transactional asymmetry'. The 'manner and form' of enacting the entrenchment provision was politically less difficult to achieve than the degree of entrenchment provided for.

Conversely, an entrenchment device could lay claim to having '*positive* transactional asymmetry' in circumstances where the lawmaking process used to introduce the entrenching device is politically more difficult to achieve than the degree of entrenchment provided for.[78]

The hypothetical entrenchment device envisaged in Johnson's Act has negative transactional asymmetry in several respects. The two most obvious and significant are the requirement of a Commons two-thirds majority at third reading and then approval (by at least 53% of votes cast) in a referendum.[79] Transactional symmetry would be met if the enhanced Commons majority requirement merely matched that achieved in the 2024 bill and/or that bill had itself been approved (by a 53% or more vote) in a referendum.

Contextual Symmetry

Transactional symmetry is, however, quite a crude device. In a purely formalistic sense, s.7A would have been transactionally symmetrical if it had – instead of deploying a referendum – made its own repeal subject to the same Assembly majority at second and or third reading as the Bavin/Peden bill had received.[80] However, even if that transactional symmetry had been achieved, there are several contextual matters which might come into play if one is seeking to assess the legitimacy of an entrenchment initiative.

The first is simply one of electoral mandate. Bavin had not made entrenchment of the Council's existence along s.7A lines a prominent issue at the 1927 Assembly election, so his government could not credibly claim any express electoral support for pursuing the policy.

The second lies in the realm of legal uncertainty. As Bavin and Boyce had made clear in the Assembly and Council during the bill's passage, they had significant doubts about s.7A's legal efficacy, to the point that both men suggested that s.7A would likely operate only as a moral rather than legal impediment to a government commanding a majority in both houses.[81] In such circumstances, legislators could have no sensibly informed idea (and nor could their electors) of the legal consequences of the measure they were approving. *McCawley* lent obvious credibility to the legal enforceability argument, but it would likely be an empirical fiction to suggest that Birkenhead's judgment was well

positive vote in a bare majoritarian referendum and would be automatically repealed if the vote was negative is certainly *asymmetrical in form* to s.7A. It may also be *asymmetrical in substance* if there might be a plausible basis to believe that voters might be more (or less) likely to vote in favour of a 'bill' than of an 'Act'.

[78] Had enactment of s.7A been subject to, for example, an enhanced majority in either or both houses, as well as being contingent in terms of its coming into effect on bare majority support in a pre- or post-assent enactment referendum.

[79] Other (minor) asymmetries are commencement in the Commons, the specification of particular words in any subsequent repealing Act and identification of time periods between different stages of proceedings.

[80] 44–32 at second reading; 41–35 at third reading (pp 46–47 above).

[81] Pp 41–46 above.

understood even by legislators – let alone the electorate – in New South Wales in 1929. Constitutional law reform premised on (perhaps ill-informed) hope (or presumed mendacity) rather than (well-grounded) expectation might readily be thought to be of questionable substantive legitimacy.

The contextual asymmetry of Johnson's fictional entrenchment device is readily apparent in an electoral mandate sense. The 2019 election – fought essentially on the basis, as Johnson put it, of 'Getting Brexit done' – would have provided an obvious opportunity to seek electoral approval for a constitutional innovation that would have taken EU re-entry beyond the reach of orthodox legislative bare majoritarianism. In effect, the Johnson government would have been inviting the 'electorate' to evaluate whether they did indeed wish to engage in a revolutionary project to constrain – on just one, but perhaps the most important, of political issues – the power of bare parliamentary majorities. A revolution by due process of election perhaps. It may be that the possibility did not cross the minds of Conservative ministers or advisers; or that it was considered but rejected as too politically unappealing a project to put before electors.

Whether there could have been any credible basis during the 2024 Act's parliamentary passage for legislators to believe that the Act would be legally effective is perhaps a more open question than it had been in Sydney in 1929 with respect to Bavin's Act, when, if *McCawley* had been properly understood, that argument was a strong one. Some members of each House likely understood the significance of *Factortame (No 2)*;[82] a smaller number were likely familiar with Baroness Hale's 'that is for another day' comment in *Jackson*. Periodic fulminations in the modern era from minister and backbenchers (during both Labour and Conservative administrations) about 'judicial supremacism' would suggest that many MPs appreciate the significant power exercised by the courts, even if they provide little evidence that the constitutional basis of that power is widely understood.[83] A government case led in the Commons by Johnson, Raab and Braverman might be thought unlikely to have been rooted in painstakingly well-informed deliberation.

The general premise emerging from this analysis is that it is difficult to envisage circumstances arising within the existing constitutional order in which significant[84] entrenchment initiatives could stake any claim to substantial legitimacy. Had the first Blair government won its Commons majority on the back of an entrenchment agenda for its devolution, human rights, House of Lords and EU integration reforms, and subsequently attracted Liberal Democrat and Scots and Welsh Nationalist support for such constitutional change, a credible case for legitimacy and subsequent judicial enforcement could perhaps have been made. That it might be done by a single-party government enjoying a modest Commons majority on the back of a minority share of the electoral vote seems entirely unlikely.

[82] On the level (miniscule) of awareness of the legal implications of EEC accession among MPs in 1972, see Nicol (2001) *EC membership and the judicialization of British politics* ch 4.

[83] See eg the episodes recounted in Loveland (2018) op cit pp 507–14, 583–86.

[84] By which I mean substantially enhanced parliamentary majorities within and/or the addition of a bare majoritarian referendum to the lawmaking process.

III. Conclusion

Given that my publisher has already been very indulgent of the way in which this project has grown beyond its original conception, these final sections have been designedly curt and rudimentary in speculating about the arguable legal issues that my hypothetical Act might throw up. Many of the 'submissions' I have offered are also designedly limited in their credibility. Whether or not that limited speculation proves to be a successful enterprise depends on the interest which legal scholars and law students might subsequently show in addressing those and other undiscussed issues more thoroughly.

As a final observation, however, and one more rooted in the political than the legal dimension of constitutional analysis, we might note a peculiarity of this hypothetical litigation – a peculiarity which would presumably be quite evident to the Starmer coalition government but which apparently did not occur to Jack Lang after his defeat in the High Court in respect of Bavin's Act.[85] The peculiarity is that for the Starmer government to lose the case would offer it remarkable opportunities to curtail the future influence of right-wing political ideologies on the UK's political landscape. If the Jennings thesis is accepted as correct by the Supreme Court – and of general application rather than limited to the *sui generis* (or 'one-off') phenomenon of EU membership – Starmer's administration, assuming it could maintain a Commons and Lords majority, would find itself sitting in power with all (to use a loaded word) manner of entrenchment devices in respect of all manner of political values within its grasp. (Re)creation of Scotland and Wales as sovereign states, the inviolability of the Human Rights Act, fundamental alteration of the identities of the House of Lords or even of the House of Commons, the structure and powers of local government, the contents of the Commons electoral system – all could be the subject of new settlements imposed by bare majoritarian legislation, which could in future only be altered by a manner and form of lawmaking which rendered them invulnerable to the self-serving opportunism of a political faction enjoying only minority electoral support.

For adherents to a Blackstonian or Diceyan perception of the sovereignty of Parliament, such a prospect might indeed seem to be 'subversive of all government'.[86] But while Blackstone was penning his soon to be received constitutional wisdom, a great many British constitutional theorists in Britain and its colonies rejected its underlying premise. As Bernard Bailyn has so eloquently put it:

> How to qualify, undermine or reinterpret this tenet of English political theory was the central intellectual problem that confronted the leaders of the American cause … To search deliberately for the seams along which the fabric of power might be divided …[87]

[85] Pp 87–88 above. The peculiarity did occur to Queensland's Labour government, albeit that the opportunity provided was not much exploited; pp 129–30 above. *Trethowan*'s potential as an entrenchment device in 1930 was likely limited to 'identity' issues within CLVA 1865 s.5 rather than to 'competence' issues more generally.

[86] Although perhaps less so if the entrenchment agenda came from a government of the political right than of the centre.

[87] (1967) *The ideological origins of the American revolution* pp 202, 209.

It took James Madison and his colleagues barely 20 years to perhaps not find, but rather sew those seams, setting a pattern that most of the Western world has subsequently followed. Nearly 250 years later, the presumption that the UK's Parliament must inevitably continue to be dressed in the coarsely grained and roughly cut constitutional cloth of bicameral bare majoritarianism seems a proposition that has become both less and less palatable in terms of political morality and less and less fantastic in terms of legal enforceability.

BIBLIOGRAPHY

Ahmed F and Parry A (2017) 'Constitutional statutes' *OJLS* 461

Allan T (2011) 'Questions of legality and legitimacy: form and substance in British constitutionalism' *International Journal of Constitutional Law* 155

Appelby G (2015) 'The Gavan Duffy court' in Dixon R and Williams G (eds) *The High Court, the constitution and Australian politics*

Bailyn B (1967) *The ideological origins of the American revolution*

Barber N (2016) 'Why entrench?' *International Journal of Constitutional Law* 325

Berriedale Keith A (1909) *Responsible government in the Dominions*

Berriedale Keith A (1916) *Imperial unity and the Dominions*

Berriedale Keith A (1933) *The constitutional law of the British Dominions*

Bridge C (1993) *Earle Page: the politician and the man*

Browne Wilkinson (Lord) (1992) 'The infiltration of a Bill of Rights' *Public Law* 397

Buckley K, Dale B and Reynolds W (1994) *Doc Evatt*

Cain F (1931) 'Jack Lang and the great depression' in Cooksey (1970a) *infra*

Clark D (2016) 'Cautious constitutionalism: Commonwealth legislative independence and the Statute of Westminster 1931–1942' *Macquarie LJ* 41

Clark M (1993) *History of Australia*

Clune D and Griffith G (2006) *Decision and deliberation: the Parliament of New South Wales 1856-2003*

Clune D and Turner K (eds) *The Premiers of New South Wales 1856–2005*

Cooksey R (ed) (1970) *Lang and socialism*

Cooksey R (ed) (1970a) *The great depression in Australia*

Cowen D (1952) 'Legislature and judiciary: part 1' *MLR* 282

Cowen D (1953) 'Legislature and judiciary: part 2' *MLR* 273

Cowen Z (1967) *Isaac Isaacs*

Craig P (2014) 'Constitutionalising constitutional law' *Public Law* 373

Crocket P (1993) *Evatt, a life*

Currey C (1943) 'The Legislative Council of New South Wales 1843–1943: constitutional changes attempted and achieved' *JRAHS* 337

Currey C (1960) 'The most recent attempt to abolish the Legislative Council of New South Wales' *The Australian Quarterly* 21

Dalziel A (1967) *Evatt the enigma*

Davy P (2006) *The Nationals: the Progressive, Country and National parties in New South Wales 1919–2006*

Dickey B (1969) *Politics in New South Wales 1856–1900*

Dixon O (1957) 'The common law as an ultimate constitutional foundation' *Australian Law Journal* 240

Dixon O (first published 1935) 'The law and the constitution' in Dixon O (1965) *Jesting Pilate*

Dixon O (first published 1955) 'Concerning judicial method' in Dixon O (1965) *Jesting Pilate*

Dixson M (1970) 'Rothbury' in Cooksey (1970a) *supra*

Dixson M (1971) 'Ideology, the trades hall reds and J T Lang' *Politics* 53

Dutton D (2011) 'Simon, John Allsebrook, first Viscount Simon' *ODNB*

Edwards C (1965) *Bruce of Melbourne*

Elliot M (2003) 'Embracing constitutional legislation: towards fundamental law' *NILQ* 25

Elliot M (2017) 'Judicial power and the United Kingdom's changing constitution' *Queensland LJ* 274

Elliot M and Young A (2019) '*Privacy International* in the Supreme Court: jurisdiction, the rule of law and parliamentary sovereignty' *Cambridge LJ* 490

Ellis U (1958) *The Country Party: a political and social history of the party in New South Wales*

Evans J and Lovelock L (2008) *Legislative Council practice*
Evatt H (1940) *Australian Labour leader*
Fitzgerald R (1995) *"Red Ted": the life of E.G. Theodore*
Friedmann W (1950) 'Trethowan's case, parliamentary sovereignty and the limits of legal change' 24 *Australian LJ* 103
Gaegler S (1987) 'Foundations of Australian federalism and the role of judicial review' *Federal LR* 162
Garran R (1924) 'The development of the Australian Constitution' *LQR* 221
Goldsworthy J (2006) '"Australia" – devotion to legalism' in Goldsworthy J (ed) *Interpreting constitutions: a comparative study*
Goldsworthy J (2007) 'Trethowan's case' in Winterton G (ed) *State constitutional landmarks*
Goodhart W (2004) 'Buckmaster, Stanley Owen' *ODNB*
Gordon (2009) 'The conceptual foundations of parliamentary sovereignty: reconsidering Jennings and Wade' *Public Law* 519
Griffith G (2006) 'Sir John Peden: representing the public interest' in Hogan M and Turner K (eds) *The worldly art of politics*
Griswold EN (1952) 'The "coloured vote case" in South Africa' *Harvard LR* 1361
Hagan J (1991) *A history of the Labor Party in New South Wales, 1891–1991*
Haldane R (1899) 'Lord Watson' *Juridical Review* 278
Hart P (1970) 'Lyons – Labour Minister – leader of the UAP' in Cooksey *supra*
Hawker G (1971) *The parliament of New South Wales 1856–1965*
Heuston R (1963) *The lives of the Lord Chancellors*
Heuston R (1970) 'Liversidge v Anderson in retrospect' *LQR* 33
Jenkyns H (1902) *British rule and jurisdiction beyond the seas*
Jennings I (1959 5th edn) *The law and the constitution*
Jowell (2006) 'Parliamentary sovereignty under the new constitutional hypothesis' *Public Law* 562
Lang J (1956) *I remember*
Lang J (1962) *The great bust*
Lang J (1970) *The turbulent years*
Laws J (1993) 'Is the High Court the guardian of fundamental constitutional rights?' *Public Law* 59
Laws J (1995) 'Law and democracy' *Public Law* 72
Laws J (1998) 'The limitations of human rights' *Public Law* 254
Lee D (2016) 'States rights and Australia's adoption of the Statute of Westminster 1931–1942' *History Australia* 258
Lentin A (2004) 'Hamilton, John Andrew, Viscount Sumner' *ODNB*
Lewin J (1956) 'The struggle for law in South Africa' *Political Quarterly* 176
Lewis G (2004) 'Atkin, James Richard, Baron Atkin' *ODNB*
Loveland I (2015 7th edn; 2018 8th edn) *Constitutional law, administrative law and human rights*
Lumb R (1961) 'The New South Wales Legislative Council abolition case' 4 *University of Queensland LJ* 23
MacCormick N (1978) 'Does the United Kingdom have a constitution? *Northern Ireland Law Quarterly* 1
Markey R (1987) 'Populism and the formation of a Labor party in New South Wales, 1890–1900' *Journal of Australian Studies* 39
Matthew H (2004) 'Haldane, Richard Burdon, Viscount Haldane' *ODNB*
McCarthy J (1974) 'A law and order election: New South Wales June 1932' *JRAHS* 2
McCarthy J (1971) 'All for Australia: some right wing responses to the depression in NSW, 1929–1932' *JRAHS* 160
Mcmair M (2008) 'Talbot, Charles, first Baron Talbot of Hensol' *ODNB*
McMinn W (1979) *A constitutional history of Australia*
Meale D (1992) 'The history of the federal idea in Australian constitutional jurisprudence' *Australian Journal of Law and Society* 25
Melbourne and Joyce R (1963) *Early constitutional development in Australia*
Millar G (2004) 'Murray, Andrew Graham, first Viscount Dunedin' *ODNB*
Morgan K (2004) 'Pritt, Dennis Nowell' *ODNB*
Morrison A (1976) 'Dominions Office correspondence on the New South Wales constitutional crisis 1930–1932' *JRAHS* 323
Morrison A (1982) 'Further documents and comments on the New South Wales constitutional crisis 1930–1932' *JRAHS* 122

Morrison W (1991) 'The future scope of Australian common law' *Sydney LR* 335
Morton D (2006) *A short history of Canada* ch 5
Murphy D (1975) *T.J. Ryan: a political biography*
Nairn B (1989) *The "big fella": Jack Lang and the Australian Labor Party, 1891–1949*
Nicol D (2001) *EC membership and the judicialization of British politics*
O'Farrell P (1958) 'The Australian Socialist League and the labor movement 1887–1891' *Historical Studies* 152
Ong B (2020) 'The ouster of parliamentary sovereignty' *Public Law* 41
Page E (1963) *Truant surgeon*
Palmer N (1931) *Henry Bourne Higgins*
Palmer R and Collier R (1864) 'Report of the Imperial Law Officers' in Blackmore E (1894) *Law of the constitution of South Australia*
Perks M (1977) 'The rise to leadership' in Radi and Spearritt *infra*
Poole T (2003) 'Back to the future? Unearthing the theory of common law constitutionalism' *OJLS* 435
Pratt E (1929) 'Proposed reform of Legislative Council in New South Wales' *The Australian Quarterly* 80
Pugsley D (2004) 'Collier, Robert Porrett, first Baron Monkswell' *ODNB*
Radi H and Spearritt P (eds) (1977) *Jack Lang*
Robertson J (1970) 'Scullin as Prime Minister: seven critical decisions' in Cooksey *supra*
Robertson J (1974) *J H Scullin: a political biography*
Ross L (1947) 'The philosophy of the Australian Labor Party' *The Antioch Review* 109
Rozkowski T and Goldsworthy J (2012) 'Symmetric entrenchment of manner and form requirements' *Public Law Review* 216
Rubin G (2004) 'Lawrence, Sir Paul Ogden' *ODNB*
Samuels A (2004) Pollock, Ernest Murray, first Viscount Hanworth' *ODNB*
Sawer G (1944) 'Injunction, parliamentary process, and the restriction of parliamentary competence' *LQR* 83
Sawer G (1956) *Australian federal politics and law 1901–1929*
Sawer G (1967) *Australian federalism in the courts*
Schedvin C (1970) *Australia and the great depression*
Sharp (1927) 'The Canadian election of 1926' *American Political Science Review* 101
Shell D (1992) *The House of Lords*
Smith R (2006) *Against the machines: minor parties and independents in New South Wales*
Smith T (1957) 'The Union of 1707 as fundamental law' *Public Law* 99
Stevens R (2004) 'Sankey, John, Viscount Sankey' *ODNB*
Stevens R (2004) 'Younger, Robert, Baron Blanesburgh' *ODNB*
Steyn Lord (2006) 'Democracy, the rule of law and the role of the judges' *EHRLR* 243
Swinton K (1976) 'Challenging the validity of an Act of Parliament': the effect of enrolment and parliamentary privilege' 14 *Osgoode Hall LJ* 345
Tennant K (1970) *Evatt: politics and justice*
Thomas P (2007) 'Yorke, Philip, first earl of Hardwicke' *ODNB*
Tobias T (2006) 'Atkinson, John, Baron Atkinson' *ODNB*
Todd A (1894) *Parliamentary government in the British colonies*
Turbeville A (1927) *The House of Lords in the eighteenth century*
Twomie A (2004) *The constitution of New South Wales*
Twomie A (2006) *The chameleon Crown*
Tyler P (2006) *Humble and obedient servants: the administration of New South Wales 1901–1960* v.2
Upton M (1989) 'Marriage vows of the elephant: the constitution of 1707' *LQR* 79
Wade HRW (1955) 'The basis of legal sovereignty' *Cambridge LJ* 172
Wade HRW (1996) 'Sovereignty – revolution or evolution?' *LQR* 568
Ward R (1978) *The history of Australia: the twentieth century 1901–1975*
Ward R (1992) *Concise history of Australia*
Wheare K (1953) *The Statute of Westminster and Dominion status*
Wickes E (2001) 'A new constitution for a new state: the 1707 Union of England and Scotland' *LQR* 109
Winterton G (ed) *State constitutional landmarks*
Wrottesley F (2008) 'Pollock, Ernest Murray, First Viscount Hanworth' *ODNB*
Young (2020) 'Fundamental common law rights and legislation' in Elliot M and Hughes K (eds) *Common law constitutional rights*

INDEX